Change Management H

Leadership of Change® Volume 3

By

Peter F Gallagher

Change Management Handbook
This handbook contains over fifty concepts, models, figures, assessments, tools, templates, checklists, plans, a roadmap and glossary structured around the ten-step **a2B Change Management Framework® (a2BCMF®)** each with a practical case study.

Change Management Body of Knowledge Volume 3

Enabling the Leadership of Change®

Change Waits for No Leader

Leadership of Change®

If more employees were better leaders of change, the organisational benefits would be endless. We enable the Leadership of Change®

The **Leadership of Change®** encompasses practical change management concepts, models, depictions, assessments, tools, templates, checklists, plans, a roadmap and glossary structured around the ten-step **a2B Change Management Framework®**. The delivery vehicles are change management books, change management gamification manuals, change management gamification workshops (face-to-face/virtual), leadership alignment workshops and masterclasses.

The **Leadership of Change®** is both thought leadership and a suite of tools to propel you from where your organisation is right now, the current 'a' state, to where you want to be, the future 'B' state. The **Leadership of Change®** will help you to implement your organisation's change or improvement and achieve a 100% return on investment (ROI) with full employee adoption, enabling you to secure future profit and remain ahead of your competitors. Truly great **Leadership of Change®** combines thoughtful strategy alignment of your leadership team and change leadership skills to lead employee change adoption and employee behaviour change.

Leadership of Change® Volumes: The Change Management Body of Knowledge volumes are intended to be leading practice in organisational change management and implementation, which supports strategy execution. They are based on the author's work, with over thirty years of organisational change implementation, transformation, and business improvement experience in over thirty countries.

Volumes 1 - 7 focus on learning about the practical implementation of change management. The books cover Change Management: Fables, Pocket Guide, Handbook, Leadership, Adoption, Behaviour and Sponsorship.

Volumes A - C are workshop manuals that focus on using change management gamification to learn about change leadership, employee change adoption and employee behaviour change.

Change Management Handbook - Leadership of Change® Volume 3

Change Management Handbook: This change management handbook contains over fifty concepts, models, figures, assessments, tools, templates, checklists, plans, a roadmap and glossary, structured on the ten step **a2B Change Management Framework®** (**a2BCMF®**) each with a practical case study.

About the Book:

This handbook is for growth mindset leaders, senior managers, students, HR professionals and change management practitioners who want to deliver organisational change while their organisation continues with day-to-day operations. **Leadership of Change®** Volume 3 is based on over thirty years of experience implementing change, transformation and improvements into some of the world's largest and most successful organisations across many countries and cultures. It provides deep insights into change programme delivery using the **a2B Change Management Framework®** (**a2BCMF®**). It starts by aligning the change with the organisation's strategy and vision, moving through to successfully closing and sustaining the change. It covers ten key change management implementation concepts in detail, which include sponsorship, change history, communication, change planning, readiness, resistance, developing the new skills and behaviours, as well as adoption. It also includes the **AUILM® Employee Change Adoption Model** and the **a2B5R® Employee Behaviour Change Model**.

Disclaimer

Descriptions and other related information in this document are provided only to illustrate the methods covered. You are fully responsible for the use of these methods. peterfgallagher.com and a2B.consulting assumes no responsibility for any losses incurred by you or any third parties arising from the use of these methods or information.

We have used reasonable care in preparing the information included in this book, but peterfgallagher.com and a2B.consulting does not warrant that such information is error free. We assume no liability whatsoever for any damages incurred by you resulting from errors in, or omissions from the information included herein.

peterfgallagher.com and a2B.consulting does not assume any liability for the infringement of patents, copyrights, or other intellectual property rights of third parties by or arising from the use of peterfgallagher.com and a2B.consulting information described in this document. No license, express, implied or otherwise, is granted hereby under any patents, copyrights or other intellectual property rights of peterfgallagher.com and a2B.consulting or others.

The document contains statements that are general in nature and do not constitute recommendations to the reader as to the content's suitability, applicability or appropriateness.

PFG Publishing has no responsibility for the persistence or accuracy of URLs for external or third-party internet websites referred to in this publication and does not guarantee that any content on such websites is, or will remain, accurate or appropriate.

The following case studies contained within this book/e-book/pdf are fictional and do not depict any actual person or event

Disclaimer and Copyright

Copyright ©

Change Management Handbook
Leadership of Change Volume 3

All rights reserved. No part of this work may be used or reproduced by any means: graphic, electronic, mechanical, including photocopying, recording, taping or by any information storage retrieval system without the written permission of the publisher, except in the case of brief quotations embodied in critical articles and reviews.

www.peterfgallagher.com and www.a2B.consulting

The following are registered trademarks:
a2B Change Management Framework® (a2BCMF®)
a2B AUILM® Model
a2B5R® Model

This book was created and written by Peter F Gallagher.

This book is suitable for business professionals undertaking organisational change management, transformation and improvement, or students studying change management. It is typically sold or distributed under, or as part of, a license agreement to learn the frameworks, models and concepts contained herein.

Copyright © 2019-2021 *Peter F Gallagher and a2B.consulting*
All rights reserved.
ISBN-13: 9781795878975

Publisher: PFG Publishing

Dedication

I dedicate this book to my wife Sarah and son Tiarnán who I love and treasure.

I would like to thank the brilliant people that I was fortunate enough to meet, work with and learn from, these experiences have enabled me to write this book.

Although the books took two years to write, they are in fact the result of over thirty years of work experience.

In life, never give up, rarely judge or criticise and always learn, improve and love.

In work, get up early, ignore the naysayers, work hard and never give up.

Forward

I have worked both as an internal and big four consultant, involved in general project delivery, business improvement, transformation and change programmes for nearly all of my career. When I look back at what makes a programme or project more successful than others, the main difference is the application of change management using a structured change framework to implement programme change and change models that support the employees both through the change and the development of their new required behaviours.

The ten-steps of the **a2B Change Management Framework®** outline the key success elements of organisational change management implementation. The **Change Management Handbook** is structured on these elements. The main objective in developing the **Leadership of Change® Volume 3 - Change Management Handbook** is to provide practical and detailed change implementation solutions for people who are tasked with implementing change management into their organisation. This handbook assumes that the users will be experienced in the basics of change management and its concepts. I hope that this book and our other **Leadership of Change Volumes** will help to provide the user with information on how to successfully implement change into their organisation.

Through my career, I have observed change teams, sponsors and leaders meandering through change implementation programmes. So much energy and resources are wasted on a change or improvement that will not be fully implemented or adopted by the organisation, and a strategic execution opportunity will therefore be missed. By following this framework, supported by over fifty concepts, figures, assessments, tools, templates and plans, a roadmap, glossary and ten case studies, I hope you can successfully deliver your organisation's change or improvement.

Make your organisation's change magnificent!

Who is this Handbook for?

All too often, change management implementations fail to deliver the expected organisation benefits or gain employee adoption. **Volume 3 - Change Management Handbook** is targeted at all employees going through an organisational change. It will help them to understand why organisations need to change, and why they need to learn new skills and behaviours. It will also explain why becoming involved in shaping the change can be more fulfilling for them and their organisation.

This handbook is of particular interest to change practitioners, HR professionals, students studying change management, and project managers, including organisational managers and leaders.

This book can also be used as part of a self-study programme or as a reference before, during, and after training to learn change management concepts, assessments, tools, templates, checklists and plans, as well as the roadmap and glossary.

Acknowledgements

In a career that spans over thirty years, I've worked for some wonderful people in great locations, both on and offshore. You have helped me learn so much, and for that I am very grateful. There was never a dull moment.

Contents

Enabling the Leadership of Change®..iii
Leadership of Change®..
Change Management Handbook - Leadership of Change® Volume 3............i
Disclaimer..
Copyright ©..i
Dedication...ii
Forward..iii
Who is this Handbook for?...iv
Acknowledgements..v
Contents...vi
List of Figures...x
How to use this Handbook..xii
Section 1: Change Management Introduction..1
1.1 Organisation Change Disruption..2
1.2 What is Change Management?..4
1.3 Organisational Change Challenges...6
1.4 The Benefits of Change Management...10
1.5 Organisation Change Capability...12
1.6 Change Management Leadership..14
1.7 Incremental Change Versus Transformation..20
Section 2: a2B Change Management Framework®...23
2.1 a2B Change Management Framework®..24
2.2 a2B Change Management Framework® Icons...26
2.3. a2B Change Management Framework® Benefits.....................................28
Section 3: Change Delivery..31
Section 3A: Plan - a2BCMF® Steps 1 - 4..33
3.1 Change Definition...34
3.1.1 Change Definition - Overview...34
3.1.2 Case Study - Fish Food Versus Safety Strategy......................................36
3.1.3 The Importance of Change Definition...41
3.1.4 Strategy Alignment..42
3.1.5 Strategic Portfolio Prioritisation Funnel..42
3.1.6 Organisation Change Capacity and Workload.......................................44
3.1.7 Business Case...46
3.1.8 Change Roadmap - Guide..47
3.1.9 Benefits Plan and Tracker - Guide..52
3.1.10 Change Elevator Speech - Guide...55
3.1.11 Stakeholder Analysis - Guide...56
3.1.12 Stakeholder Mapping - Guide..60

- 3.1.13 Governance 61
- 3.1.14 Review and Checklist 62
- 3.2 Secure Sponsorship and Resources 64
- 3.2.1 Sponsorship and Resources - Overview 64
- 3.2.2 Case Study - Nobody Told me I was the Sponsor 66
- 3.2.3 The Importance of Sponsorship and Resources 71
- 3.2.4 Key Elements of Sponsorship 71
- 3.2.5 Change Sponsor Assessment - Guide 76
- 3.2.6 Core Change Team Resources 79
- 3.2.7 Cascading Change Throughout the Organisation 80
- 3.2.8 Leadership and Management Change Support 82
- 3.2.9 Change Agents 84
- 3.2.10 Change Agents and the Trusted Adviser 87
- 3.2.11 Review and Checklist 88
- 3.3 Assess Previous Change 90
- 3.3.1 Assess Previous Change - Overview 90
- 3.3.2 Case Study - Gambling with Organisation Finances 92
- 3.3.3 The Importance of Assessing Previous Change 94
- 3.3.4 Change and Learning Organisations 94
- 3.3.5 Change History Assessment© - Elements 95
- 3.3.6 Change History Assessment© - Guide 98
- 3.3.7 Assessment Results 101
- 3.3.8 Review and Checklist 104
- 3.4 Develop Detailed Change Plan 106
- 3.4.1 Project Change Plan - Overview 106
- 3.4.2 Case Study - Fail to Plan, Plan to Fail 108
- 3.4.3 The Importance of a Project Change Plan 117
- 3.4.4 Project Change Plan - Key Elements 118
- 3.4.5 Project Change Plan - a2BCMF® Steps 118
- 3.4.6 Supporting Component Plans 120
- 3.4.7 Work Streams Change Support 121
- 3.4.8 Project Change Plan - Guide 121
- 3.4.9 Master Project Plan Alignment 124
- 3.4.10 Review and Checklist 126
- Section 3B: Execute - a2BCMF® Steps 5 - 8 129
- 3.5 Communicate the Change 130
- 3.5.1 Communicate the Change - Overview 130
- 3.5.2 Case Study - The Illusion of Communication 132
- 3.5.3 The Importance of Communicating the Change 137
- 3.5.4 Communicate the Stakeholder Needs 138

3.5.5 Communication Planning - Guide 141
3.5.6 Communication Message Components 142
3.5.7 Why Are We Changing? - Guide 143
3.5.8 Communication Channels 145
3.5.9 Communication for Adoption 148
3.5.10 Change Communication Plan - Guide 149
3.5.11 Review and Checklist 152
3.6 Assess Readiness 154
3.6.1 Assess Readiness - Overview 154
3.6.2 Case Study - Preparation Generates Readiness 156
3.6.3 The Importance of Assessing Readiness 160
3.6.4 Change Readiness Elements 161
3.6.5 Change Readiness Assessment - Guide 164
3.6.6 Change Readiness Assessment - Results 166
3.6.7 Change Readiness Assessment - Interventions 167
3.6.8 Review and Checklist 168
3.7 Manage Resistance 170
3.7.1 Change Resistance - Overview 170
3.7.2 Case Study - Employees with Different Agendas 172
3.7.3 The Importance of Change Resistance 176
3.7.4 Resistance Standpoints 177
3.7.5 Individual Reasons for Resistance 179
3.7.6 Actions to Reduce Resistance 182
3.7.7 Finding the Tipping Point 186
3.7.8 Change Implementation Approaches 187
3.7.9 Change Resistance Planning - Guide 189
3.7.10 The Fixed Versus Growth Mindset 191
3.7.11 Change Resistance Costs 193
3.7.12 Review and Checklist 194
3.8 Develop New Skills and Behaviours 196
3.8.1 Develop New Skills and Behaviours - Overview 196
3.8.2 Case Study - No Behaviour Change, No Change 198
3.8.3 The Importance of New Skills and Behaviours 201
3.8.4 Employee Training 202
3.8.5 Developing the New Skills 202
3.8.6 a2BDNS© Developing the New Skills Model 203
3.8.7 The Behaviour Change Challenge 206
3.8.8 Developing the Behaviours 207
3.8.9 a2B5R® Employee Behaviour Change Model 208
3.8.10 Change Management Training 210

3.8.11 Review and Checklist 212
Section 3C: Sustain and Close - a2BCMF® Steps 9 - 10 215
3.9 Adoption 216
3.9.1 Adoption - Overview 216
3.9.2 Case Study - Easy Solutions are Not Always Adopted 218
3.9.3 The Importance of Adoption 223
3.9.4 Change Adoption - Day One Consideration 224
3.9.5 Employee Change Transition Feelings and Stages 224
3.9.6 AUILM® Model and Tactics 225
3.9.7 Culture and Change 228
3.9.8 Review and Checklist 230
3.10 Sustain and Close 232
3.10.1 Sustain and Close - Overview 232
3.10.2 Case Study - 'Tell' Change is More Effective 234
3.10.3 The Importance of Sustain and Close 240
3.10.4 Sustain 241
3.10.5 Benefits Delivery, Transition and Sustainment 242
3.10.6 Balanced Scorecard 242
3.10.7 Individual Performance Plan 243
3.10.8 Close 243
3.10.9 Transfer of Ownership 244
3.10.10 Lessons Learned - Guide 245
3.10.11 Knowledge Transfer 248
3.10.12 Celebration 249
3.10.13 Review and Checklist 250
Section 4: Other Information and Support 253
4.1 References 254
4.2 Glossary 258
4.3 Bibliography 272
4.4 Index 280
4.5 About the Author 287
4.6 Other Leadership of Change Volumes 288
4.7 Connect with us online 290

List of Figures

Plans, Tools, Templates and Assessments

Figure 1.1.1 Industrial Revolution Timeline 2

Figure 1.1.2 Normal Day-to-Day Operations and Disruption 3

Figure 1.2.1 Change Management Definition 4

Figure 1.3.1 Organisational Change Management Challenges 8

Figure 1.4.1 Change Benefit Realisation 11

Figure 1.5.1 Developing Change Organisation Capability 13

Figure 1.6.1 Change Leader and Sponsor Activities 17

Figure 1.7.1 Incremental Change Versus Transformation 21

Figure 2.1.1 a2B Change Management Framework® 24

Figure 3.1.1 Aligning Strategy and Change 41

Figure 3.1.2 Strategic Portfolio Prioritisation Funnel 43

Figure 3.1.3 Organisation Change Capacity 45

Figure 3.1.4 Change Programme Business Case 46

Template 3.1.5 Roadmap Input Data 49

Roadmap 3.1.6 Change Roadmap 50

Template 3.1.7 Benefits Plan and Tracker 54

Tool 3.1.8 Change Programme Elevator Speech 55

Assessment 3.1.9 Stakeholder Analysis 59

Template 3.1.10 Stakeholder Map 60

Figure 3.2.1 Key Elements of Sponsorship 72

Assessment 3.2.2 Change Sponsorship Assessment 77

Figure 3.2.3 Change Team Structure and Roles 80

Figure 3.2.4 Cascading the Change 81

Figure 3.2.5 Change Agents - Internal versus External 85

Figure 3.2.6 Trusted Adviser Equation 87

Figure 3.3.1 Gambling Organisation Finances on Change 94

Figure 3.3.2 Change History Elements 96

Assessment 3.3.3 Change History Assessment© 99

List of Figures, Plans, Tools, Templates and Assessments

Figure 3.3.4 Change History Question Result 101

Figure 3.3.5 Change History Comparison 103

Plan 3.4.1 Project Change Plan 122

Figure 3.5.1 Stakeholder Communication Needs 139

Template 3.5.2 Communication Planning 140

Figure 3.5.3 Communicate Message Components 143

Template 3.5.4 Why Are We Changing? 144

Plan 3.5.5 Change Communication Plan 150

Figure 3.6.1 Change Readiness Elements 162

Assessment 3.6.2 Change Readiness Assessment 165

Figure 3.6.3 Change Readiness Assessment Results 166

Figure 3.7.1 Change Resistance Standpoints 177

Figure 3.7.2 Employee Resistance 186

Figure 3.7.3 Tell and Sell Change Approaches 188

Template 3.7.4 Change Resistance Planning 190

Figure 3.7.5 Fixed versus Growth Mindset 192

Figure 3.8.1 Developing the New Skills 206

Figure 3.8.2 a2B5R® Behaviour Change Model 208

Figure 3.8.3 Change Management Training Modules 211

Figure 3.9.1 Change Adoption 223

Figure 3.9.2 Employee Change Transition 225

Figure 3.9.3 a2B AUILM® Adoption Model 226

Figure 3.10.1 Sustain the Change 241

Figure 3.10.2 Balanced Scorecard 243

Figure 3.10.3 Close Change Programme 244

Template 3.10.4 Change Lessons Learned 247

Figure 3.10.5 Knowledge Transfer Process 249

How to use this Handbook

Leadership of Change® Volume 3 - Change Management Handbook is organised into four main sections:

Section 1: Introduction

This section starts by introducing the fourth industrial revolution and change disruption. After an overview of change management, it focuses on the important wider enablers for successful organisational change; understanding change challenges, achieving benefits, building change capability, the importance of leadership and incremental change versus transformation.

Section 2: a2B Change Management Framework® (a2BCMF®)

This section introduces the **a2BCMF®** and its ten key steps which are central to section 3. The benefits of using the **a2BCMF®** are outlined and these help to address some of the main organisation implementation challenges listed in section 1.

Section 3: Change Delivery

This section provides detailed concepts, models, tools and assessments in each of the ten-steps of the **a2BCMF®**. The first page of each subsection provides a definition, business benefits, business objective and key stakeholders for each **a2BCMF®** step. The second page contains a table on enablers and barriers. Each subsection concludes with a summary and a checklist of the main change activities.

Section 3A: Plan. a2BCMF® Steps 1 - 4

Step 1 - Change Definition.
Step 2 - Secure Sponsorship and Resources.
Step 3 - Assess Previous Change.
Step 4 - Develop Detailed Change Plan.

Section 3B: Execute. a2BCMF® Steps 5 - 8

Step 5 - Change Communication.
Step 6 - Assess Readiness.
Step 7 - Manage Resistance.

Step 8 - Develop New Skills and Behaviours.

Section 3C: Sustain. a2BCMF® Steps 9 - 10

Step 9 - Adoption.

Step 10 - Sustain and Close.

Section 4: Other Information and Support

This section includes the references, glossary, bibliography and index, as well as supporting information about the author, other books in this series and how to connect with us online.

Notes:

Case Studies: Each **a2BCMF®** step includes a pertinent short case study* that highlights typical problems that organisations might encounter when implementing change. Insights and potential solutions will be included in the subsequent text.

Change Management Concepts: The handbook contains over fifty concepts, figures, assessments, tools, templates, checklists and plans, as well as a roadmap (depictions) and glossary. These cover the main change concepts such as sponsorship, communications, readiness, resistance and adoption.

Depiction Numbering: Depictions are numbered by the section, subsection and then sequence number. e.g. figure 2.2.2 can be found in section 2, subsection 2 and is the second figure in this subsection.

Assessments: Each assessment will outline the creation steps with numbered instructions. The assessments use the five-point Likert (1932) scoring range: Strongly agree (5 points), agree, neutral, disagree, strongly disagree (1 point). Scores of 5 would be considered as a positive prognosis for successful change implementation. Scores of 4 or lower would indicate potential challenges. The assessments contain a limited number of example questions, however, for more complex changes more questions might be required.

*Extracts from **Leadership of Change® Volume 1 - Fables.**

Section 1: Change Management Introduction

1.1 Organisation Change Disruption

Change disruption is the order of the day. Rapidly changing customer buying habits, access to new technology, and social media accelerate the way organisations need to adapt to change to remain competitive or even survive.

The first industrial revolution in the eighteenth-century allowed production to be mechanised. This revolution drove social change as people became increasingly urbanised (**Figure 1.1.1**). The second industrial revolution developed mass production, and the third, beginning in the 1950s, saw the emergence of computers and digital technology. This led to increased automation through digitisation and computers.

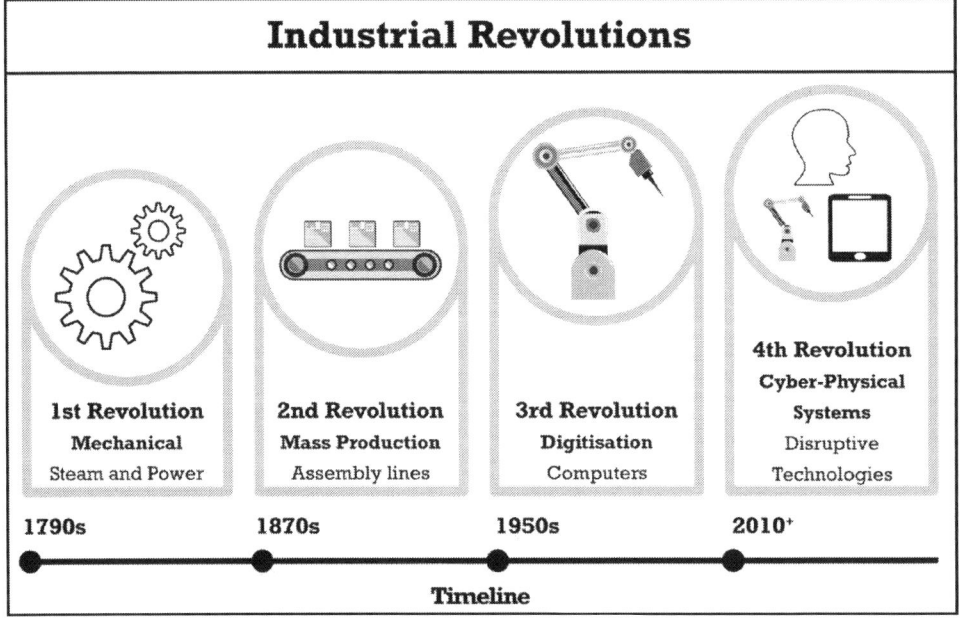

Figure 1.1.1 Industrial Revolution Timeline

We are currently in the middle of the fourth industrial revolution (4IR) and a time of major disruption. 4IR is differentiated by the speed of technological breakthroughs and its widespread scope. It has had an incredible impact, changing the way organisations operate and how we live and relate to one another. 4IR includes technology breakthroughs in fields such as artificial intelligence, robotics, the Internet of Things, autonomous vehicles, 3D printing, 5G, genetic modification and energy storage. *"What I consider to be the fourth industrial revolution is unlike anything humankind has experienced before"* (Schwab, 2017).

Change will impact nearly every organisation like an explosion, continually disrupting how the organisation delivers normal day-to-day operations. How organisations react to this change explosion will become a source of competitive advantage. Their ability to reduce the internal period of disruption and negative performance to deliver positive operating performance and future state benefits will be critical (**Figure 1.1.2**). Reasons for organisational change may include; 4IR, mergers and acquisitions, financial crises, political factors, etc. *"Change is the law of life. And those who look only to the past or the present are certain to miss the future"* (Kennedy, 1963).

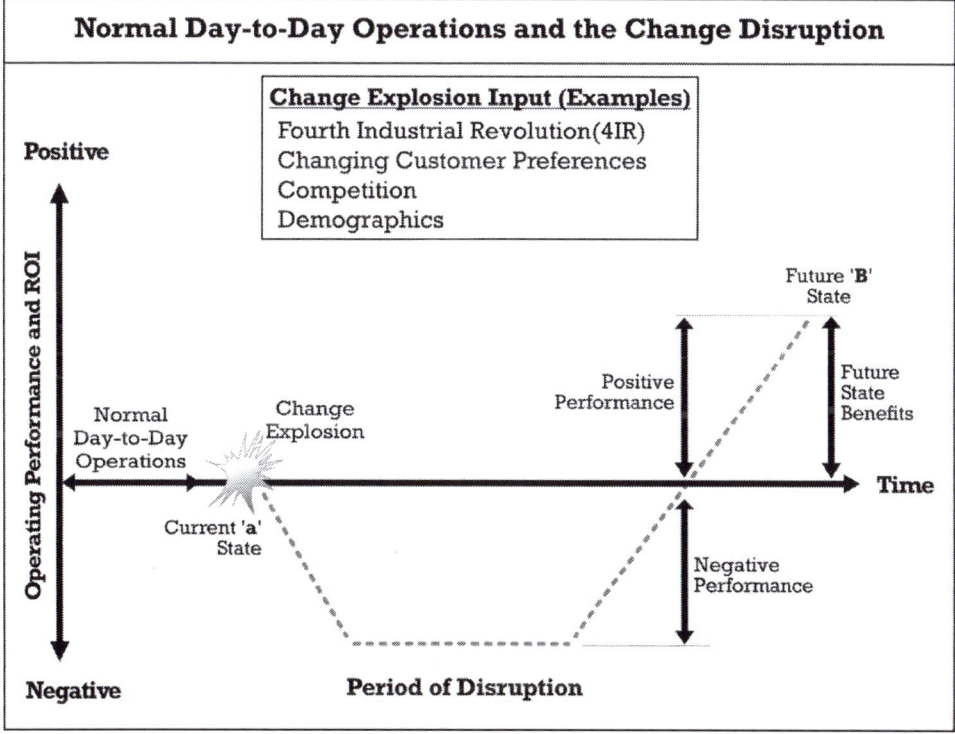

Figure 1.1.2 Normal Day-to-Day Operations and Disruption

1.2 What is Change Management?

Change management is the process, techniques and tools to support organisations, leadership teams and employees going through a change transition from the current 'a' state to the improved future 'B' state.

Organisational change management has evolved over the last few decades. Change management used to be about communications and training delivered just before a new change was implemented. The soft and fluffy people thingamajig. The project manager perceived change management as a tick box exercise on the project plan, an optional extra and a fragmented activity not directly related to project success or measurable results.

Today, in times of change disruption, change management is seen by leading organisations as critical strategic capability. It will enable an organisation to keep ahead of their competition or potentially even help them to survive. An organisation's strategic portfolio sets out multiple programmes and projects that need to be implemented to meet changing customer requirements, stay ahead of the competition, utilise new technology, etc. But in order to adapt and reap the benefits of the new technology we need our employees to change and adopt the new way of working. Change management is the enabler for this (**Figure 1.2.1**).

Leadership of Change® - Change Management Definition
Change management is the process, techniques and tools to support organisations, leadership teams and employees going through a change transition from the current 'a' state to the improved future 'B' state. It minimises organisation disruption and maximises benefits

Figure 1.2.1 Change Management Definition

The objective of change management is to minimise organisation disruption (any impact on day-to-day operations and growing change resistance) and maximise organisation benefits (employee adoption and improved operating performance). Change management specifically helps employees to become aware of the change, to understand the business needs, become involved, and develop the new skills and behaviours so they can adopt the new way of working. It also motivates employees to commit to sustaining the change, ensuring the organisation achieves their benefits and return on investment.

Three Key Focuses of Change Management

Leadership of Change focuses on the three basics of organisational change implementation:

1. **Programme Change Delivery:**
   - ❖ **A Change Management Framework:** A disciplined and structured programme approach to deliver business change.
   - ❖ **Change Processes, Tools and Techniques:** Important change concepts used while driving and delivering change.

2. **Employee Change Support:**
   - ❖ **Change Adoption Support:** Change success is highly dependent on employees adopting the new way of working. Employees should be supported throughout the change with an employee change adoption model (**AUILM®**).
   - ❖ **Behaviour Change Support:** Often critical to change success is behavioural change. Employees should be supported to develop the new behaviours with an employee behaviour change model (**a2B5R®**).

3. **Organisational Change Alignment:**
   - ❖ **Leadership:** Leaders lead the change. This is a fundamental element in change success because of their position and influence in the organisation.
   - ❖ **Organisational Structure Alignment:** The structure of the organisation, its business processes and systems must be aligned with the change.

1.3 Organisational Change Challenges

There are many challenges that organisations consistently face before implementing change, such as leadership alignment, normal day-to-day operations, and organisation change capability.

Lots of statistics show organisational change and transformations failing to deliver their intended benefits. You can argue about the true percentage of success, but the fact is that many organisations do not achieve full benefits realisation, and in many cases, they fail to attain a return on investment (ROI). Equally unacceptable to shareholders is that the vision is not realised, meaning the organisation's strategy has not been executed. Even when the organisation and its leadership team agree the changes are necessary for the future of the organisation, they still face a number of consistent and specific challenges (**Figure 1.3.1**). *"Implementing change. The phrase sounds reasonable enough, and yet managing change is probably one of the most troubling and challenging tasks facing organisations today"* (Kanter, et al., 2001).

There will be many challenges and barriers for organisations. These can be listed into two categories: consistent challenges throughout change implementation, and specific challenges throughout change implementation.

Consistent Challenges Throughout Change Implementation:

- ❖ **Normal Day-to-Day Operations:** Balancing urgent daily operational activities that need to be completed against important strategic change management activities.

- ❖ **Leadership:** Leaders not fully supporting the change in terms of their responsibilities: '**Articulate**' the change vision, '**Model**' the new behaviours and '**Intervene**' to reinforce the change.

- ❖ **Organisation Change Capability:** Organisations constantly facing change recognise they need to use internal capabilities and have a standard approach, a change framework, models, processes and tools.

Specific Challenges Throughout Change Implementation:

- **Too Many Change Initiatives:** Not enough capacity to deliver ongoing and new change programmes.

- **Inactive or Invisible Sponsorship:** Lack of visible support usually leads to change failure.

- **Poor Previous Change History:** This increases the likelihood of repeating past mistakes.

- **No Detailed Project Change Plan:** Implementing change with only a communication plan and not aligning it to the master project plan.

- **Poor Communication:** Lack of engagement and communication.

- **Ignoring Change Readiness Input:** If the change readiness assessment indicates the organisation is not ready then the change should not be implemented.

- **Thinking there is No Resistance:** There will always be resistance even if it is not overt!

- **Ignoring the Importance of Behaviours:** If you do not change employee behaviour, you will not get organisational change.

- **Thinking Employees will Adopt the Change:** Employees will need to be supported throughout the change by the leadership team so adoption is maximised.

- **Not Transferring Ownership:** Not closing the change properly by using a structured process to ensure sustainment and benefits delivery.

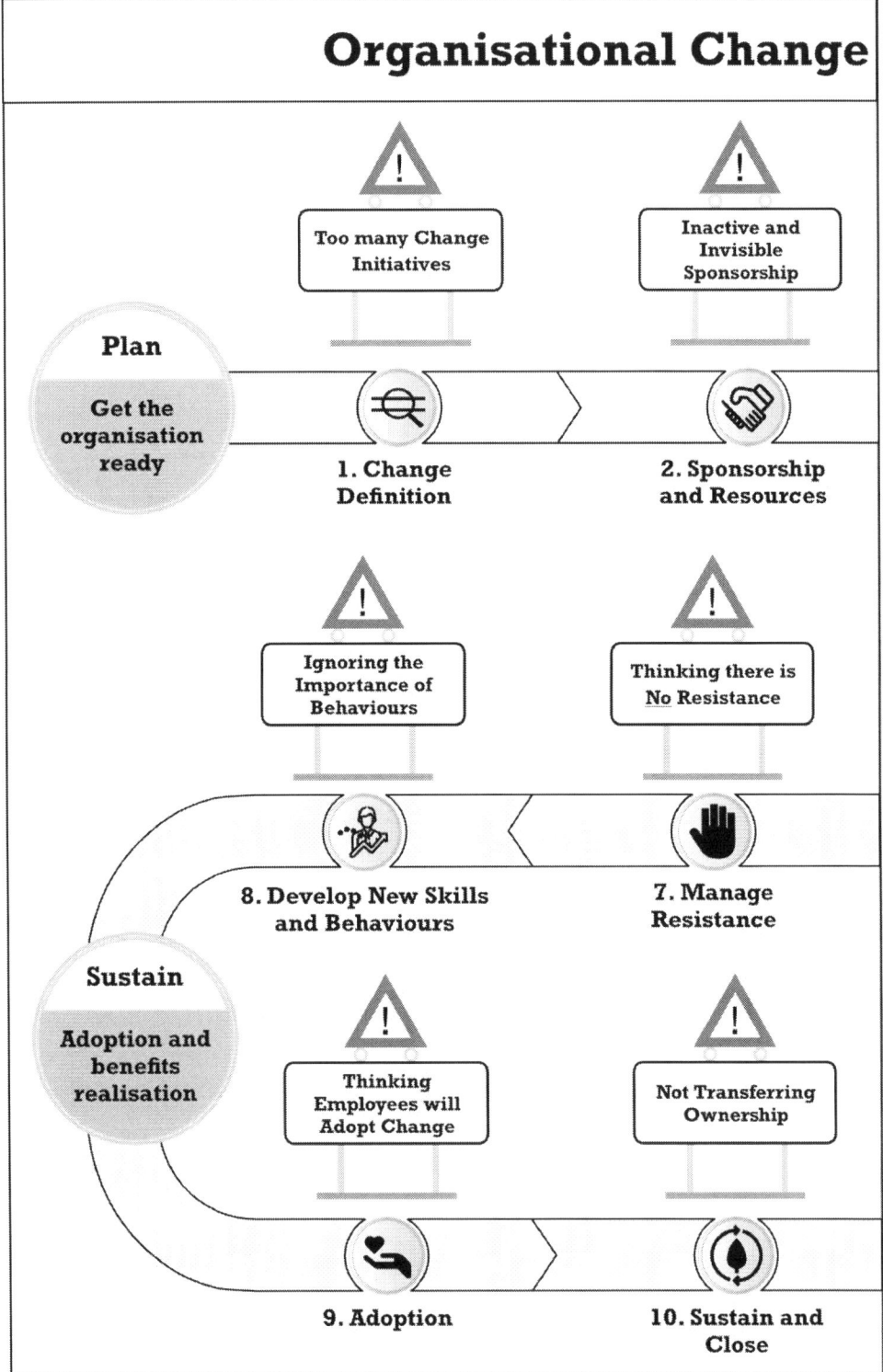

Figure 1.3.1 Organisational Change Management Challenges

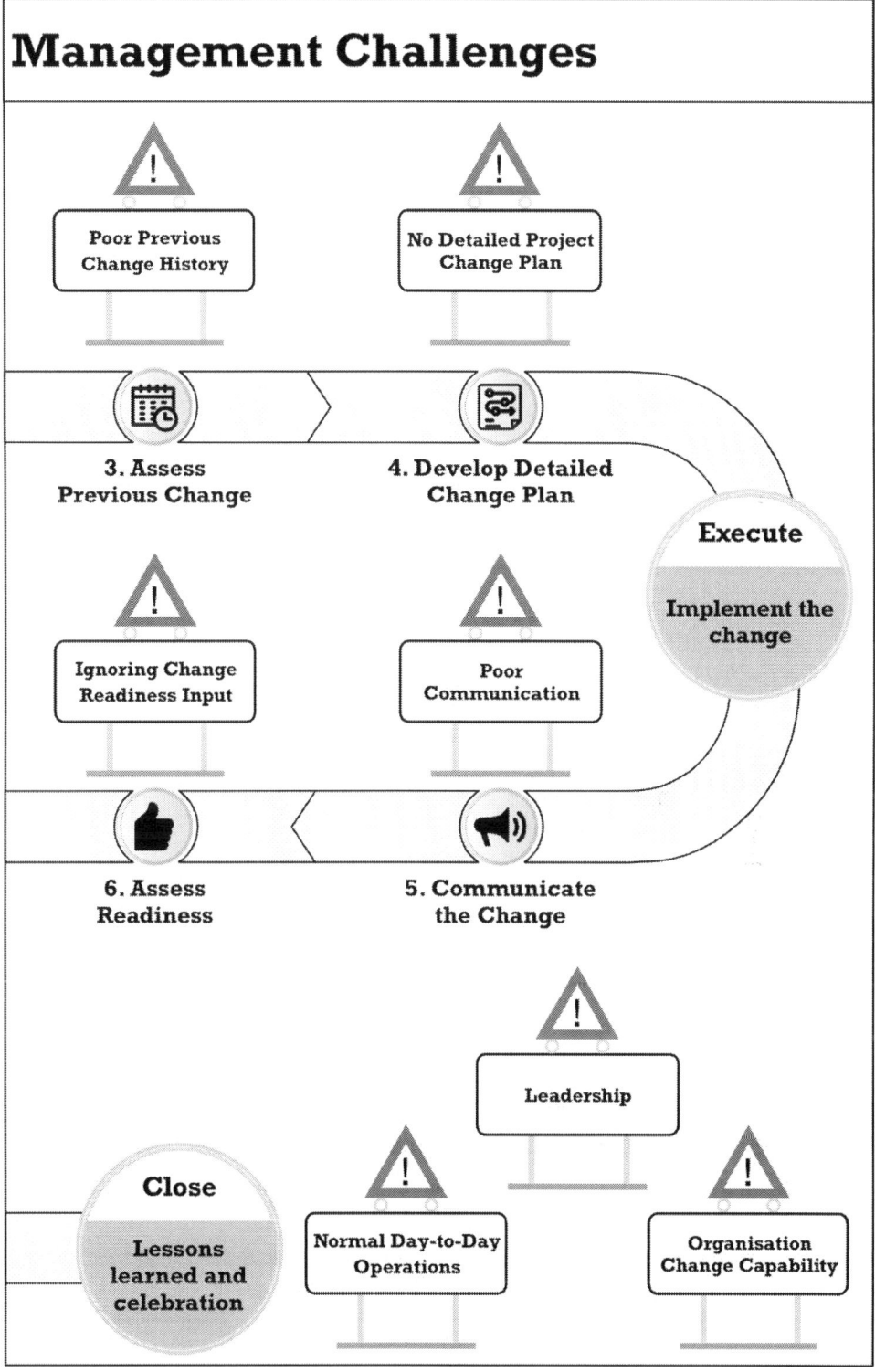

1.4 The Benefits of Change Management

While change and transformation programmes focus on strategy execution to improve organisation performance, shareholders, at a minimum, expect benefits delivery.

Too many organisational change, improvement and transformation programmes fail, which that means that objectives are not achieved and the organisation fails to execute their strategy. These failed approaches do not usually have a planned and systematic approach to preparing, communicating and implementing change into the organisation. The key to effective implementation of change programmes is to develop and deploy structured approaches that will help organisations, leaders, teams and employees understand, accept and work with change, to minimise resistance and disruption. This structured approach supports change adoption and benefits realisation (**Figure 1.4.1**).

The main benefits of using a structured approach to change management are to deliver successful change and meet targets:

- ❖ Time.
- ❖ Budget.
- ❖ Scope.
- ❖ Change Adoption.
- ❖ Improved Business Performance.

Benefits Realisation and Period of Disruption
- ❖ **Unmanaged Change - High Disruption - Low Benefits:** With unmanaged change, the organisation's leaders push the change into the organisation but continue to focus on normal day-to-day operations. This usually results in a long period of disruption to the organisation, negative performance, low benefits realisation and a failure to get a return on investment.

- ❖ **Reactive Change - Medium Disruption - Medium Benefits:** With reactive change, the organisation's leaders push the change into the organisation but keep both a focus on normal day-to-day operations and on the change. They react to poor change implementation progress by moving some of their people onto the change. This usually results in medium disruption, medium benefits realisation and a small improvement in operating performance.

- ❖ **Supported Change - Low Disruption - High Benefits:** With supported change, the organisation's leaders push the change into the organisation, agreeing that the success of this change is important to ensure the organisation's strategy is executed. They understand that today's operations provide revenue for now, but the successful implementation of the change will ensure revenue for tomorrow. So, they allocate some of the best people to lead the change whilst leaving others to focus on operations. This usually results in a shorter period of disruption, higher future performance and benefits realisation, and a return on investment.

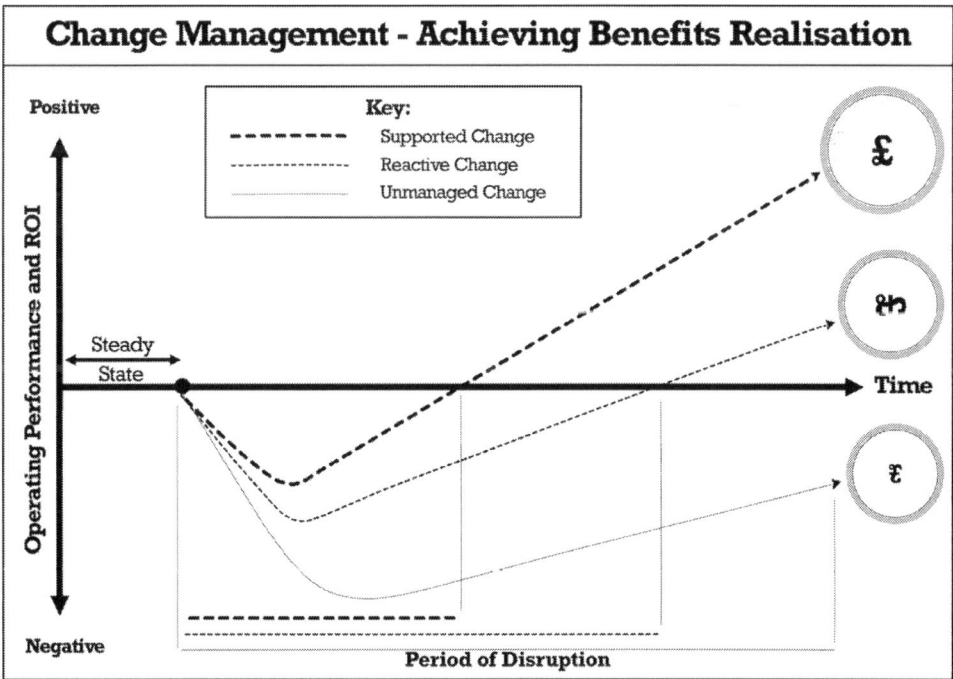

Figure 1.4.1 Change Benefit Realisation

1.5 Organisation Change Capability

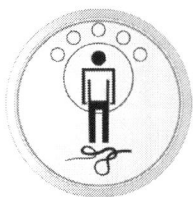

Rapidly changing customer buying habits, access to new technology and social media accelerate the way organisations need to change and build internal change capability so they can quickly adapt to change to remain competitive or even survive.

Organisational change management, transformations and improvements have become permanent features of the business landscape. Until recently, an organisational leader or manager could just focus on normal day-to-day operations, handing off change management and implementation responsibilities to other people.

Corporate thinking about change management has evolved in recent years and it is considered as a core competence by some leading organisations (Prahalad and Hamel, 1990). Varying degrees of change capability, low employee adoption, lack of sustainability and low benefits realisation have become the drivers to develop corporate change capability. There is now a recognition that delivering each change programme or project using the same change methodology and approach is less confusing and more effective for the organisation. An even more effective and efficient way is to have a single approach to change using a corporate change management framework, models, processes, tools and techniques.

Developing internal change capability requires structure and intent. Organisational leaders should develop internal change management capability, a change framework that supports programme change delivery, and models to support employee change adoption and behavioural change (**Figure 1.5.1**). In addition, change capability requires change processes, tools and techniques, competent and motivated resources, and is strengthened by training and coaching to deliver ongoing change.

For the value of this investment to be realised it should be treated like a change programme and, like any change, it must be sustained so the developed capabilities are utilised and there is a return on investment.

Figure 1.5.1 Developing Change Organisation Capability

- **Leadership and Sponsor Commitment:** Change programmes will not be successful without effective and proactive leadership and sponsorship. Specific workshops, masterclasses or coaching can prepare leadership teams to lead change.

- **Change Management Framework and Models:** A change management framework can support structured change delivery. Change models can support employees through the change as well as helping to develop new skills and behaviours.

- **Change Processes, Tools and Techniques:** These can help the change team through the **Plan**, **Execute** and **Sustain** phases, explain concepts, communicate with stakeholders, perform assessments, etc.

- **Competent and Motivated Resources:** Move away from putting 'available' employees onto a change initiative (they are available for a reason). Invest in high potential employees to build competence.

- **Training and Coaching:** These are required to develop the new skills and behaviours so employees can adopt the change. Training and coaching should also be considered for the change team and the change agents as early in the process as possible.

1.6 Change Management Leadership

Leaders go about their daily task of delivering normal day-to-day operations when all of a sudden there is a change explosion. The leadership paradox is implementing organisational change management versus delivering normal day-to-day operations.

Leadership can be defined as the process of influencing others to understand and agree about what needs to be done and how to do it, and the process of facilitating individual and collective efforts to accomplish shared objectives (Yukl, 2012). This is very much the case for leaders when their organisation is implementing a change programme or project. Leaders go about their daily task of implementing the organisation's strategy to deliver financial results, when all of a sudden there is a change explosion that disrupts operations and results. They face the leadership paradox: implementing change versus delivering day-to-day operations. Leaders then need to adjust their focus to implement the change, so that the organisation stays ahead of the competition and continues to deliver revenue to its shareholders. That means the change has to ensure a return on investment (ROI), full employee change adoption, and sustainable change.

The technology revolution shows no sign of slowing, and future leaders will have to be equally skilled at simultaneously leading operations and change implementation. Until recently, an organisational leader or manager could just focus on normal day-to-day operations, handing off change management and implementation responsibilities to other people. Their responsibility was to approve the budget, send an email announcing the programme, and confirm who they had made accountable for delivery. Unfortunately, they kept their best people around them to support day-to-day operations, with the change programme being run by people who were 'available' at the time. No consideration was given to why those people were available, nor to the longer-term missed opportunity of not putting the best people on the organisation's key strategic investment for future success. It is too late to wait until the technology implementation goes live and fails before the leader intervenes. By this point the damage may be done, and the situation may not be recoverable. Even if it is recoverable, there will be delays in implementation, user adoption rates might be lower than planned, and the ROI may never be fully realised. There is also the damage to reputation, employee resistance might have grown, and the success of future change could be tarnished.

The days when a leader could announce a new change programme by email with an attached presentation are numbered. The twenty-plus page PowerPoint presentation may cover the change objectives, timelines, and business case, but it is a one-way communication tool that does not check for employee understanding, nor does it collect feedback.

Organisational change management, transformation, and improvement have become permanent features of the business landscape. The owners and shareholders of organisations are now starting to demand that the leaders they select have both day-to-day operational and change implementation skills. The leader of change needs to go well beyond sending out an email. They need to ensure that the change is aligned with strategy, provide proactive sponsorship, engage and communicate with employees to reduce resistance, support user adoption, and ensure sustainable benefits. It is critical that they engage all levels of the organisation to ensure that both the organisation and the employees have capacity for the change. Change comes so constantly and quickly that if leaders don't focus on properly balancing normal day-to-day operations with change implementation there may be no day-to-day operations tomorrow. Leaders must also get today's changes right.

Leading change can be one of the most difficult burdens of a leader's role, especially when normal day-to-day operations continually throw up urgent activities that must be dealt with. Effective leadership is essential for successful change. Change management will become one of the most important factors of successful leadership and management capabilities (Hayes, 2010). The three leader responsibilities for the successful leadership of change are '**Articulate**', '**Model**' and '**Intervene**' (**Figure 1.6.1**).

Leadership Element 1: 'Articulate'

A critical responsibility for leadership is to articulate the vision for change, explaining how it is aligned to the organisation's strategy, vision, mission and objectives. Leaders should outline why the programme is important to the organisation, why the organisation has chosen this vision for change, the benefits and what the disadvantages are of not implementing this change successfully. The change vision should be articulated in such a way as to motivate and align the organisation. Leadership is a process whereby an individual influences a group of people to achieve a common goal (Northouse, 2015), in this case the common goal is successful change programme implementation.

- ❖ **Resource Balance:** An enabler of realising the change vision will be resourcing the change with competent staff. Leaders cannot be a driving force for change without ensuring this happens. Leaders must ensure that the organisation's resources can achieve the balance between normal day-to-day operations and the change programme. They must avoid a pure focus on the urgent operational activities.

Leadership Element 2: 'Model'

Leaders push change implementation into the organisation, but they must set the standards for new skills and behaviours, visibly role modelling them effectively at all times. Leaders should do what they expect of their employees. The leader who pro-actively role models the new skills and behaviours has earned the moral right to expect others to do the same. When employees see their leaders attending training and modelling the new behaviours, they are much more likely to adopt the same behaviour.

- ❖ **Engage:** The enabler to modelling the new skills and behaviours is for leaders to engage the employees throughout the change. It cannot be done by sending an e-mail or through a social media post. Leaders must continually engage employees with two-way communication. An organisation with low employee engagement is intrinsically change resistant. The more that leaders engage with their employees, the more they will understand and accept the need for the business change. It will also reduce resistance and start the positive process of getting them involved. The ability to engage others with integrity are the qualities that distinguish outstanding leaders (Thomas, 2008).

Leadership Element 3: 'Intervene'

Intervention by leaders is critical to reinforce the new way of working and behaviours to ensure adoption. Leaders must be active and visible, intervening, communicating and reinforcing the change. There should be positive consequences for adopting the new desired behaviours and negative consequences for failing to do so. Intervention and reinforcement are about making adoption of the new behaviours easier, while making it harder to maintain the status quo. Positive reinforcement can include visible rewards, such as promotion, recognition, and bonuses, should they be needed. Negative reinforcement can include sanctions if change success is critical, such as legal compliance or health and safety.

❖ **Ownership:** A key enabler of change is for leaders to proactively take ownership of the change as the programme progresses. Leaders should not be waiting until the change team has completed the implementation before getting involved. Leaders need to be involved right from the start of the change, not waiting until the change team has dissolved and then blaming them for lack of change adoption.

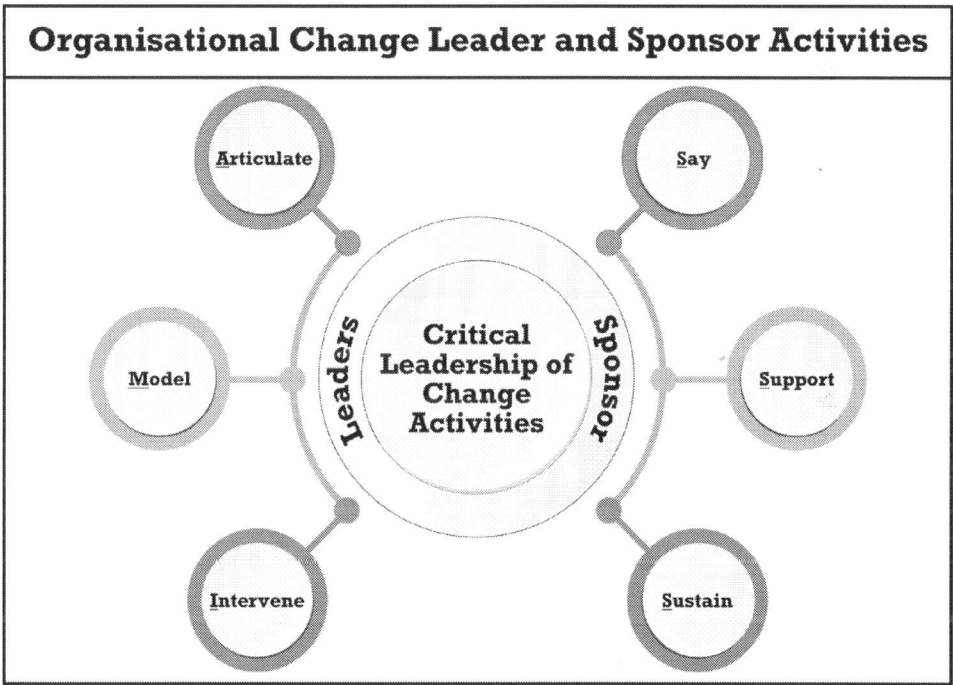

Figure 1.6.1 Change Leader and Sponsor Activities

Leaders need to support the sponsor and the change team, provide resources, and not act negatively against the change. While the leaders of change should exhibit the above three elements ('**Articulate**,' '**Model**' and '**Intervene**'), they face challenges and barriers themselves. Kruger (1996), likens the factors involved in organisational change to an iceberg. When implementing change, many leaders and managers only consider the tip of the iceberg, which focuses on cost, quality, and schedule. However, much more challenging are the perceptions, beliefs, power and politics that lie below the surface. These, and the private competing agendas of leaders, must also be managed in order for change to succeed. Of course, the above three elements are useless if the leader has another agenda that puts him or herself before the change programme. Guidance from Dwight David Eisenhower, the 34th US President would be, *"The supreme quality for leadership is unquestionably integrity. Without it, no real success is possible, no matter whether it is on a section gang, a football field, in an army, or in an office."*

Level 5 Leadership

The concept of Level 5 Leadership was created by J Collins (2001), in his book, 'Good to Great'. As part of his research, he found that leaders with humility, not seeking success for their own glory, understand that success is necessary in order for the team and organisation to thrive. Level 5 leaders share credit for success and they are the first to accept blame for mistakes. Collins also says that level 5 leaders are often shy but fearless when it comes to making decisions, especially ones that most other people consider risky. These are the traits that organisations involved in change implementation would greatly benefit from.

Change Implementation is not 'Just-Do-it'

Some leaders believe that change management implementation requires a just-do-it (JDI) approach. This is a less sophisticated change implementation approach chosen by fixed mindset leaders or managers who think that everyone has the same shared vision of success. '**Tell**' is the default approach for fixed mindset leaders. Winning the hearts and minds of the employees is redundant thinking. The fixed mindset approach does not support the employee through **A**wareness, **U**nderstanding, **I**nvolvement, **L**earning, and **M**otivation, as a way to achieve adoption. The fixed mindset leaders and managers will blame slow adoption or compliance issues on the employees and their limited capability. Rarely will they admit that their JDI approach failed. This approach is short-sighted, and it is likely to be repeated for the next change.

Organisational change management happens in a system. This impacts employees and other parts of the organisation and is much more complex than the JDI approach. Studies from our change history assessment© (CHA©) usually show low scores of change success when this JDI leadership approach is evident in the organisation. This concept is developed in **Section 3.3**. When JDI leaders are presented with low scores for the employee's belief in future change success, they quickly dismiss the scores and insights. This qualitative data and information are seen by a growth mindset leader as an opportunity to learn and grow, but fixed mindset leaders stick to what they know. A good analogy here is that fixed mindset leaders see the change as a simple task of herding sheep into a pen with a sheepdog. Instead, what transpires is more akin to herding cats, which is futile. While we can laugh at that, we cannot laugh at the way that some of the JDI leaders attack people whose thinking is opposed to theirs. They are not part of the rarely blame the employee (RBtE) philosophy. At their very worst, JDI fixed mindset leaders will prevent true change. They will quickly contaminate an organisation by killing growth and creativity, as well as promoting incompetence based on their likeness (Gallagher, 2019A).

The Illusion and Deception of Leadership

While we hope our change programmes are supported by level 5 leadership, the reality can be quite different. While technology and education have improved most of our lives, the same cannot always be said of our choice of leader or their leadership skills. Too often the change team will engage a leader with success delusion, this look is obvious on their face when you enter their office. They think to themselves, *'Who is this plebeian and dullard before me?'* This delusion becomes a liability when they have to change (Goldsmith and Reiter, 2007).

While delivering organisational change or improvements, one cannot be sure whether the main challenge is narcissistic and deluded leaders or the sheep that follow in abundance. A major weakness of narcissists is that they surround themselves with 'yes men' who are no threat but also no good (Maccoby, 2003). Deluded leaders and the 'yes men and women' that follow are barriers to successful organisational change and improvement.

1.7 Incremental Change Versus Transformation

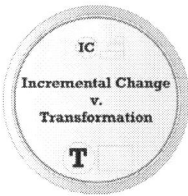

An organisation's ability to survive is determined by its capability to implement incremental change or to transform.

Winston Churchill is credited for the quotation, *"to change is to improve, to improve often is to perfect."* An organisation's ability to survive is determined by its capability to implement incremental change or to transform. The terms 'change' and 'transformation' are used interchangeably, and although both are about improving an organisation's performance they differ in terms of complexity and effort.

The **Leadership of Change**® defines that an organisation can improve performance in one of two ways:

- ❖ **Incremental Change:** Small strategic improvements or adjustments that will improve organisational performance but will not alter the organisation's core.

- ❖ **Transformation:** Fundamental change which takes the organisation in a different direction. This could alter the structure, processes, systems, culture or strategy to improve long-term performance or market position. Transformations are usually driven by the C-Suite as they could include a change to the operating model which would fundamentally alter the way an organisation operates.

It should be noted that these definitions will vary from organisation to organisation, as will the reasons for incremental change or transformation. However, both incremental change and transformations will require change management support in terms of a change framework, models, processes and tools, including internal capability (**Figure 1.7.1**). These two change types are developed further below:

Incremental Change

Small strategic improvements or adjustments might include:

- Continuous or business improvement initiatives to make incremental improvements to manufacturing processes.
- Implementation of new computer systems to increase efficiencies.
- Reorganisation of a department to reduce the head count.
- Outsourcing the marketing department because it is no longer considered a strategic core capability.

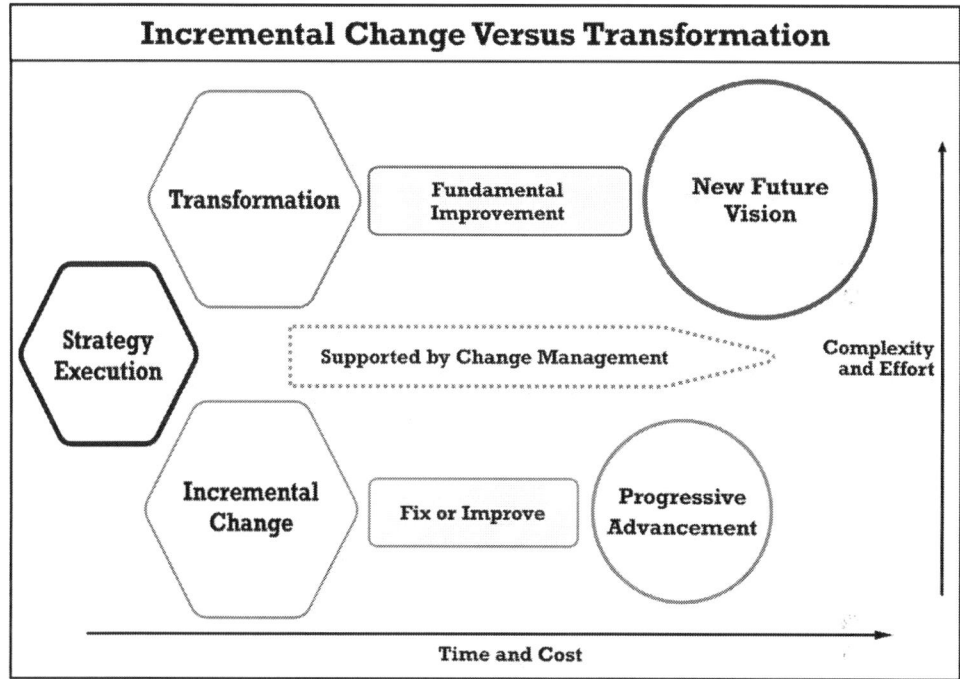

Figure 1.7.1 Incremental Change Versus Transformation

Transformation

Fundamental changes to the organisation might include:

- Digital transformation to integrate digital technology across the organisation.
- The addition or removal of a product or service within the market.
- Altering the distribution model, for example, a manufacturer starts to sell to the customers directly using e-commerce channels.
- A shift in the business culture of an organisation.
- Making the organisation more future-proof to align with technology, competition, consumer trends, etc.

Section 2: a2B Change Management Framework®

2.1 a2B Change Management Framework®

a2B Change Management Framework®

3 main programme delivery phases — 10 steps tailored to suit each client

- 01 Change Definition
- 02 Secure Sponsorship and Resources
- 03 Assess Previous Change
- 04 Develop Detailed Change Plan
- 05 Communicate the Change
- 06 Assess Readiness
- 07 Manage Resistance
- 08 Develop New Skills and Behaviours
- 09 Adoption
- 10 Sustain and Close

Phases: Plan, Execute, Sustain

.ıla2BCMF® Enabling the Leadership of Change

Steps may have iterations — Strategy and leadership alignment

Figure 2.1.1 a2B Change Management Framework®

The **a2B Change Management Framework®** (**a2BCMF®**) is a structured and disciplined approach to support organisations, leadership teams and individuals going through a change, the transition from the current 'a' state to the improved future 'B' state. The **a2BCMF®** (**Figure 2.1.1**) has three phases and ten key process steps. Each phase provides change strategies, principles, analysis and tactics to move from one phase to the next.

The framework is based on over thirty years of international change experience and brings together leading practice in change, people and programme management. The structured programme approach, processes, techniques and tools focus on overcoming the failures of previous change by incorporating ten key steps and success elements for achieving organisational change. It supports strategic change implementation in terms of context, content and process (Pettigrew and Whipp, 1991). The framework is a comprehensive management model that allows executives, managers and change practitioners to successfully deliver and achieve organisational change. It requires a holistic approach and some steps can be performed simultaneously.

Three Phases

Plan: Setting the programme up for success by aligning it with the organisation's strategic portfolio, ensuring there is a business case, sponsorship and resources, as well as a detailed plan for delivery that considers previous organisational change history weaknesses.

Execute: Implementing the change by assessing if the organisation is ready for the change, constantly communicating the change, developing the new skills and behaviours, and managing resistance.

Sustain: Sustaining adoption and ensuring benefits realisation by linking them to the organisation's balanced scorecard (BSC) and each employee's individual performance plan (IPP). This phase also involves the controlled and approved governance closure, transfer of ownership of the programme to operations as well as administrative tasks, such as capturing lessons learned.

Main Benefits

The main benefits of using the **a2B Change Management Framework®** are to deliver successful change and meet targets:

- ❖ Time.
- ❖ Budget.
- ❖ Scope.
- ❖ Change Adoption (***Behaviours***).
- ❖ Improved Business Performance.

2.2 a2B Change Management Framework® Icons

Step 1 - Change Definition: Ensure that the change is properly defined and is aligned to the strategy.

Step 2 - Secure Sponsorship and Resources: Identify the sponsor and other change resources.

Step 3 - Previous Change: Assess previous change to enable future change management success.

Step 4 - Develop Detailed Change Plan: Document the actions, timelines, milestones and resources needed.

Step 5 - Communicate the Change: Simple, repeated communication with a feedback loop.

Step 6 - Assess Readiness: Assess if the organisation and employees are ready for the change.

Step 7 - Manage Resistance: Manage the negative reaction of the organisation or individuals.

Step 8 - Develop New Skills and Behaviours: Ensure the employees can perform their new role.

Step 9 - Adoption: Leave the old ways behind and adopt the new way of working.

Step 10 - Sustain and Close: Governance to formally close the change and ensure sustainment.

2.3. a2B Change Management Framework® Benefits

The change management framework provides an approach for dealing with consistent and specific challenges an organisation encounters when implementing change.

Consistent Challenges Throughout Change Implementation

1. **Normal Day-to-Day Operations:**
    - The **a2BCMF®** continually stresses the balance that is needed between change and normal day-to-day operations.
2. **Leadership:**
    - The **a2BCMF®** continually outlines how leadership support is critical for change success.
3. **Organisation Change Capability:**
    - The **a2BCMF®** and supporting techniques provide organisations with change concepts and guidance on how to use tools, assessments etc.

Specific Challenges Throughout Change Implementation

Each step of the framework focuses on specific challenges faced by organisations when implementing change. This includes change concepts, models, processes, tools and techniques, plans and assessments.

1. **Too Many Change Initiatives:**
    - **a2BCMF® Step 1 - Change Definition:** This step ensures that change initiatives pass through the strategic prioritisation funnel. This guarantees that only approved initiatives, those that the organisation has capacity for, and those that add value, go ahead.
2. **Inactive or Invisible Sponsorship:**
    - **a2BCMF® Step 2 - Secure Sponsorship and Resources:** This step stresses the importance of sponsorship in change success. It also provides insights into other change team resources, including change agents.
3. **Poor Previous Change History:**
    - **a2BCMF® Step 3 - Assess Previous Change:** This step assesses the previous change history of the organisation to mitigate any previous weaknesses in future change.

4. **No Detailed Project Change Plan:**
   ➢ **a2BCMF® Step 4 - Develop Detailed Change Plan:** This step provides guidance on how to prepare a project change plan (PCP) and link it with the wider master project plan.

5. **Poor Communication:**
   ➢ **a2BCMF® Step 5 - Communicate the Change:** This step provides guidance on how to create a change communication plan (CCP) and insights into the importance of communication.

6. **Ignoring Change Readiness Input:**
   ➢ **a2BCMF® Step 6 - Assess Readiness:** This step provides guidance on how to create a change readiness assessment (CRA) and explains why this is critical to achieving sustainable change.

7. **Thinking there is No Resistance:**
   ➢ **a2BCMF® Step 7 - Manage Resistance:** This step outlines three typical employee resistance standpoints to change, reasons for change resistance and actions to reduce resistance.

8. **Ignoring the Importance of Behaviours:**
   ➢ **a2BCMF® Step 8 - Develop New Skills and Behaviours:** This step defines the processes to develop the new skills and behaviours required for the new way of working. This step is supported by both the **a2BDNS© Developing the New Skills Model** and the **a2B5R® Employee Behaviour Change Model**.

9. **Thinking Employees will Adopt the Change:**
   ➢ **a2BCMF® Step 9 - Adoption:** This step outlines the **AUILM® Employee Change Adoption Model** to support employees as they go through the change transition.

10. **Not Transferring Ownership:**
    ➢ **a2BCMF® Step 10 - Sustain and Close:** This step provides detailed processes on how to sustain and close the change programme, including the transfer of ownership in a controlled way with governance approval.

Section 3: Change Delivery

Section 3A: Plan - a2BCMF® Steps 1 - 4

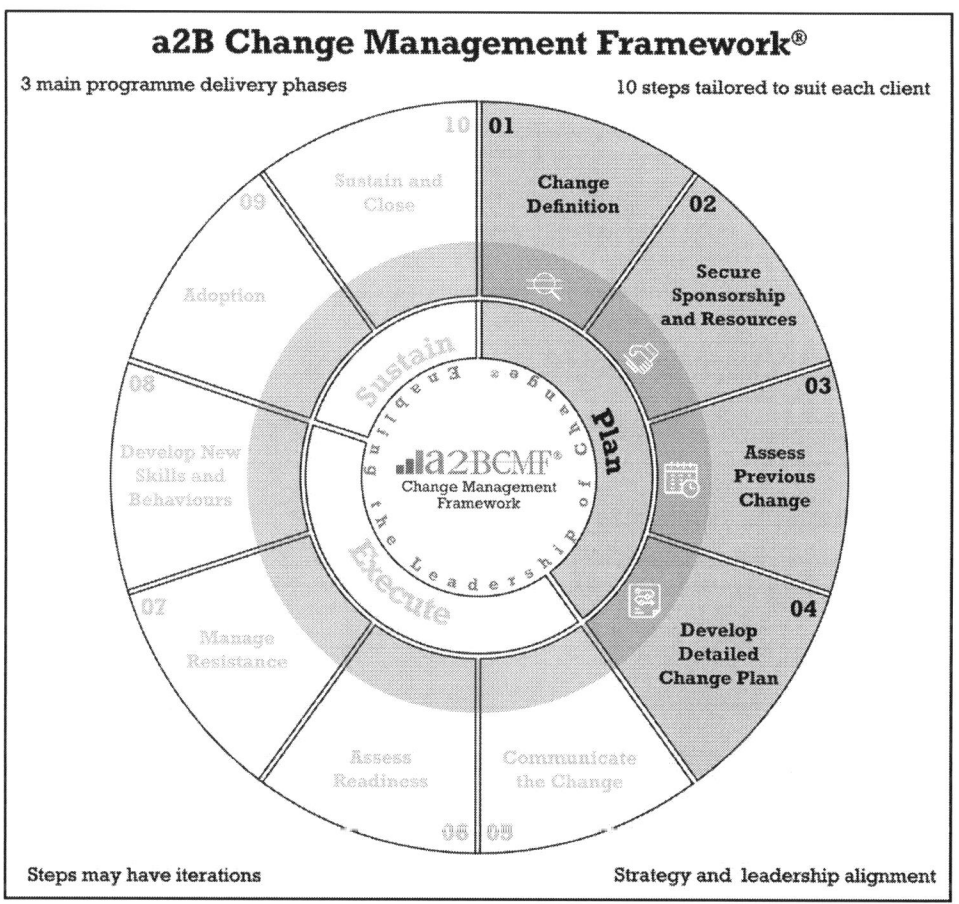

Plan: Setting the change programme up for success.

3.1 Change Definition

Unless the change programme is continually aligned to the organisation's strategy and capacity it will not deliver speedy benefits or value to the organisation.

3.1.1 Change Definition - Overview

Definition: This step is about **Defining the Change** and aligning the change programme within the portfolio to the organisation's strategy. This step ensures there is a business case and resources to deliver value, an understanding of the stakeholder impacts, proper governance and high-level timing and milestones.

Business Benefits: Too many change programmes and transformations fail to deliver the business benefits and value on which they are justified. This step identifies the key foundations that need to be in place to deliver the benefits. This step ensures proper due diligence by assessing estimates of costs, benefits and risks, go/no go decision, etc.

Key Stakeholders and Elements: All key stakeholders are involved in the change. Like risks, stakeholders should be identified, categorised and tracked as they can have either have a positive or negative impact on the outcome of the programme. This **a2BCMF®** step initiates stakeholder identification, analysis and mapping processes that are critical to change programme success.

Business Objective: To assess if the change is aligned with the organisation's strategy, it should have a business case and resources to deliver value, clear stakeholder impacts, proper governance, a high-level timeline and milestones. An important deliverable that could differentiate this change programme from other projects will be benefits planning and tracking.

Enablers and Barriers

Enablers	Barriers
Aligning the change programme with the organisation's strategy so it is prioritised and has resources.	Being perceived as just another change programme or initiative that the organisation has launched.
Early consideration of employee change adoption and understanding how employee behaviours are linked to change success.	Not having a structured approach to support employee change adoption, **AUILM®** or changing behaviours, **a2B5R®**.
Ensuring the change programme has passed through the strategic portfolio prioritisation funnel (due diligence).	The change programme has been launched without any assessment criteria or comparison to other initiatives.
Understanding the organisation's change capacity and if this change programme is the best use of available capacity.	Not assessing the organisation's capacity for change in terms of normal day-to-day operations and mandatory change.
Developing a business case for the change with defined cost benefits.	Ignoring alternative solutions, risks and business operational impacts.
A roadmap that communicates the high-level change plan and deliverables.	Inability to communicate the high-level plan with key stakeholders.
Taking the time to create a benefits plan and tracker (BPT) that is linked to the **Execute** and **Sustain** phases.	Expecting to compete against other initiatives without having quantified benefits.
Having a change elevator speech that communicates the change succinctly and quickly, gaining change support.	Failing to communicate a change message which allows rumours to flourish and resistance to grow.
Understanding that stakeholder analysis and mapping is critical to manage potential stakeholder resistance.	Thinking that stakeholder analysis and mapping is an unnecessary luxury.
Governance, providing effective oversight throughout the life cycle.	Thinking the sponsor and leadership will ensure the change is delivered.

3.1.2 Case Study - Fish Food Versus Safety Strategy

An international energy organisation was rolling out a global portfolio of ten critical transformation programmes. Four of these critical programmes were related to health and safety. This was slightly before the Deepwater Horizon drilling rig explosion in April 2010, which resulted in eleven fatalities.

Priority was given to projects aligned with the four safety transformation programmes. Our team supported these globally, with a focus on implementing safety improvements at the processing plant locations onshore and offshore. The general objective was to instil a culture of safety across the organisation and reduce fatalities.]

On a processing plant, supervisors perform a vital role in operations and are key to safety leadership and performance. They are responsible for multimillion-pound operations and many people on-site. While they are responsible for the technical aspects of running the plant, their focus needs to be on the safety and leadership of people. They have to be a visible presence on the processing plant. Previous health and safety incident investigation findings and other improvement project analysis indicated that actual time spent by supervisors on the processing plant was limited. Our investigations suggested that both supervisors and managers worked long hours but were mainly involved in administrative tasks. While other safety improvements had reduced the number of fatalities, the processing plants were still not achieving the zero-target defined by the four critical transformation programmes. As a result, I became involved in the supervisor time improvement project.

It was early morning, and as I drove up the access road I could see the large, sturdy security fence separating me from the processing plant on my right. For obvious security reasons, access to the plant was more complex than entry to a typical workplace. First, I had to announce myself using the intercom to speak to the security guard, and they in turn checked that I was an authorised visitor before granting me access through the turnstile.

The security guard greeted me and checked me in. He pointed at the safety sign and asked me to give him anything that was listed. I handed over my electronic car key and mobile phone and was given a security badge.

"Peter, I've called your sponsor. Please take a seat until he arrives. You must have an escort at all times."

A few minutes later, James, the plant manager, entered the security cabin from the plant side.

"Hello, Peter. Good to see you again. How are the transformation programmes going?"

"Hi James. We're making steady progress on change and business improvement, especially across this asset. However, we are still killing people who work for us, either as a contractor or as an employee, and that is why I'm here for the next few days."

We walked to James's office via the main office block, through the clean and tidy corridors, and past the company transformation posters and other current information. Standard procedure for new visitors and the first task on-site was to watch the site induction video and answer the questionnaire, but as I'd visited the plant before this was not necessary. We sat down in James's office to finalise the project approach and the plan we'd begun a few weeks earlier.

Over the next working day we would use a lean technique called 'Day In the Life Of' (DILO). The DILO study would provide insights into the operational tasks that add value in day-to-day work and highlight those that do not. Simply put, it offers insights into a standard working day. It provides an independent eye and, if properly conducted, it can provide fantastic insights into what really happens in the workplace, as opposed to in the job description.

I was to be the observer, objectively watching work activities, and I would ask questions to ascertain why certain activities were performed. It is critically important that the observer makes no judgement or criticises what they see. We rarely blame the employee (RBtE), as it could be any of us in the same position. Typically, a DILO is started first thing in the morning but due to logistics this one would start slightly later.

We made the decision to apply the DILO study to a selected supervisor, shadowing them for a full shift and recording all tasks and activities. James introduced me to the selected supervisor and left to get on with managing the plant. The supervisor's name was Lucy. My role was to quickly put Lucy at ease about the process and thank her for agreeing to be part of the exercise. Part of my task was to quickly build a rapport and make Lucy feel at ease. I explained that I was not there to judge or criticise, but to identify activities or tasks that she should not be doing. I concluded that the key objective was to remove tasks that prevented supervisors in critical safety roles from performing their role, so their main time was focused on people, safety, and efficient plant operations. I shared the data record sheet with Lucy and explained that she would approve all the data and comments captured over the next full working day. We agreed that we would start the DILO right after the morning tea break.

After the 11:00 break we began, and Lucy's first task was to review and expedite invoices. Between inspecting the invoices on the system, phoning people to progress matters, and checking the spreadsheet, this activity took thirty minutes. I noted the detailed activities on the DILO record sheet, along with my comments.

At 11:30 Lucy walked up the stairs to meet the maintenance team to get feedback from the morning meeting and updates on progress. Twenty minutes later, we walked to the canteen to have a short lunch. After a quick walk back to the office, the next ninety minutes was spent progressing emails, invoices, and answering queries, both over the phone and in the office. We also walked over to the store to have a discussion with the storeman about a critical part and the recruitment of a new buyer.

At 14:00 Lucy returned to her office to further respond to emails and voice messages. At 14:48 Lucy went out to inspect the site, but with the next meeting booked in for 15:00 it was a very short inspection and we arrived two minutes late to meet with two pipe inspectors. Fifteen minutes later, we walked over to get a coffee and then returned to Lucy's office. This took less than seven minutes. The rest of the afternoon was spent making headway on maintenance issues, a small number of invoices, and answering queries directly from the main on-site maintenance contractor.

At 16:15 Lucy and I walked over to James's office and we debriefed him on progress to date. At this point, I did not dare to make any conclusions or judgements, but what stuck in my head was that in over five hours we had only been on the processing plant for fourteen minutes. Three observations resonated in my mind during the debriefing. Firstly, we had only been on the plant a very short period of the working afternoon, but I would have expected to see greater safety focus, especially when our four latest safety transformation programmes were well into the execution phase. Secondly, walking around the plant perimeter itself would have taken in excess of thirty minutes, and that would not have included any of the processing areas where critical maintenance takes place. Thirdly, based on the body language and conversation, this was nothing out of the ordinary for this site. We concluded the debrief and agreed to meet in Lucy's office the next morning at 07:30.

Lucy signed me in the next morning and we went directly to her office to put on our Personal Protective Equipment (PPE). I asked whether she was still comfortable with the process we were following, she said she was. At 07:45 Lucy logged on to her computer and started to review emails that had accumulated since the night before. Just before 08:00 we walked up the stairs to join the wider maintenance team for the morning meeting. The meeting covered the main highlights for the day and was completed in less than ten minutes.

Over the next two and a half hours there was a period of ten or more interruptions as Lucy tried to answer emails, log on to various systems to expedite tasks, or provide approvals. While trying to reply to one of the more complex emails, there were three phone calls and two interruptions from contractors. There also seemed to be a constant stream of both employees and contractors knocking on the office door with queries or requests for help. Lucy was further disturbed by the constant ringing of the phone. On several occasions Lucy had to leave the office, the first time to go to the permit office to countersign a work permit and the next to the inspector's office to get a signature. As well as dealing with all this, Lucy also attended the 09:00 production meeting.

It was coming up to 11:00 and there was a slight lull in activities, so we quickly took the opportunity to grab a cup of coffee. We arrived back at the office and sat in our chairs for a brief moment to rest and reflect.

Great, I thought. Now is the chance to go out to the processing plant to check on critical maintenance activities, review workplace safety, speak with the maintenance crews, and review some of the work permits.

Lucy raised her finger to her head (a light bulb moment). She pulled the keyboard closer to her, logged on to SAP, and then on to the procurement system. As usual, I observed and asked questions so I could record the details on to the DILO record sheet.

"Lucy, which procurement order are you checking?"

"Peter, I'm not checking an order. I need to raise an urgent and important order for the plant and then we can try and take a walk across to the processing area to assess safety and maintenance progress." I continued to record my notes and watched the monitor.

"OK. What is the urgent order for?" I asked.

"Fish food," Lucy replied. I was surprised by her response and it was at this moment that I had to remind myself of the little DILO rule, 'Do not judge or criticise'.

I maintained my poker face as I asked,

"Why is the fish food order so urgent and important?" Lucy continued to type into the required fields.

"The role of the person who used to place this order back at the central office was made redundant, as part of a cost-cutting initiative last year. As a result, it seems to be me who is responsible for performing this task, or it will not get done."

Hoping to drill down and find out more, I asked my second 'why'.

"But why do we need fish food in a gas processing plant?"

"Peter, we need fish food for the fish in the pond beside the processing plant" she responded, as if it was a natural requirement.

I asked my third 'why'.

"Why do we have a pond in the processing plant?"

Lucy again answered quickly, in a matter-of-fact way,

"The pond plays a very important safety role within the plant, as it is used to supply water in on-site emergency situations to the fire service. We need to have a large independent source of water, should there ever be a fire on-site that could risk people, the plant, or the gas supply to the National Grid."

A great snippet of information, I thought to myself.

I continued to drill down further and asked my fourth 'why'.

"I understand why you need a pond in case there is a fire, but why are there fish in the pond?"

Lucy again answered quickly,

"Peter, the fish eat the algae and help to keep the water in good condition."

I knew I was getting closer to the reason for the fish food, so hoped the fifth 'why' (5 Whys) would give me the answer I needed.

"Lucy, sorry. I think this is my last question. Why do we need the fish to eat the algae?"

Lucy patiently responded.

"Well, without the fish eating the algae, the algae would get into the water pipes and block the fire hoses. I can't think of anything worse in terms of employee health and safety than having a fire on an oil and gas plant and not being able to use our water supply. Can you imagine the damage to life and to our assets if we had a fire, followed by explosions, with no way of controlling it?"

Wow. She had a great point, and I thought about a fire taking hold of a processing plant without access to water. The dilemma for Lucy was balancing her time between being on-site, to ensure safe and normal operations, against doing additional tasks that should have been done by someone else, such as ensuring the plant had an independent water supply for the fire service, should there be an emergency situation on-site. We continued with the DILO up until lunchtime to ensure that we had a completed a full working day with enough data to provide good analysis.

Over the next few weeks, we presented our findings, including the solution developed to support the supervisors to get more time on-site in the processing area. The solution was about implementing a structured day for the supervisor, with allocated times to be on-site and at key meetings. Tasks like writing purchase orders for fish food would be reallocated to the on-site procurement team, who were given extra budget and resources to manage the tasks that were previously completed by the central office. There would be uninterrupted time for emails, phone calls, and the approval of work permits and contracts. The supervisor would be available for two open-door sessions per day, for anyone on-site who had non-urgent queries or needed support. Obviously urgent queries would receive priority, especially for safety-critical issues. The solution was presented to the plant managers and management team to gain their buy-in, input, and approval. A pilot solution was then launched with Lucy and, once proven, was rolled out to other supervisory functions and to other processing plants.

Case Study - Insights:

- ❖ **Organisation Change Capacity:** An organisation only has so much capacity for change while normal day-to-day operations continue. Pushing ten different transformation programmes into the organisation will limit successful change implementation.

- ❖ **Individual Capacity:** Employee workload and capacity for change should also be a big consideration. If new and additional work is created by the change, then leaders need to remove some of employee's original workload to enable them to have enough capacity for new activities.

3.1.3 The Importance of Change Definition

Defining the change is about aligning the change programme within the portfolio to the organisation's strategy, ensuring it has a business case and resources to deliver value, there is an understanding of the stakeholder impacts, proper governance and a high-level timeline and milestones. It is extremely important that the change is aligned to the organisation's strategy and is part of the strategic portfolio. At the very least, the benefits should clearly be identified. Equally important is the organisation's and the employee's capacity to deliver the change programme while delivering normal day-to-operations.

This is the point where the change leaders start to engage employees and the other key stakeholders and begin to make them aware of the change. They should listen to the employees and remove obstacles to enable them to understand, and hopefully become involved in the change. As a business leader, they should also check that the change programme or project is aligned to the organisation's strategy, the business case is solid, the risks have been assessed, the benefits are clear, the roadmap is logical and challenges, such as behavioural change or culture, have been considered.

Figure 3.1.1 Aligning Strategy and Change

3.1.4 Strategy Alignment

An organisation's strategy is a result of the strategic planning cycle, where the mission and vision are translated into a strategic plan within the restrictions of organisational values. Organisations build a strategy to define how their vision will be achieved. The strategic plan is subdivided into a set of organisational initiatives (**Figure 3.1.1**). These are influenced in part by customers, disruptive technology, strategic partners, market dynamics and shareholder requests, as well as government regulations and the plans and actions of competitors. These initiatives should be grouped within the organisation's strategic portfolio, containing the many programmes and projects which will be executed in the future, once authorised.

The goal of linking portfolio management to the organisational strategy is to establish a balance between change programmes and normal day-to-day operations outlined in the operating plan. According to Lester Thurow, *"A competitive world offers two possibilities. You can lose. Or, if you want to win, you can change"* (Steers, et al., 2013). Having too much change could inhibit the organisation from achieving its wider goal. Failing to achieve the resource balance could impact both efforts to successfully execute change programmes and normal operations.

3.1.5 Strategic Portfolio Prioritisation Funnel

Portfolio management is a coordinated collection of strategic processes and decisions that together enable the most effective balance of organisational programmes and projects. Organisations that do this effectively achieve the right balance between normal day-to-day operations and organisational change. In getting this capacity balance right, the organisation will usually deliver both the annual operating plan and the strategic portfolio.

Portfolio management includes the selection, prioritisation and control of programmes and projects which are aligned with the organisation's strategy and objectives. The person responsible for portfolio management should ensure the organisation's leadership team decides which programmes and projects to execute and resource. Execution is the key to a strategy's success and is as flawed as it is popular (Martin, 2010). The objective is to align the right programmes and projects with an organisation's business strategy to achieve a compelling competitive advantage (Moore, 2010). The selection of the programmes and projects to be executed should follow predefined organisational assessment criteria (**Figure 3.1.2**). Typical assessment criteria include:

- ❖ **Revenue Potential:** What are the potential future profits and benefits?
- ❖ **Investment Requirements:** How much capital is required?
- ❖ **Strategic Fit:** Does this opportunity fit with the organisation's current strategy?
- ❖ **Implementation Effort:** How much effort will this opportunity need, and do we have capacity to execute it?

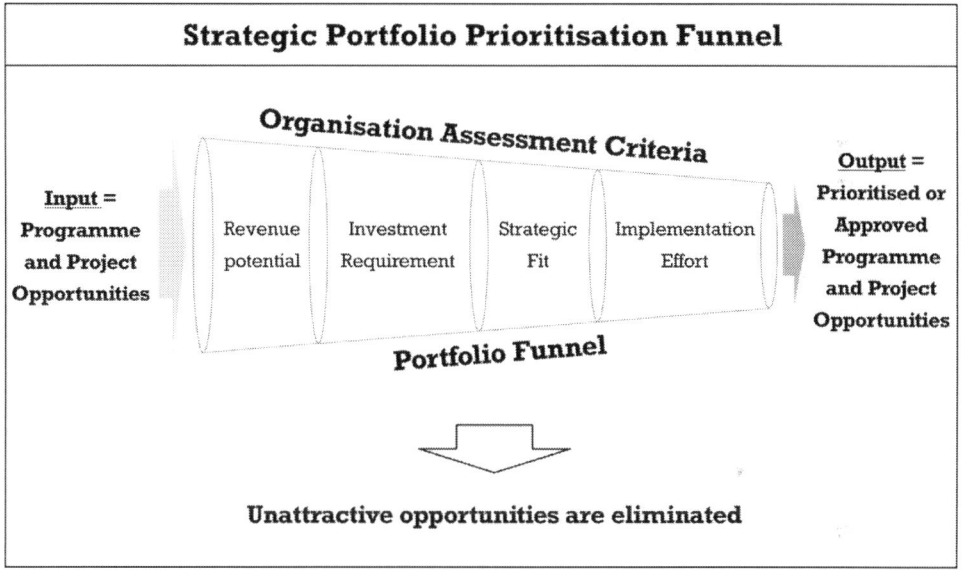

Figure 3.1.2 Strategic Portfolio Prioritisation Funnel

It is important that the change sponsor and team ensure that their change programme or project is clearly aligned to the organisation's strategy. If it is not and other programmes or projects are better aligned, they will tend to get more support within the organisation. They will get the critical resources, time and energy of the business leaders and will have more chance of success. Even if the team believes that they have secured the critical resources and support to launch the change, this will become more challenging as the change progresses through each **a2B Change Management Framework®** step. The complaint about how much time it takes to perform an effective strategic portfolio prioritisation funnel exercise will quickly be surpassed by a change programme or project being abandoned mid-cycle.

3.1.6 Organisation Change Capacity and Workload

An organisation's capacity can be defined as the organisation's total workload for delivering normal day-to-day operations and change activities. If the organisation does not have change capacity it is unlikely the employees will be able to take on any extra workload. Getting this balance right can mean the difference between successfully delivering both, however the data from the change history assessment© (CHA©) constantly highlights this as a challenge (**see Section 3.3.5**). The feedback from employees is that their workload is not considered when the organisation is implementing change. Specific feedback indicates that workload is not taken into account when learning new software, technology, systems, methods or processes. This change overload (Harrington and Voehl, 2014) not only causes workforce stress but also creates resistance to the change that would otherwise have been accepted.

Capacity and workload are serious considerations. Not only should the organisation have a strategic planning process, the output in terms of available capacity should be an important input factor to change sponsors and their teams when planning their change programmes. So, how much capacity should an organisation have for change as it delivers normal day-to-day operations? There are typically four key organisational capacity components (**Figure 3.1.3**):

- ❖ **Normal Day-to-Day Operations:** Normal business operations are the activities that a business and its employees engage in on a daily basis for the purposes of generating a profit. They are permanent endeavours that produce repetitive outputs, as opposed to change programmes or projects which are usually temporary endeavours.

- ❖ **Unplanned Work or Rework:** No matter how good an organisation's planning process is, new or unplanned work will enter the organisation. In some cases, it may have to be prioritised. Worse still, scrap or rework are often overlooked, unmeasured or even denied, but they can take up quite a lot of time.

- ❖ **Mandatory Change Capacity:** This type of change is a mandatory requirement that the organisation must complete. This could be to meet legal requirements such as a government law, financial reporting, health and safety requirements or European Union (EU) regulations, such as General Data Protection Regulation (GDPR).

❖ **Strategic Change Capacity:** This is optional change the organisation can select to do. Most organisations prioritise normal operations and any capacity left after unplanned work or mandatory change is available for change or improvement programmes and projects.

The percentage splits of the four key organisational capacity components will vary from organisation to organisation and from year to year. The important concept is that organisation and change professionals might live in a world where they see their change programme or project as the most important thing. In reality however, their change programme is only small in comparison to normal day-to-day operations. Another important consideration is that the organisation's leaders tend to think that successful change implementation will not take much effort and because it is important everyone will support delivery. Good-to-great companies don't just focus on what to do to become great, but also what not to do, and what to stop doing (Collins, 2001). It is important to have the discipline to only start the change programmes or projects that will drive the organisation's economic engine.

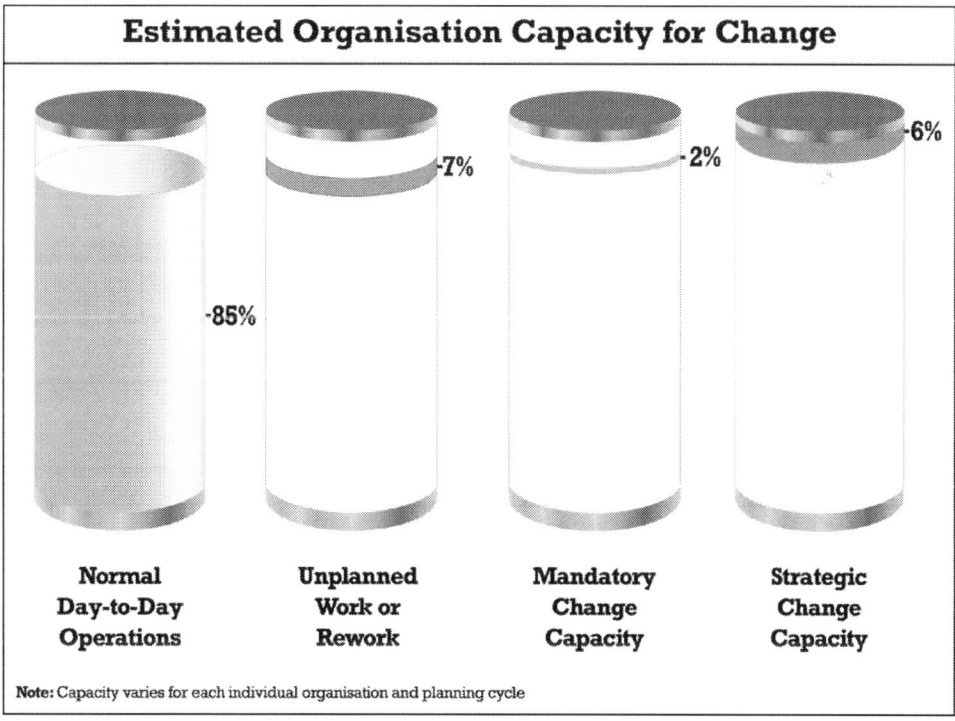

Figure 3.1.3 Organisation Change Capacity

3.1.7 Business Case

The business case is developed to assess the change programme's balance between costs and benefits. The business case may either be basic and high-level or detailed and comprehensive. The business case includes key parameters used to assess the objectives and constraints for the intended change programme. The business case may include details about problems or opportunities; business and operational impacts, cost benefit analysis; alternative solutions and risks. The business case establishes the authority, intent and philosophy of the business need. It also serves as a formal declaration of the value that the programme is expected to deliver and a justification for the resources that will be expended to deliver it. The four typical components of the business case are (**Figure 3.1.4**):

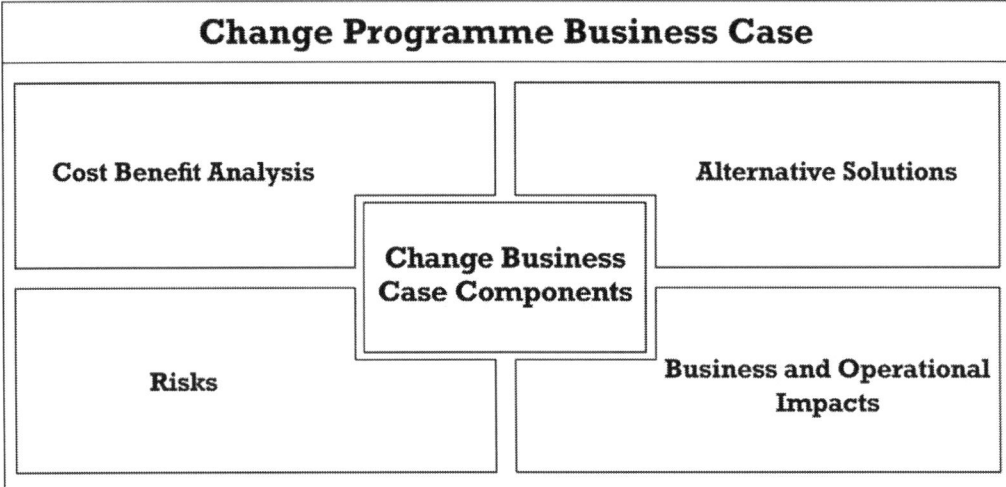

Figure 3.1.4 Change Programme Business Case

* **Cost Benefit Analysis:** A technique used to compare the total costs of the change programme against its benefits, using common metrics (monetary units, market share, etc.). Change programme decisions are based on whether there is a net benefit or cost to the approach, i.e. total benefits minus total costs.
* **Alternative Solutions:** Assessing other possible courses of action, solutions or change programmes. It is about asking an independent and challenging question, 'Are there alternatives and have they been investigated?'
* **Risks:** The probability of occurrence of a specific event that affects the pursuit of change objectives. Risks are not negative by definition. Risks are potential external events that could have a negative impact

(although not always) on the change programme if they occur. Risk also refers to the combined likelihood of the event occurring and the impact on the change programme if the event does occur.

- ❖ **Business and Operational Impacts:** This relates back to organisational change capacity. The analysis of business and operational impacts could provide invaluable insights to the sponsor and change team. It is about performing a systematic process to determine and evaluate the potential impacts on normal day-to-day operations.

The business case may contain other relevant documents such as the programme charter, but this varies from organisation to organisation. The programme charter is a short document formally issued by the organisation which describes the change programme in its entirety. It provides the programme sponsor with the authority to apply organisational resources, it will also contain the objectives and constraints, solution direction, identified stakeholders, risks, statements about scope, etc.

3.1.8 Change Roadmap - Guide

The change roadmap is a graphical time order representation of the programme's intended direction and a set of documented success criteria for each of the scheduled events. It should depict the relationship between programme activities and expected benefits. It should outline the key dependencies between major milestones and communicate the linkage between the business strategy and the key activities of the change approach. The tool depicts the ten **a2BCMF®** steps and presents other information such as the:

- ❖ Strategy Statement.
- ❖ Change Objectives.
- ❖ Challenges or Risks.
- ❖ Programme Infrastructure.

The roadmap should be used as soon as it is approved, and when engaging the various stakeholder groups. When used in conjunction with the elevator speech, it becomes a powerful tool to gain buy-in and support for the change programme, while simultaneously reducing resistance of those impacted by the change.

Benefits: The roadmap will help to quickly communicate the high-level change plan, benefits and goals, manage stakeholder expectations and generate a shared understanding across the teams involved. It provides valuable input to help develop the detailed change and communication plans.

Creation Steps: The change roadmap (**Roadmap 3.1.6 Change Roadmap**) should not be created in isolation. The suggested creation steps are:

1. Assemble a diverse team with relevant experience.
2. Allocate roles and agree the objectives of the roadmap.
3. Recreate a draft outline of **Template 3.1.5** to work on.
4. For each of the **a2BCMF®** steps define the; 'deliverables', 'assumptions', 'benefits', 'start date' and 'finish date'. The dates may be estimates at this stage and will become more accurate during **a2BCMF® Step 4 - Develop Detailed Change Plan**.
5. Review the completed **Template 3.1.5 - Roadmap Input Data**.
6. Recreate a draft outline of **Roadmap 3.1.6** as a template to work on.
7. Brainstorm, filter and rank the key ideas.
8. Insert the 'deliverables', 'assumptions' and 'benefits' for each of the **a2BCMF® Roadmap** steps captured in **Template 3.1.5**.
9. Develop the 'timeline' and key 'milestones' for each step.
10. Add other supporting information such as the 'strategy statement', 'change objectives', 'challenges and risks' and the 'programme infrastructure'.
11. Prepare a first draft roadmap, review and improve.
12. Test with a wide range of selected stakeholders and collect feedback.
13. Refine, rehearse and present.
14. Align and link with all change communications.
15. Use as input into the detailed project change and communications plans.

Change Roadmap - Insights:

❖ The roadmap appeals to all stakeholders as it provides a quick visual display of the change programme and helps gain change support.

❖ The roadmap should be updated regularly throughout the change programme, and openly displayed and shared with all stakeholders.

Template 3.1.5 - Roadmap Input Data

#	a2BCMF® Steps	Deliverables	Assumptions	Benefits	Start Date	Finish Date
1	Change Definition					
2	Sponsorship and Resources					
3	Assess Previous Change					
4	Develop Detailed Change Plan					
5	Communicate the Change					
6	Assess Readiness					
7	Manage Resistance					
8	Develop New Skills and Behaviours					
9	Adoption					
10	Sustain and Close					

Template 3.1.5 Roadmap Input Data

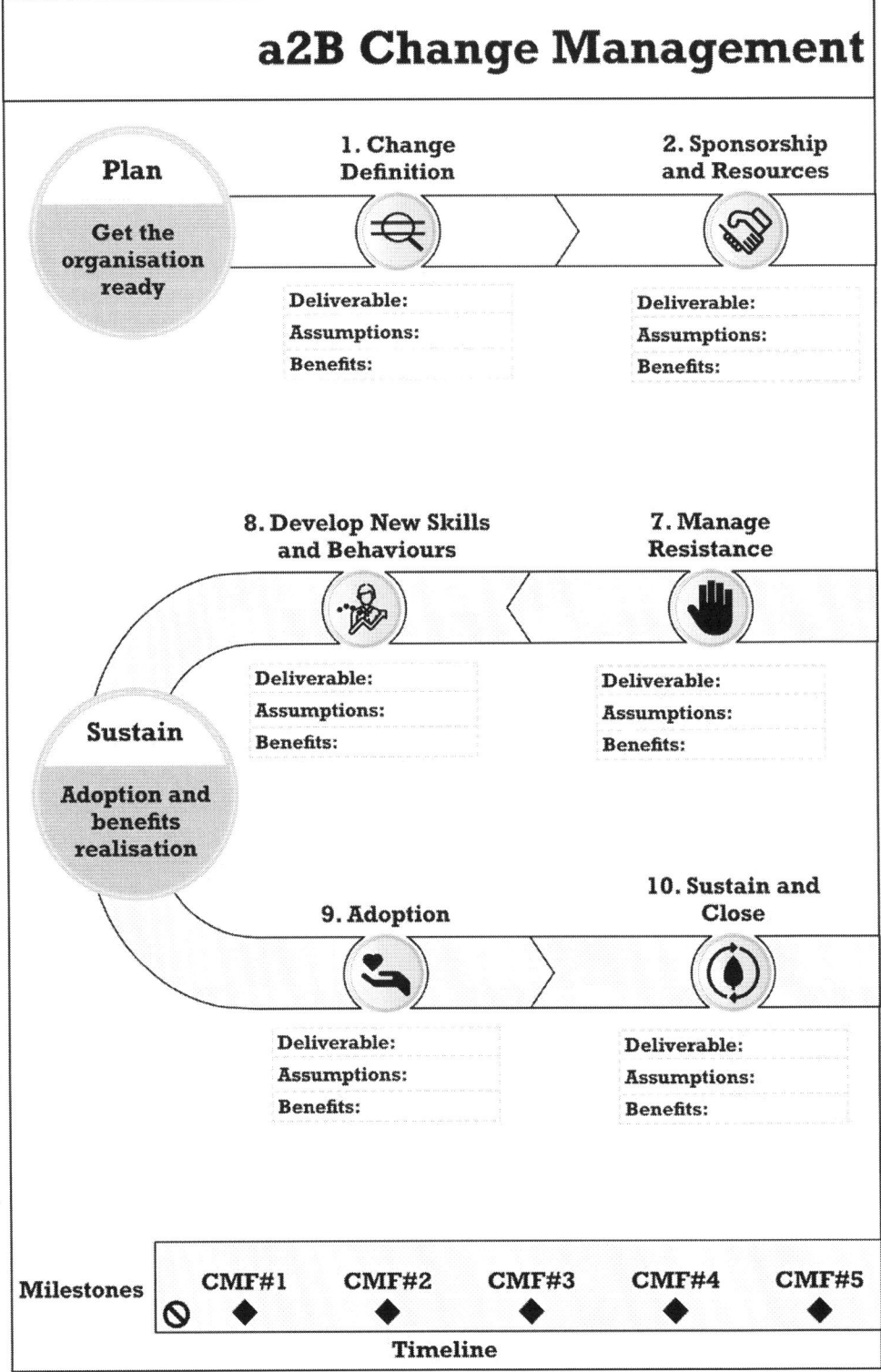

Roadmap 3.1.6 Change Roadmap

a2BCMF® Step 1 - Change Definition

Framework® Roadmap

3. Assess Previous Change

Deliverable:
Assumptions:
Benefits:

4. Develop Detailed Change Plan

Deliverable:
Assumptions:
Benefits:

Execute

Implement the change

6. Assess Readiness

Deliverable:
Assumptions:
Benefits:

5. Communicate the Change

Deliverable:
Assumptions:
Benefits:

Close

Lessons learned and celebration

Change Programme Key Elements

Strategy Statement: _____

Change Objectives: _____

Challenges and Risks: _____

Programme Infrastructure: _____

Key

🚫 Start   ◎ Close

◆ Milestone   **a2BCMF®#** = Change Management Framework Step®

| CMF#6 | CMF#7 | CMF#8 | CMF#9 | CMF#10 |
| ◆ | ◆ | ◆ | ◆ | ◆ |

Timeline

3.1.9 Benefits Plan and Tracker - Guide

The reason that organisations have change programmes and invest time, resources, money and effort is to realise benefits and add value to the organisation. Benefits realisation is an integral part of change management but is often overlooked or becomes less of a priority when the change team is distracted by the other urgent activities of delivering the change. Each organisation will have its own inherent processes for benefits realisation and in some change programmes a finance professional may join the team and have accountability for this activity. Whatever the process, the objective is to successfully deliver quantifiable and meaningful business benefits to the organisation. Benefits realisation includes the following processes:

- ❖ **Identification:** Identify and qualify the business benefits or value to the organisation. Identification should start at the portfolio level and be developed through the completion of the business case.

- ❖ **Analysis and Planning:** This stage will normally require input from other functions within the organisation, and the analysis and planning can become very detailed depending on the value of the change programme. This will probably include establishing measures or metrics, a baseline and schedule, as well as potential and associated risks.

- ❖ **Delivery:** Depending on the type of change programme, the benefits can start to happen during the **Execute** phase or after the change is implemented and the programme closes. Either way, there should be a benefits delivery schedule to track estimated savings against actual savings.

- ❖ **Sustainment:** One of the biggest challenges of any change programme is how the benefits will be sustained long after the team has moved on. Three key elements of **Sustain** are:
  - ➢ **Benefits Delivery Transition and Sustainment:** Establishing a responsible party after the change team has dissolved.
  - ➢ **Balanced Scorecard (BSC):** Linking the change benefits realisation to specific organisation performance measures.
  - ➢ **Individual Performance Plan (IPP):** The IPP can be used as means to support change success by aligning employee

performance to benefits realisation. This is covered in more detail in **a2BCMF® Step 10 - Sustain and Close.**
- ➢ **Adoption:** Without full employee adoption of the new way of working it is unlikely the change will realise the benefits targeted in this step. This is also covered in more detail in **a2BCMF® Step 9 - Adoption.**

Creation Steps: The benefits plan and tracker (**Template 3.1.7 Benefits Plan and Tracker**) should not be created in isolation. The suggested creation steps are:
1. Align with the strategy department and their portfolio for input.
2. Recreate a draft outline of **Template 3.1.7** to work on.
3. Involve the finance function for input and guidance.
4. Assemble a diverse team with relevant experience.
5. Brainstorm, filter and rank ideas.
6. Starting with the largest benefits, populate the template moving from left to right; 'title and description', 'metrics baseline and risks', etc.
7. Share the first draft with the sponsors, executives and actionees to gain acceptance.
8. Review the second draft with the finance function and strategy office.
9. Gain sponsor and governance approval.
10. Use as input into the project change plan and communication plan.
11. Use the benefits plan and tracker to monitor benefits through the **Execute** and **Sustain** phases of the change programme.

Benefits Plan and Tracker - Insights:
- ❖ The benefits plan and tracker is a minimal approach which, depending on the magnitude of the benefits, will become more complex. More detailed plans and trackers will include monthly or quarterly columns for comparing estimated budget spend versus actual, mitigation plans, etc.
- ❖ If the benefits of the change programme are not properly articulated or communicated, they will not receive the attention of the organisation or stakeholder support and will most likely fail.
- ❖ The benefits should be included in the elevator speech, detailing why this change is important.

Template 3.1.7 Benefits Plan and Tracker (BPT)

#	Benefits Information			Actions and Responsibilities			Progress Tracking		
	Title and Description	Metrics Baseline and Risks	Sponsor or Executive	Prerequisites and Key Actions	Actionee	ECD	Saving to Date	Progress (Budget vs. Actual)	Status
1									
2									
3									
4									
5									
6									
7									
8									
9									
10									

Template 3.1.7 Benefits Plan and Tracker

3.1.10 Change Elevator Speech - Guide

The change elevator speech should be a clear, brief business message, the 'commercial' or 'advertisement' of the change programme. It communicates the 'What', 'Why' and the 'Benefits' of the change programme. The elevator speech should be no longer than eighty to a hundred words or eight to ten sentences. The concept is that you can share the information about the change with anyone quickly within an elevator trip lasting no longer than thirty seconds (**Tool 3.1.8 Change Programme Elevator Speech**).

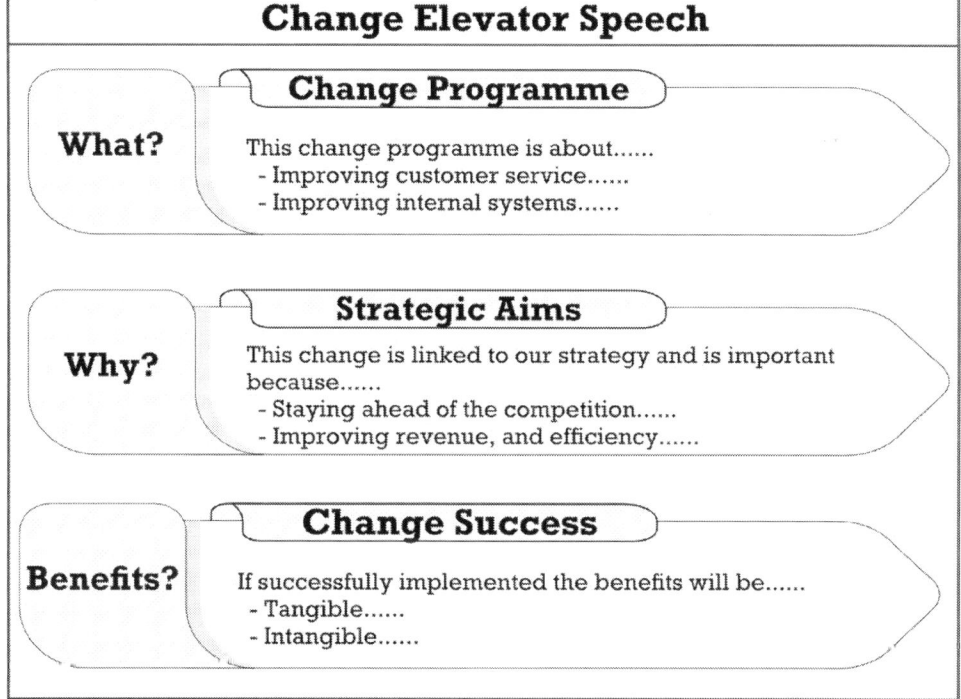

Tool 3.1.8 Change Programme Elevator Speech

A well-constructed change elevator speech will:
- ❖ Communicate the change to gain stakeholder support and buy-in, as well as help to sell the change case to secure critical organisation resources.
- ❖ Communicate the most important aspects of the change programme within a short amount of time.
- ❖ Be used as part of all stakeholder communications.
- ❖ Help to communicate a consistent change message.

❖ Help prevent rumours from starting and resistance from building.

Creation Steps: The change programme elevator speech (**Tool 3.1.8 Change Programme Elevator Speech**) should not be created in isolation. The suggested creation steps are:
1. Align with the organisation's general communications team.
2. Assemble a diverse team with relevant communications and change experience.
3. Recreate a draft outline of **Tool 3.1.8** as a template to work on.
4. Brainstorm, filter and rank ideas.
5. Develop the 'what', 'why' and the 'benefits'.
6. Prepare first draft, review and improve.
7. Test with an impartial audience and collect feedback.
8. Use the feedback to improve the first draft.
9. Present to the sponsor and gain approval.
10. Align and link with all future communications.

Elevator Speech - Insights:
❖ **Avoiding Change Resistance:** The importance of the change elevator speech cannot be overstated. It helps to reduce early resistance and prevent rumours from building momentum, potentially damaging the change before it begins.
❖ **Acquiring Company Resources:** All company programmes, projects and initiatives compete for resources and capacity. A well constructed elevator speech could make the difference between securing those critical resources or failing to do so.

3.1.11 Stakeholder Analysis - Guide

No matter how good the change team are, how hard you work and how important the change programme may be to the organisation, without good stakeholder engagement you will hit major barriers. Stakeholders can be defined as any group or individual who can affect or is affected by the achievement of the organisation's objectives (Freeman, 1984). Detailed stakeholder analysis and mapping is critical to ensure the change team understands and manages resistance throughout the change programme.

Stakeholder Engagement

It is always advisable to understand the organisation's culture prior to engaging stakeholders. Stakeholders represent all those who will interact with the change, as well as those who will be affected by the implementation of the change programme. Stakeholders, like risks, should be identified, categorised and tracked as they can have either a have positive or negative impact on the outcome of the programme. The objective is to capture and understand stakeholder needs, desires and expectations. This facilitates the analysis of change impacts on the various groups, departments and individual standpoints, it will help to maintain stakeholder support, tailor communications and mitigate resistance.

Rebels, Observers and Advocates

The **Leadership of Change**® categorises stakeholders into three simple groups:

- ❖ '**Rebels**' tend to resist change blindly, sometimes this can be a natural reaction even if the change is to their benefit. The default reaction is that change is a bad thing and will put them at a disadvantage.
- ❖ '**Observers**' will monitor the '**Advocates**' and assess if the change is benefiting them. If this appears positive, they will tend to move towards being receptive to the change.
- ❖ '**Advocates**' are similar to the change agents with their positivity towards change. Their energy should be harnessed as they can play an effective role in leading and implementing the change.

Section 3.7 develops this concept further.

Stakeholder Analysis

Stakeholder analysis is the first step in stakeholder management. It is an important process that successful change teams perform to win support for their project. Effectively and efficiently managing stakeholders helps to ensure that projects succeed where others might fail. The analysis should not preclude the interests of some stakeholders overriding the interests of the other less powerful stakeholder groups. It is not always possible to assess stakeholder motivation, however a systematic approach will help to gain a better understanding.

Stakeholder analysis is essential for the success of a project. Engaging with key stakeholders will also help the change team gain invaluable insights about the various stakeholders. It establishes the interests of stakeholders in relation to the change objectives and highlights who will be directly affected by the change. It also identifies those stakeholders who are less impacted and who may require less attention during the change programme. Stakeholder analysis should be performed as early as possible in the change programme, and definitely before any stakeholder communication or engagement begins.

Assessment Steps: The creation of the stakeholder assessment should not be performed in isolation. Any contentious information should be treated confidentially. The suggested steps are:

1. Assemble a diverse team with relevant experience and knowledge of the organisation and the impacted stakeholders.
2. Recreate a draft outline of **Assessment 3.1.9** as a template to work on.
3. Brainstorm to identify the key stakeholder's 'name' and record their organisation 'role'.
4. Prioritise and rank their 'current 'a' level of influence' and resistance.
5. Discuss and define their 'desired 'B' level of cooperation'.
6. Define and record 'comments and actions' to move the identified stakeholders to more desirable positions, if required.
7. Use the stakeholder assessment output as input into the stakeholder mapping template (**Template 3.1.10 Stakeholder Map**).

Stakeholder Analysis - Insights:

- ❖ **Objective Exercise:** The stakeholder assessment should be conducted as an objective exercise. Every effort should be made to dispel any previous negative interactions the sponsor or change team may have had with a stakeholder prior to the change programme.
- ❖ **Challenging Key Stakeholders:** Although the stakeholder assessment and mapping exercise is confidential, it can be advantageous to sit down with some high influence stakeholders and have an open and honest conversation about their required support.
- ❖ **Tread with Caution:** The change team members and change agents should tread with caution when engaging powerful, ambitious and zealous stakeholders, as (in some occasions) the change programme could be against these individual's best interests!

Assessment 3.1.9 Stakeholder Analysis

#	Stakeholder Information (Confidential)			Current 'a' Level of Influence			Desired 'B' Level of Cooperation		
	Name	Role	Comments and Actions	Rebel	Observer	Advocate	Rebel	Observer	Advocate
1									
2									
3									
4									
5									
6									
7									
8									
9									
10									

Assessment 3.1.9 Stakeholder Analysis

3.1.12 Stakeholder Mapping - Guide

Stakeholder mapping is the visual representation of the stakeholder analysis. It organises the impacted stakeholders according to the key criteria defined in the earlier analysis (**Assessment 3.1.9 Stakeholder Analysis**). Stakeholder mapping is essential for the success of a change programme and will help in better managing potential resistance and expectations. Mendelow (1991), suggests we analyse our stakeholder groups based on **Power** (the ability to influence our organisation's strategy or project resources) and **Interest** (how interested they are in the organisation or change succeeding). For the purposes of change implementation, we are more focused on the stakeholder's level of **Cooperation** as opposed to **Interest** (Template 3.1.10 Stakeholder Mapping).

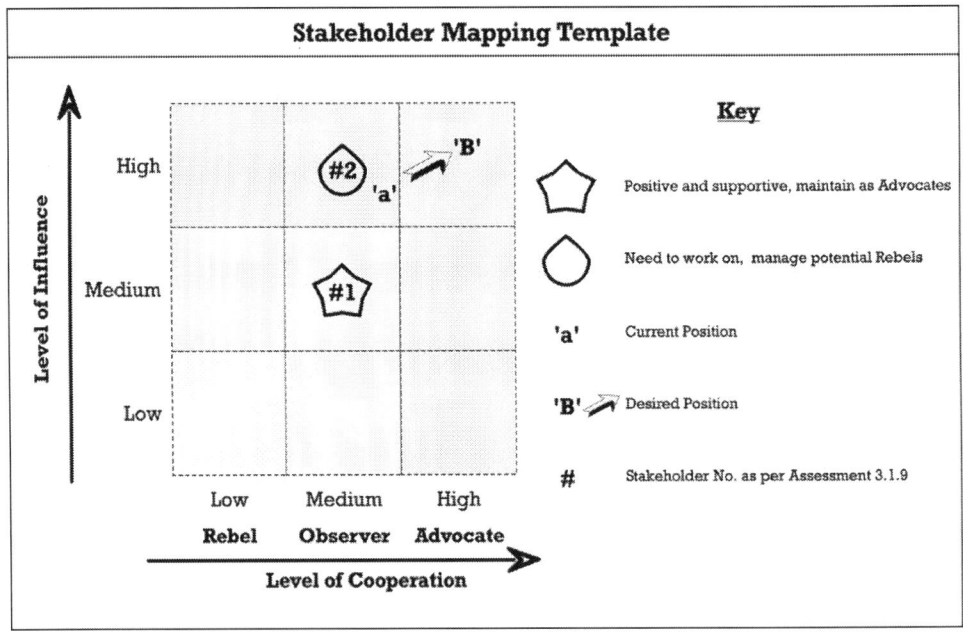

Template 3.1.10 Stakeholder Map

Creation Steps: Use the stakeholder analysis (Assessment 3.1.9 Stakeholder Analysis) as input. The suggested creation step are:

1. Assemble an experienced change team and selected stakeholders.
2. Recreate a draft outline of **Template 3.1.10** to work on.
3. First, map the 'current position 'a'' of each of the stakeholders listed in the assessment onto the template.
4. Second, establish the 'desired position 'B''.

5. Update the stakeholder assessment 'comment and actions' column (**Assessment 3.1.9 Stakeholder Analysis**).
6. Align the actions with the detailed project change plan (PCP).
7. Update the stakeholder map periodically or when there is a change in stakeholders throughout the **a2BCMF®** life cycle.

Stakeholder Mapping - Insights:
- ❖ **Contentious Information:** The output of this exercise should be treated as confidential as it can tarnish or be used to tarnish selected stakeholders.
- ❖ **Factual Data:** All of the analysis, assumptions, data and actions should remain factual without bias. The objective is to successfully deliver the change, not attack or expose undesirable elements.

3.1.13 Governance

Governance covers the systems and methods of how the change programme will be authorised, monitored and supported by its sponsoring organisation. Programme governance refers to the structure, practices and processes which ensure that the change programmes are managed effectively and consistently throughout their life cycle. Governance is achieved through the actions of a review and a decision-making body that is responsible for approving recommendations made during the change implementation. Effective governance includes:

- ❖ Establishing a clear procedure and structure as to how the sponsoring organisation will oversee the change and its degree of autonomy.
- ❖ Ensuring that the goals of the change programme are aligned with the strategic vision, business case and resources.
- ❖ Identifying and nominating the sponsor and assessing continued programme support.
- ❖ Authorising the programme budget and resources (change agents).
- ❖ Creating a link between the change benefits and the balanced scorecard (BSC).
- ❖ Ensuring the employee's individual performance plan (IPP) is aligned with the BSC.
- ❖ Creating a process for communicating programme issues and risks to the organisation.
- ❖ Conducting periodic organisational reviews of progress and benefits.
- ❖ Approving the formal closure of the change programme or the authority to close it early, should the necessary conditions arise.

3.1.14 Review and Checklist

Change Definition: The process of defining the change focuses on aligning the programmes within the portfolio to the organisation's strategy, ensuring it has a business case, resources and benefits.

Change Definition Importance: This ensures proper due diligence by assessing estimates of costs, benefits and risks, go/no go decision, etc.

Case Study: Organisations launch many change and transformation programmes. If employee health and safety is prioritised, the leadership team must ensure that there are no workload constraints impeding on critical on-site safety activities, such as ordering fish food!

Strategy Alignment: Ensuring that the change programme is aligned with the organisation's strategy is critical to obtain resources and gain buy-in.

Strategic Portfolio Prioritisation Funnel: Has the change being assessed against other initiatives using predefined criteria?

Organisation Change Capacity: After normal day-to-day operations, unplanned work and mandatory change there is usually little capacity left for other change initiatives.

Change Roadmap: Appeals to all stakeholders as it provides a quick visual display of the change programme and helps gain change support.

Benefits Planning and Tracking: Achieving benefits is the reason that organisations do change programmes, they should be planned and tracked.

Elevator Speech: A well constructed change elevator speech will help to communicate the change and gain stakeholder support and buy-in,

Stakeholder Analysis and Mapping: Both are essential to help ensure successful change by managing stakeholder expectations and concerns.

Governance: The change programme should be reviewed by an independent body to ensure it is managed effectively throughout the **a2BCMF®** life cycle.

a2BCMF® Step 1 - Checklist

#	a2BCMF® Questions	Complete Yes/No
1	**Strategy Alignment:** Does the change programme clearly align with the organisation's strategy and will it successfully complete against other programmes for resources?	
2	**Strategic Portfolio Prioritisation Funnel:** Has the change being assessed for; revenue potential, investment requirements, strategic fit and implementation effort?	
3	**Organisation Change Capacity:** Does the organisation have the change capacity to undertake this change programme to achieve benefits realisation?	
4	**Change Roadmap:** Has the change roadmap been prepared (deliverables, assumptions, benefits and key dates), socialised with the stakeholders and approved?	
5	**Benefits Planning and Tracking:** Have the benefits been identified, the actionees agreed and the tracking plan approved? Do the benefits align with the business case?	
6	**Elevator Speech:** Has a well-crafted elevator speech been approved and will it communicate a consistent change message and its benefits?	
7	**Stakeholder Analysis and Mapping:** Have the impacted stakeholders been identified and mapped accordingly; **'Rebels'**, **'Observers'** and **'Advocates'**?	
8	**Governance:** Does the change programme have an independent body to ensure it is managed effectively and consistently throughout the **a2BCMF®** life cycle?	

Notes:

3.2 Secure Sponsorship and Resources

Without effective and proactive sponsorship, the change programme will eventually fail, the change will not be adopted by the employees or sustained, and it will not deliver the intended benefits.

3.2.1 Sponsorship and Resources - Overview

- ❖ **Sponsorship:** The sponsor is a senior executive who is responsible for delivering change success. They are accountable for the delivery of all ten-steps of the **a2B Change Management Framework®**.
- ❖ **Resources:** The sponsor will need the support of a competent and motivated change team, a supportive CEO, the organisation's leadership team and change agents to help them implement the change.

Business Benefits: Sponsorship is the single most important factor in organisational change success. Without effective and proactive sponsorship, the organisation's investment in its portfolio of change programme or projects will not provide a return on investment (ROI).

Key Stakeholders: The sponsor and change resources will be set-up and structured to work with the CEO, the leadership team, change agents and the impacted stakeholders to deliver the change programme.

Business Objective: The sponsor and the change resources will work with the stakeholders through the **a2BCMF®** to deliver the change benefits, ensuring both a ROI and the intended strategy are achieved.

Enablers and Barriers

Enablers	Barriers
The sponsor is aware that they are the sponsor of the change programme and they have the motivation and capacity to perform the role.	The sponsor is not fully aware that they are the sponsor of the change programme or understands what the role entails.
The sponsor understanding and following the three key elements of sponsorship; 'Say', 'Support' and 'Sustain'.	Lack of understanding of the difference between sponsorship and leadership.
A core change team has competent resources to support the sponsor to implement the change programme to achieve sustainable change.	The CEO and leadership team thinking that change implementation is a part time activity.
Cascading change is similar to a multi-level fountain, water flows from the top, soaking each layer of the organisation. This is an activity led by the CEO and sponsor.	Individual leaders thinking that they can effectively cascade the change down through each part of their organisation.
Both the leader and manager coaching and influencing employees through the change process.	Leaders and managers expecting the change team to coach and influence employees through the change.
The CEO has the change programme as a prioritised item on the organisation's agenda.	The CEO and leadership team leaving the sponsor and the change team to deliver the change.
Nominated and trained change agents supporting the sponsor, the change team and their department.	Leaders thinking that they can be the main and only change agents within their organisation.
The CEO, sponsor and leadership team understanding that without trust you will not change the employees or the organisation.	Leaders not utilising change agents across the organisation to find the **'Tipping Point'**.

3.2.2 Case Study - Nobody Told me I was the Sponsor

Sponsorship is the single most important success factor in any change, transformation or business improvement project. It is apparent that the portfolios, programmes, and projects that deliver a higher ROI, get employee change adoption, and provide sustainable performance improvement have one thing in common: Effective and proactive sponsorship.

If success is to be achieved, the sponsorship role has to be understood and agreed before any project work begins. The sponsor should be a trusted senior executive with many years of experience and widely accepted organisational creditability. They should free up time during their normal working day to perform the duties of the sponsor, and that is likely to mean looking after one large change or transformation project. They should lead the kick-off meeting and ideally be involved through to the successful closure of the programme.

An international oil company was on an operational excellence journey, launching ten new global Must Win (MW) strategic transformation programmes. I was asked by my boss to support the business and to provide change management expertise and business improvement resources to enable success on three of these initiatives across Europe. One of these key initiatives was top quartile (TQ) performance of the assets, both onshore and offshore. The objective was to deliver TQ performance in production reliability and unit operating costs (UOC) on the majority of the company's assets.

TQ methodology is a structured and disciplined approach to perform a bottom-up detailed analysis of an asset's direct operations expenditure (opex). This data can be used to measure the gap between actual and TQ performance by using independent external benchmarks and internal comparisons. The methodology follows a rigorous ten-step process and starts with looking at the context of the asset. It defines where the asset is in its production life, its location, and its specific design. The other nine-steps examine elements such as operational performance gaps, key value drivers, potential improvement opportunities, performance management, and sustainable change.

I launched the planning activities for all three transformation programmes at the same time. This was helped by the fact that I had a good working relationship with the asset sponsor. As a result, the safety initiative was now an integral part of the asset business improvement plan and this initiative was at an advanced stage. The CO_2 initiative was also now starting to get traction.

As for the TQ initiative, I can't think of an occasion when it was more difficult to get an initial meeting with a sponsor. I allowed the first meeting to move down my priority list, but after three months it had still not happened. I gradually increased the frequency of my requests to try to schedule the meeting. Finally, I tried the personal touch and made weekly trips to the sponsor's office and spoke with his PA to try to get time in his schedule. This eventually resulted in a sixty-minute meeting with the sponsor, which would be adequate time to achieve a good first meeting and ensure time for planning TQ activities.

I walked up to Frank's door and knocked. I could hear, "Come in," so I entered his office.

He finished reading his document, set it down on the desk, got up, and made his way over to me. He didn't smile, so I decided to break the rising tension.

"Hi, Frank. I'm Peter. Thank you for seeing me."

"Hi. Before we start, I just need to point out that you've been pushy with my PA in trying to get this meeting." His voice became louder as he spoke.

"Well, then let me apologise if that was the way it appeared. I have been trying to get a meeting with you for three months and my frustration may have slipped out."

"I've had more important things to deal with over the last three months" he responded, slightly aggressively.

"Frank, I understand that. I am very aware of the issue and I realise it would not have been a pleasant situation to deal with." Frank looked up at me, raised his arm, and waved it at the chair as a signal to take a seat at the conference table.

"Now, how I can I help you, Peter?" Frank asked in a more relaxed tone, with a small smile.

I introduced myself properly.

"I work with the business transformation team. We are supporting the global transformation programmes as they are implemented across Europe. I assist the sponsor to lead and support their transformation programmes. Our wider resources serve the asset leadership teams, by providing change management and business improvement expertise to deliver and implement the programmes. I am here to talk about the TQ project and your role as the sponsor." I gave a short pause, "I am also supporting two of the other transformation programmes. They are doing quite well but this one is behind."

Initial sponsor meetings are always difficult and can sometimes be awkward conversations. The main challenge with a new sponsor is that they don't usually know what sponsorship means, or much about the responsibilities that come with it. Change management can be a new concept to some, and the perception is that change management is done far away from the office. For me, leadership is about delivering the strategy, building and maintaining the team, and developing the individual. Sponsorship goes much further than a leadership role. The sponsor's role is to own and lead the change.

"Ah, Peter. Nobody told me that I was the sponsor of this TQ programme, although I am involved in safety, which covers technical integrity and process safety."

Wow. This was the first time a nominated sponsor had told me this in a sponsorship conversation, especially three months after the announcement had been widely documented and communicated. We continued to discuss a wide variety of business improvement and safety challenges, and I was left in no doubt that Frank cared passionately about the business and wanted to improve it. What I was less sure about was his ability to sponsor the TQ programme. He didn't have either the capacity or the passion for this subject. We agreed that Frank would talk to his boss about being the sponsor and I would see how the TQ project was progressing from within the assets.

As the sponsor was not yet in place, I decided to just go along to some of the asset TQ meetings to observe the meeting structure and format. After attending several, it was clear that the TQ process was independently run by each individual asset. What was missing was the structured governance meeting that was attended by the asset leaders, so that comparisons could be made against each asset using internal and external benchmarks to gain insights. I asked if these governance meetings had happened in the past and was told that they had. However, these meetings had disintegrated into intellectual debates between the leaders on how their assets were different. The only way the organisation would get a TQ initiative that improved organisation performance was through proactive and effective sponsorship, where the sponsor would ensure strong governance and the leaders would be challenged to deliver and be held accountable for results.

After attending the TQ meetings, I went along to my business improvement boss to discuss the challenges I was facing on this project. I started to talk about the TQ programme and advised him it was well behind schedule. I shared the conversation that I'd had with Frank in detail. I asked Johan whether Frank had been told that he was the sponsor for the project. I told him that I was unsure how to proceed, as without a sponsor supporting this MW initiative it would fail.

"Peter, leave it alone until we sort out the sponsor. Your other two projects are going well, so concentrate on them."

I wanted to find the balance between implementing a strategic change that would help the organisation improve performance versus not being exposed by pushing an initiative with weak sponsorship. This was an important project for the organisation if they wanted to improve medium and long-term performance, and I felt that everyone should make sacrifices to achieve that goal. I debated the pros and cons with Johan, telling him it was difficult to accept his advice to just 'leave it', and as change agents we needed to challenge the current culture. As I did not yet have the support of the sponsor or my boss, pushing the TQ initiative across all the assets would simply not have worked.

Soon after the MW transformation programme with this organisation, I began working on a new HR transformation programme, which focused on improving eight global employee life cycle processes. The sponsorship discussion for the employee life cycle project would be taking place within a more supportive function, a totally different environment to some of the earlier MW projects. The senior sponsor of the HR transformation programme understood the sponsorship role and the culture of the organisation, and he was highly motivated to ensure that the programme would be a success. Even better, he'd discussed and agreed on each project sponsor for the eight global processes. Hans was leading the 'employee onboarding process'.

"Hi, Hans, I'm Peter. It is a pleasure to meet you and work on this project together."

"Likewise, Peter. I am really looking forward to it."

"So, Hans, there are a few reasons why this transformation has been highly successful so far. First, it has a great programme sponsor, and the sponsor has embraced the sponsorship role. Second, the programme is important for the wider organisation's strategy. And finally, it is highly supported by motivated HR professionals. I'm here to talk to you about the sponsorship role, what it means, and its importance."

Hans looked slightly confused.

"But, Peter, I have been a leader in this organisation for over twenty-five years and led many global and senior programmes, as well as projects over the years."

"Hans, there is no doubt that you have led some great programmes and those leadership skills will still be required. For me, leadership is about delivering the strategy called 'Task or Programme', building and maintaining the 'Team', and developing the 'Individual'. However, sponsorship goes further than a leadership role. The sponsorship role is about leading and owning the change. It involves the three key elements: **'Say'**, **'Support'**, and **'Sustain'**."

Hans listened thoughtfully.

"Hans, do you watch football?" I asked as I changed my approach.

"Yes, of course," responded Hans, looking at me slightly surprised.

"Please allow me to use a football analogy to explain the concept." Hans smiled and nodded.

"The first element of sponsorship is **'Say'**. Imagine you are watching your football team on the big colour TV at home, sitting on your soft, comfortable sofa. It is great for you, but your team cannot see or hear you and they are getting very little, if any, revenue from you. If they are lucky they might get a very small amount of money via the TV licence or cable subscription." I stopped and looked at Hans as he started to smile.

"OK, so the leader is basically sitting in his office away from his project team." I winked at Hans and smiled back as I sipped my water, giving him time to reflect.

"The next element is sponsor **'Support'**, which is ten times more important than **'Say'**. So back to the football analogy. You are still sitting on the lovely sofa in the comfort of your warm home, but at least you are paying a sports subscription which, in some way, goes to your team directly." I gave a short pause and looked at Hans.

"So, Peter, I am not just sitting in my office. I am now providing resources?"

"Yes, Hans, but your team can now hear you when things are not going to plan. So now the third element: '**Sustain**'. This is a challenge in any organisation, but more so with us. We have so many initiatives it is easy not to complete the current one before moving on to the next.

"You're not sitting on the sofa in your warm house watching the TV and seeing the rain and sleet pour down on the players any more. You have put on your winter coat, hat, and gloves and made your way through the turnstile to take your seat in the stand. The sleet turns to snow and it's blowing in your face. You are cold and wet. You can make out the scoreboard and you see that your team is getting beaten 2-0, but you keep cheering them on as they launch an attack on the opposition's goal. You know one goal could turn this around for your team. There is still a chance. So, what is the difference now? Well, you have bought a season ticket and the money goes directly to the club and the team. The players can see you and hear you, and you can cheer and drive them on to success." I looked at Hans and he gently nodded.

"Peter, I get it."

"Great, Hans. This is probably my last question. Do you have you the time, passion, and energy to deliver this employee life cycle project?"

His response was instant.

"Ja."

"Great," I responded. "Now we can start some high-level planning."

Case Study - Insights:

- ❖ **Sponsorship is Different from Leadership:** The leaders of organisations typically associate the role and traits of a change sponsor with those of a leader. However, while these leadership traits are important foundations, the role of the sponsor goes beyond the role of a leader. A sponsor's role is to be personally involved in leading and owning the change, this involves the three key elements: '**Say**', '**Support**', and '**Sustain**'.
- ❖ **Sponsor's Capacity:** As well as considering organisational capacity, sponsor capacity must also be taken into account. The **Leadership of Change**® does not stipulate that a sponsor can only do one change programme at a time, but it does warn of potential conflicts. The biggest conflict is time. How does a leader balance their time (when that time is limited), especially when they might have a preference for one change programme over another? The second conflict is around visibility and resources. How does the sponsor ensure that both change programmes get equal resources and time on the organisation's agenda? Does having a separate sponsor for each change programme provide the best opportunity for success? The CEO and the leadership team must consider the capacity challenges of not only the organisation and its employees but also the sponsors. Effective and proactive sponsorship can be the difference between being able to execute an organisation's strategy or failing to do so.

3.2.3 The Importance of Sponsorship and Resources

Simply put, without a proactive and effective change sponsor, most change programmes or initiatives will fail to achieve the targeted objectives. To be effective, the sponsor will need to have a good team behind them. That team will need to be dedicated, motivated with a strong understanding of people, and have change and communication skills. As mentioned in **Section 3.1.6**, strategic organisational change capacity is not something that most organisations have in abundance. Without even considering the competing forces from other change or improvement initiatives, it will be difficult to get enough competent or motivated resources. However, accepting a resource that is *available* could be more problematic than you might think. As with all change programmes and general projects, they are a temporary endeavour, and acquiring and developing the sponsor and change resources is a critical success factor.

A distinction must be made between sponsorship and leadership, or even management. The action-centered leadership (ACL) model focuses on achieving the task, managing the team or group and managing individuals (Adair, 2006). However, change management sponsorship is different from leadership and is much more important in terms of delivering and implementing successful organisational change. In terms of change management, the task is to successfully deliver organisational change and this cannot be achieved without the full support of the organisation's leaders who '**Articulate**' the change vision, '**Model**' the new behaviours and '**Intervene**' to reinforce the change (**See Section 1.3**).

3.2.4 Key Elements of Sponsorship

Identification of the appropriate change sponsor should be one of the first tasks within any change programme, and it should happen as soon as possible after the '**Change Definition**' is completed. Delivery of the change programme is a strategic element of the organisation's portfolio and a capital investment in terms of organisation resources, time and effort. This investment should provide a return to the organisation through improved financial performance.

Without effective and proactive sponsorship, the change programme will eventually fail, the change will not be adopted by the employees nor be sustained, and it will not deliver the intended benefits. Getting the right person and character to be the sponsor is extremely important. **Figure**

3.2.1 outlines the three key elements of successful sponsorship: **'Say'**, **'Support'** and **'Sustain'**.

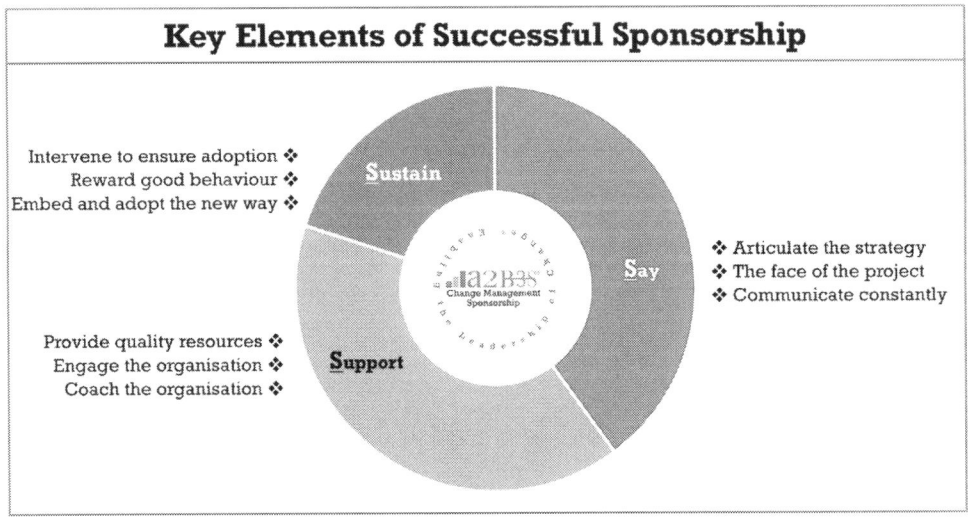

Figure 3.2.1 Key Elements of Sponsorship

Sponsorship Element 1: 'Say'

❖ Articulate the strategy
❖ The face of the project
❖ Communicate constantly

'**Say**' is the foundation and is all about communicating the business case for the change to all affected stakeholders. Within this element the sponsor has three key activities:

1. **Articulate the strategy:** All change programmes should be aligned to the organisation's strategy, vision, mission and objectives, as they are all fundamental in delivering organisational value through the portfolio. This is the responsibility of the change sponsor.

    ❖ It is essential that the sponsor ensures a compelling vision is in place throughout the change programme. The vision defines what the organisation will be like once the change has been implemented. The strategy and vision should be articulated in such a way as to stretch, motivate and align the organisation.

2. **The Face of the Project:** Everyone in the organisation should know who the sponsor is, the '**face**' of the change programme or project. They should engage the stakeholders face-to-face as the brand of the change, passionately promoting why its success is important.

   ❖ If an organisation has prioritised an important change programme and will use its critical strategic change capacity and limited financial resources, then it is essential the programme delivers the intended benefits. The sponsor should be both responsible and accountable to the organisation for delivery, there should be no hiding if the change is not delivered.

3. **Communicate Constantly:** The sponsor should be constantly communicating the case for change. Simple messaging could include 'What's In It For Me?' (WIIFM) and what is expected of each employee.

   ❖ Throughout the change programme, the impacted stakeholders and employees will be looking to hear a consistent and constant communication about the change and its progress. This communication should come directly from the sponsor and have a feedback loop.

Sponsorship Element 2: 'Support'

> **Provide quality resources** ❖
> **Engage the organisation** ❖
> **Coach the organisation** ❖

Having built the foundation of communication, '**Support**' builds on '**Say**'. It is in this element that the sponsor starts to actively and overtly support the change, providing resources and coaching the organisation.

1. **Provide Quality Resources:** One of the key issues that causes conflict on most programmes is resources. Sponsors must secure competent and capable resources that are committed to the programme and successful change delivery.

❖ The sponsor is able to allocate funds, change management capability, and their own time to ensure the change programme has every chance of being successful. Experienced and successful sponsors will also ensure the change team has adequate equipment and facilities throughout the programme. A strong argument for a sponsor to only lead one change programme at a time is balance, how can they impartially allocate critical resources or their time to different initiatives?

2. **Engage the Organisation:** The sponsor's role is to ensure that every level of the organisation impacted by the change has been engaged, and the change message has not missed any level of the organisation when cascaded from the top to the bottom.

❖ The organisation, especially the impacted stakeholders, are engaged directly by the sponsor. This should make the employees feel passionate about the change and be committed to its success. The message has been cascaded throughout the organisation and there are no vacuums. This concept is developed further in **Section 3.2.7.**

3. **Coach the Organisation:** The sponsor should have the ability to act both as an organisation and personal coach, this will start to move the organisation from the current '**a**' state to the improved future '**B**' state.

❖ Change management capability provides an important competitive advantage for organisations, especially during the fourth industrial revolution (4IR). The sponsor and organisational leaders should therefore develop internal change management capability. There is no greater time to do this than during a change programme.

Sponsorship Element 3: 'Sustain'

Intervene to ensure adoption ❖
Reward good behaviour ❖
Embed and adopt the new way ❖

'**Support**' is much more important than '**Say**', but '**Sustain**' is critical for the organisation to deliver value and achieve its strategic goals.

1. **Intervene to Ensure Adoption:** One of the most difficult roles as a leader or manager is to intervene and provide feedback to employees with poor performance. If the sponsor does not make a quick intervention when first spotted, the chances of change success will dissolve.

   ❖ The interventions by the sponsor should be completed in a consistent and respectful way to achieve the desired result. The leadership team, manager and members of the change team should replicate these interventions to reinforce the change and the new behaviours.

2. **Reward Good Behaviour:** It is hard to find an individual that does not like to be praised when performing well, everyone likes to be told they are doing a good job. Praise acknowledges positive action and reinforces the new behaviours.

   ❖ A successful recognition and rewards strategy should be designed into the change programme and communicated and implemented throughout its life cycle. The value and contribution an employee adds to the change and the team should be celebrated. It should be remembered that employees tend to look for meaningful recognition.

3. **Embed and Adopt the New Way:** The main objective of any change programme is to get the organisation to adopt the new ways of working and to change behaviours, to create the new culture.

   ❖ A change programme only succeeds when the new way of working becomes embedded in normal day-to-day operations. To make it stick, the sponsor needs to get the critical mass of impacted stakeholders and employees to adopt the new way of working.

Other Sponsor Responsibilities

The sponsor is primarily concerned with ensuring that the change programme delivers the agreed upon business benefits and acts as the representative of the organisation. They play a vital leadership role and the bigger the change programme the more senior the sponsor should be. The sponsor does not need to have project management skills, but they should understand the basics, such as the triple constraint; time, cost and scope. The sponsor should also be ready to cancel the change programme, either because its charter is fulfilled or conditions arise that bring the programme to an early close, such as the change is no longer aligned with the organisation's strategy.

The sponsor is not just a figurehead role and the role will vary from organisation to organisation. Other sponsor activities may include:

- Programme governance - ensuring control mechanisms and reviews are in place, with interventions if required.
- Financial control and oversight - ensuring benefits delivery.
- Ensuring risks and programme changes are managed properly and sufficiently.
- Developing and maintaining a supporting coalition of leaders and impacted stakeholders across multiple functions within the organisation.
- Ensuring timely decisions and the approval of deliverables.
- Role modelling the new behaviours, adhering to new process and using the new systems.
- Approving stakeholder communications, content and channels.
- Arbitrating and mediating between impacted stakeholders.

3.2.5 Change Sponsor Assessment - Guide

The change sponsor assessment is used to assess if the sponsor is performing their duties and if they are committed to the success of the change programme. The assessment should be transparent and focus on how the sponsor is performing their role with regards to **'Say'**, **'Support'** and **'Sustain'** activities. The assessment will identify the strengths, weaknesses and any potential corrective actions, should they need to be put in place. It should be completed at least four weeks after the sponsor has started their new role and periodically throughout the change programme.

Assessment 3.2.2 - Change Sponsorship

#	Assessment Questions	Likert Scale Scoring				
		Strongly Agree	Agree	Neutral	Disagree	Strongly Disagree
1	**General:** Has the change management lead had the 1:1 face-to-face conversation with the sponsor to explain the role of sponsorship and how it differs from leadership?					
2	**General:** Does the sponsor understand their role as the change sponsor with regards to 'Say', 'Support' and 'Sustain' activities?					
3	**General:** Has the sponsor implemented change programme governance, ensuring control mechanisms and reviews are in place with interventions if required?					
4	**General:** Has the sponsor implemented financial control and oversight to ensure benefits delivery?					
5	**Say:** Is there verifiable evidence that the sponsor articulated the strategy for change and the importance of the change programme being implemented for future organisation success?					
6	**Say:** Is there verifiable evidence that the sponsor communicated the change project constantly and consistently at every meeting they have attended?					
7	**Say:** Is there verifiable evidence that everyone in the organisation knows who the sponsor is, the 'face' of the change? Are they passionately promoting why the programme's success is important?					
8	**Say:** Is there verifiable evidence that the sponsor communicated the 'What's In It For Me?' (WIIFM) message and what is expected of each employee?					
9	**Support:** Is there verifiable evidence that the sponsor obtained committed and competent resources for the change programme?					
10	**Support:** Is there verifiable evidence that the sponsor coached both the organisation and individuals to move the organisation from the current 'a' state to the improved future 'B'?					
11	**Support:** Is there verifiable evidence that the sponsor engaged every level of the organisation, ensuring that the change message has not missed any level of the organisation?					
12	**Support:** Is there verifiable evidence that the sponsor is developing internal change management capability, a change framework and models that support programme delivery?					
13	**Sustain:** Is there verifiable evidence that the sponsor intervened when they became aware of change resistance?					
14	**Sustain:** Is there verifiable evidence that the sponsor developed a recognition and rewards strategy and, if applicable, rewarded employees who adopted the change?					
15	**Sustain:** Is there verifiable evidence that the sponsor had a plan(s) to ensure change sticks and the change will be embedded into normal day-to-day operations?					
16	**Sustain:** Is there verifiable evidence that the sponsor has a plan(s) to get the critical mass of impacted stakeholders and employees to adopt the new way of working?					

Assessment 3.2.2 Change Sponsorship Assessment

Performing the sponsor assessment can be a challenging task and it is best completed face-to-face with the sponsor. The person carrying out the assessment should be cognisant that on some occasions the nominated sponsor is reluctant to perform the role in full and may then blame the change team on any poor performance. Normally the better assessment outcomes are performed by senior member of the change team in a relaxed one-to-one atmosphere. It should be positioned as a rich and open conversation to discuss current progress and explore improvement opportunities rather than as an interrogation.

Assessment Steps: The suggested assessment process steps are:

1. Ensure the sponsor has been briefed face-to-face by the change management lead about the role of the sponsor in terms of '**Say**', '**Support**' and '**Sustain**'.
2. Agree who will perform the assessment interview and who will take notes, if another person is attending.
3. Recreate a draft outline of **Assessment 3.2.2** to work on.
4. A pre-sponsor assessment (**Assessment 3.2.2 Change Sponsorship**) should be performed with the change team to assess and understand how the sponsor is performing.
5. Book a meeting in the sponsor's schedule, preferably in a neutral and relaxed location. The timeslot should allow for a rich and relaxed conversation. A rushed and short appointment should be rejected as this will be counterproductive to the assessment process.
6. The assessment should be carried out as a comfortable conversation, recording a score and comment against each of the questions.
7. The results and any potential intervention(s) should be discussed with the sponsor and shared with the change team.

Change Sponsor Assessment - Insights:

❖ The initial assessment with the sponsor should be about obtaining a baseline. Actions or interventions should be agreed with the sponsor to improve on the initial results.

❖ This is the most important assessment within the **Leadership of Change®**. Any score in the neutral to strongly disagree categories should be considered a serious risk to the change programme and interventions should be urgently actioned.

3.2.6 Core Change Team Resources

If the change programme is important to the organisation's strategy and future success, a dedicated change team may be needed. This dedicated change team may include seconded organisation leaders or specifically recruited and experienced change professionals. The team will define the change management strategy, tools, plans and then support implementation.

On a larger change programme, a change management lead will work with the sponsor and change agents, playing a key role to ensure the change meets schedule and budget objectives and employee adoption targets. Consideration should also be given to the team make up, successful teams are diverse by nature. A much-needed role in any change team is the Belbin 'completer finisher' (**See Section 3.10.3**). Team performance is helped when its members come from different skill pools, countries, industries and have different experience (Kearney, Gebert and Voelpel, 2009). The change team structure and size will vary from organisation to organisation based on change complexity (**Figure 3.2.3**).

Typical change roles include:

Change Leader: Responsibilities tend to vary from organisation to organisation, but their main role is to support the sponsor in delivering the change programme. Typically, the change leader is responsible for leading the planning, designing and change implementation, as well as managing the change team. Specific tasks will include:

- Ensuring the change team is trained and coached on change management and facilitation skills.
- Applying the change management framework, following all the **a2BCMF®** steps and applying applicable change models.
- Leading the roadmap, assessments, planning and communications sessions, engaging impacted stakeholders throughout.
- Applying the **AUILM® Employee Change Adoption Model**.
- Applying the **a2B5R® Employee Behaviour Change Model**.

Change Process Leader: Responsible for ensuring that the change implementation process is successfully designed and implemented. This may include tailoring the change management framework approach, its models and assessments.

Change Communications Leader: Responsible for developing and implementing a communication plan to support the change programme and engage stakeholders.

Change Work Stream Lead: Responsible for leading one of the change initiatives - this will vary greatly from change to change. Typical work stream leads could include; user system adoption, process adoption, training needs analysis, training, coaching, leadership alignment, etc.

Change Consultants: Can either lead, co-deliver or advise an organisation on their change implementation. Effectively they can support any of the **a2BCMF®** steps.

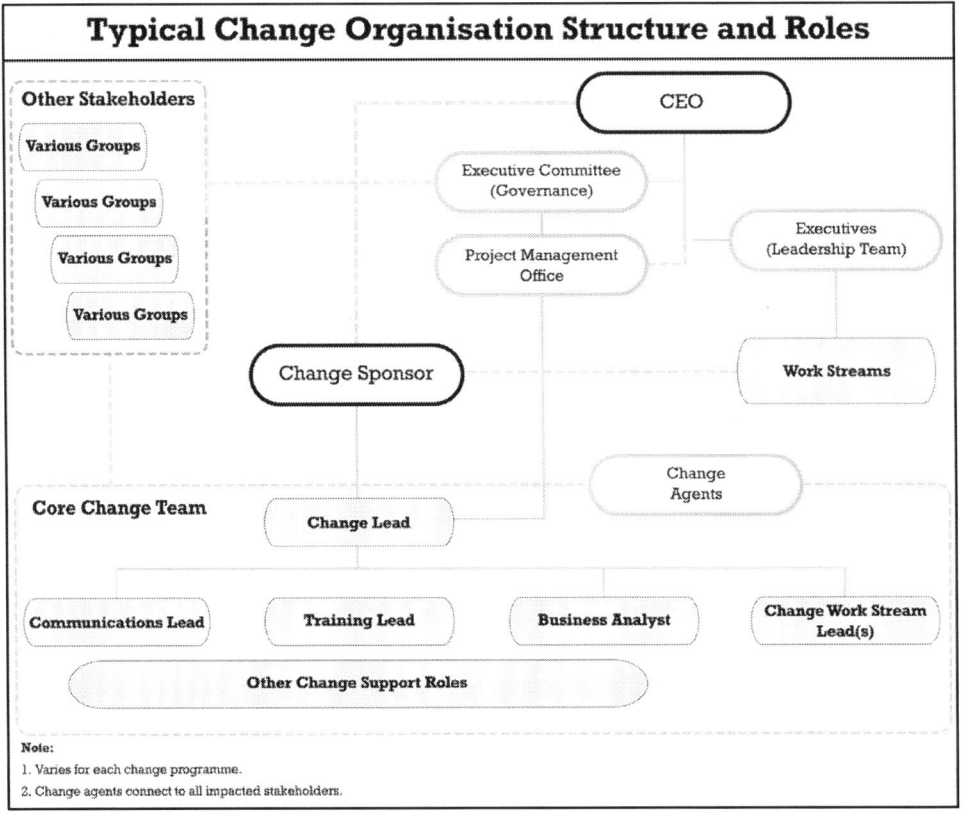

Figure 3.2.3 Change Team Structure and Roles

3.2.7 Cascading Change Throughout the Organisation

A multi-level fountain is a great metaphor to show how change should cascade down through the organisation. This concept is equally important when communicating the change. The water flows from the top, soaking each layer of the organisation until it reaches the pool at the bottom and then it is pumped back up to the top as part of a continuous loop. The water is the change business case, vision, expectations, responsibilities and business benefits (**Figure 3.2.4**).

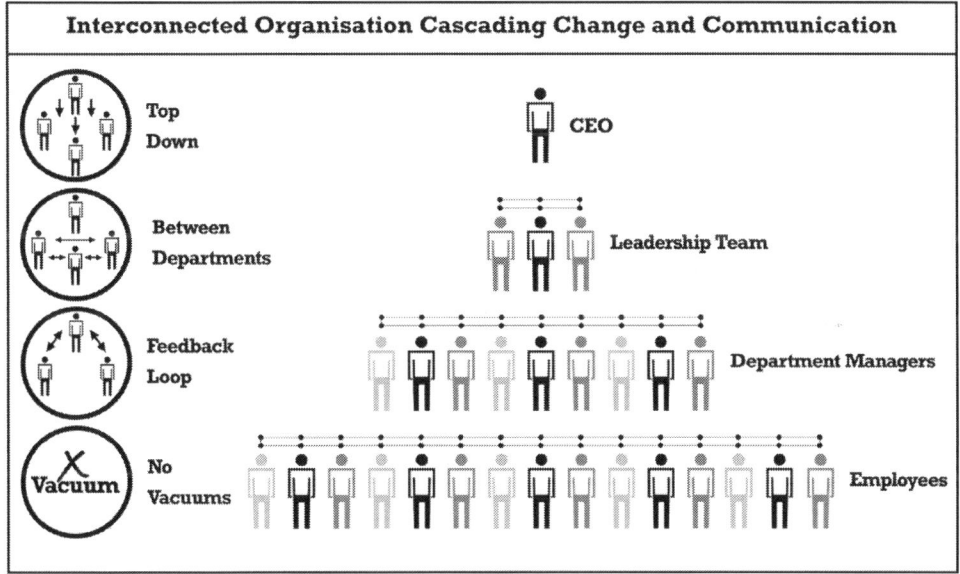

Figure 3.2.4 Cascading the Change

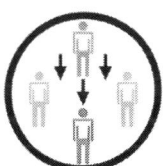

Top Down: The cascade approach should start top down from the CEO and sponsor, be passed to and from the executive team to the department managers and finally to all other employees. Like the water in the fountain, no level should be missed or bypassed.

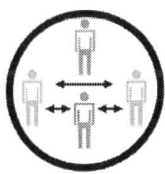

Between Departments: Horizontal and diagonal communication flow is also important to ensure departments are aware of what each other are doing. Benefits include collaboration, coordination, problem solving and resource sharing.

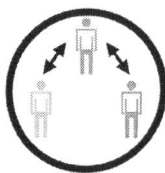

Feedback Loop: In the fountain, the water must be returned to the top to ensure a continuous flow. Similarly, the organisation needs feedback from the employees in the organisation. The feedback loop should provide insights into what is/is not working and what needs to be adjusted.

No Vacuum: Vacuums will always exist when change is being cascaded. There may be resistance ('**Rebels**') where some employees have other priorities, do not understand the change or do not agree with it. The vacuum should be quickly filled, and any resistance should be addressed.

3.2.8 Leadership and Management Change Support

Effective leadership and management involvement, as well as support, are essential to successful change. Both the leader and manager are positioned to coach and influence employees through their own change process. Specific support includes:

CEO: Successful organisational change starts with, and is highly dependent on, the CEO starting the change cascade down through the organisation. If a CEO stakes their reputation on the change, ensures finances and organisation resources, and allocates time to the change, then it has a high chance of success. Delivery of the change should be a priority on the CEO's agenda. As well as supporting the sponsor, other CEO change responsibilities include:

- ❖ **Involvement and Communication:** If the impacted stakeholders and employees see the CEO getting involved in the change and communicating its significance, they will soon realise this is an important topic. Continually articulating an actionable business case for change in a meaningful way for employees and stakeholder groups will go a long way to ensuring buy-in. Linking how the change strategy will impact the organisation, employees, processes and technology can start reducing resistance.

- ❖ **Model the New Behaviours:** Employees are generally sceptical and tend to judge leaders on actions, not just their words. Thus, the best approach is to lead by example. CEO's can gain greater employee acceptance with a 'walk-the-talk' approach.

- ❖ **Provide Organisation Capacity:** If the change programme does not secure organisation capacity in terms of agenda space and competent resources, it is highly unlikely to be successful. It will be in competition with normal day-to-day operations, unplanned work and mandatory change. The CEO, because of their power and authority within the organisation, can ensure the change programme obtains strategic change capacity, competent resources and time on the organisation's agenda.

- ❖ **Release the Best Resources:** A change programme is not only a financial investment for the organisation but, more importantly, it is about strategy execution, to ensure the organisation has a long-term and profitable future. Collins (2001) suggests that *"The best method to success is to put your best people in the biggest opportunities. It doesn't matter what kind of strategy you're pursuing if you have the wrong people in the wrong places."* All too often CEOs put the leaders of their organisation on to important initiatives because they are 'available'. Little or no thought is given to why these resources are available.

Leadership Team: Executives and senior leaders play an essential role in times of change, as key stakeholders and employees look to them for guidance. They are an extension of the change team but their role in achieving successful change is critical. The employees will assess if their leaders are demonstrating strong support for the change and the sponsor.

The leadership team needs to ensure the momentum started by the sponsor builds, and shows there is a real benefit to the organisation in implementing the change. They need to play their part in intervening when they identify any resistance to reinforce the change. Failure to become actively involved or intervening will fuel resistance.

Department Managers: Department managers will play a day-to-day role during the change by coaching their direct reports, providing encouragement and the appropriate resources during the transition to the new way of working. They will cascade communications from the CEO and leadership team, as well as supporting the sponsor to uncover and address resistance.

3.2.9 Change Agents

Change agents can be an organised group, leaders or individuals that undertake the task of leading, communicating and facilitating change in an organisation. They are the nominated advocates for change and can be internal or external to the organisation. Both internal and external change agents have advantages and disadvantages (**Figure 3.2.5**). Change agents tend to embrace and lead change, moving the organisation towards adoption and sustainable change. They work primarily with the sponsor, leadership team, their function or department and the change team. The change agents and '**Advocates**' can be a powerful coalition, they can have a considerable positive impact on the other groups. Working together, they can help to find the '**Tipping Point**', convincing the '**Observers**' to join them. Equally, the change agents can help reduce '**Rebel**' resistance, moving the '**Rebels**' to become '**Observers**'. This concept is developed further in **Section 3.7.7**. (**Figure 3.7.2**).

The leaders of the organisation should be some of the organisation's change agents as they are in key positions to influence change and have the authority to make a significant impact. HR are also in a good position to play a proactive role in change management. As change agents, they can replace resistance with resolve, planning with results, and fear of change with excitement about its possibilities (Ulrich, 1997). Working and developing the change agents across their different functions or departments can be one of the biggest levers in the transition of the organisation and its employees from their current state 'a' to the desired and improved state '**B**'.

Change Agents - Internal Versus External

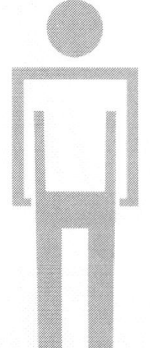

Internal Change Agents

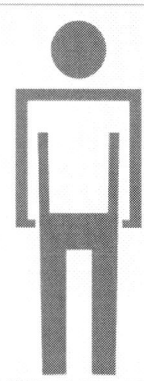

External Change Agents (Consultants)

Advantages:
- Can be released to the programme immediately and be ready to start
- Have internal organisational knowledge and cultural understanding
- Have access to company sensitive information and systems
- Can quickly establish rapport and trust with the stakeholders
- Cost less than an experienced external consultant

Advantages:
- Fills expertise gap that is unavailable internally
- Broader perspective and experience: clients, markets and sectors
- Bring a more objective perspective into the organisation development process
- Ability to probe difficult issues and to question the status quo
- Wider choice when it comes to selecting the most suitable consultants

Disadvantages:
- Will not usually have change management skills, tools or a framework to use
- Can lack objectivity and wider organisational change experience
- May hold biased views and not challenge the status quo
- Can be overly cautious when challenging stakeholders with power
- Reintegrating challenges post change adoption and change closure

Disadvantages:
- Extra time required to understand the organisation and culture
- Organisation may be wary of outsiders and building trust takes longer
- Organisation perceive outsiders negatively
- Usually more expensive, with additional travel and expenses
- Knowledge and capability leaves the organisation at contract end

Figure 3.2.5 Change Agents - Internal versus External

Characteristics and Traits

The success of any change effort depends heavily on the relationship between the change agent, the sponsor, the leadership team and the employees of the organisation. To be successful, change agents develop relationships built on trust and commitment, they become genuinely interested in other people (Carnegie, 1981).

Key characteristics and traits include:

- ❖ **People Skills:** Change is all about people and you will achieve change adoption and success when employees embrace it. The ability to show emotional intelligence during discussions will be advantageous.

- ❖ **Credibility:** Change agents must have credibility within the organisation, both in terms of their knowledge and their character.

- ❖ **Tenacity:** Change agents should not give up easily when progress is strained or when facing resistance, being patient yet persistent.

- ❖ **Listening Skills:** Ability to explore different employee perspectives and take them into account when looking for solutions.

- ❖ **Good Communicator:** Ability to communicate and articulate clearly to people in a non-threatening manner and define what is expected of them within a diverse culture.

- ❖ **Positivity:** Using positivity when communicating with employees can make a huge impact on their emotional well-being and their future adoption of the change.

Finally, the change agents should expect the leader to be focused on the change and be a more polished change agent than themselves. A leader with charisma, charm, the ability to inspire, persuasiveness, able to articulate the organisation's vision and other qualities are often associated with successful leadership. However, the change agent should be aware that they may encounter challenging leaders. There is always the potential to meet a leader with hubris syndrome disorder (Owen, 2012). A narcissistic leader with excessive self-confidence and an obsessive focus on their personal image, accompanied by contempt for anyone who thinks that the organisation's strategic change programme is more important than them. *"It ought to be remembered that there is nothing more difficult to take in hand, more perilous to conduct, or more uncertain in its success, than to take the lead in the introduction of a new order of things"* (Nicolo Machiavelli, 1469 - 1527).

3.2.10 Change Agents and the Trusted Adviser

To be an effective change agent, one needs influence in the organisation. One very important factor of influence is trust. Without trust you will not change people or be able to sell change to the organisation. The person you engage with will ask themselves one key question when you introduce yourself, *"Can I trust you?"* The trust equation (Green and Howe, 2012) provides a model for all of us involved in change (**Figure 3.2.6**).

When the change agent engages the stakeholders, they will be judged on the following factors:

- ❖ **Credibility:** The quality of being believed.
- ❖ **Reliability:** The quality of performing consistently.
- ❖ **Intimacy:** The quality of confidence and empathy.

  The above three factors should be **increased**.

- ❖ **Self Orientation:** The quality of caring.

  The above factor should be **decreased**.

"Without trust you will not change the employees or the organisation"

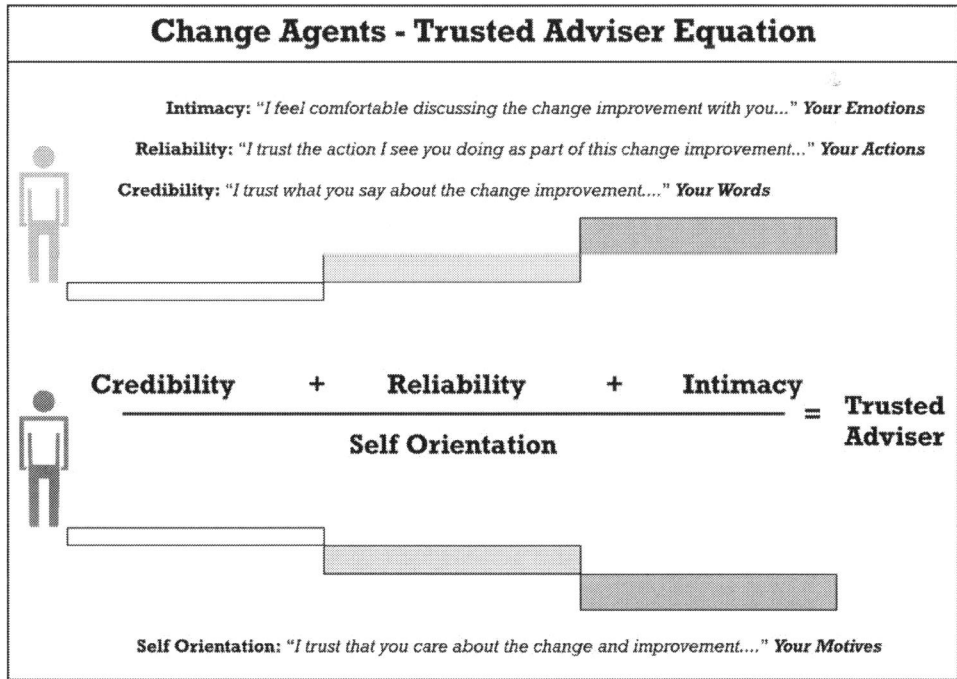

Figure 3.2.6 Trusted Adviser Equation

3.2.11 Review and Checklist

Secure Sponsorship and Resources: This process involves identifying the sponsor and other change resources who will support the change during implementation.

Sponsorship: The single most important factor in change success, without proactive sponsorship the change programme will fail. Change sponsorship involves three key elements; '**Say**', '**Support**' and '**Sustain**'.

Sponsor Assessment: This assessment is used to verify if the sponsor is performing the duties of the role and is committed to the success of the change programme. It should be transparent and focus on how the sponsor is performing with regards to '**Say**', '**Support**' and '**Sustain**' activities.

Change Team Resources: A dedicated core change team with competent resources is required to support the sponsor to deliver the change programme.

Other Change Roles: It might be worth considering other change roles, such as a change process lead, communication lead, work stream lead, training lead, etc.

Cascading Change: Similar to a multi-level fountain, water flows from the top, soaking each layer of the organisation. This is an activity led by the CEO and sponsor.

Leadership and Management Change Support: Effective leadership and management involvement, as well as support, are essential to successful change. The change programme must also be high on the CEO's agenda.

CEO Agenda: Is the change a priority for the CEO? Are they involved in the change? Are they part of the communications? Are they modelling the new behaviours and providing organisation capacity?

Change Agents: These are a nominated and organised group, leaders or individuals that undertake the task of leading, communicating and facilitating change.

a2BCMF® Step 2 - Checklist

#	a2BCMF® Questions	Complete Yes/No
1	**Previous Step:** Has the previous **a2BCMF®** step been completed?	☐
2	**Sponsor Conversation:** Has the change lead had the sponsorship conversation with the sponsor covering; 'Say', 'Support' and 'Sustain'?	☐
3	**Sponsor Assessment:** Has the sponsor assessment been completed? Have the required interventions been recorded?	☐
4	**Change Team Resources:** Are there adequate team resources to support the change? Does the team have a structure aligned to a PMO and the leadership team?	☐
5	**Cascading Change:** Are the CEO and sponsor cascading the change down through the organisation, leaving no vacuums?	☐
6	**CEO Agenda:** Is this change a priority for the CEO? Are they part of the communications, modelling the new behaviours and providing organisation capacity?	☐
7	**Change Agents:** Is there is a nomination and on-boarding process that also covers change management training?	☐
8	**Trusted Advisor:** Do those involved in the organisation's change understand the trusted adviser equation?	☐

Notes:

3.3 Assess Previous Change

To achieve future organisational change management success, analyse previous change history to mitigate previous weakness and enhance future success.

3.3.1 Assess Previous Change - Overview

Definition: This step is about **Assessing Previous Change** to achieve future change management success. This involves analysing previous organisation change history to mitigate previous weaknesses and enhance future success.

Business Benefits: Assessing previous change history can provide data and insights as to what worked well, or not so well in the past. This can provide guidance for future change implementations in order to improve adoption and benefits realisation.

Key Stakeholders and Elements: The success of assessing previous organisational change history is to first get the leadership team to agree to the assessment and then to answer the questions honestly.

Business Objective: Lessons learned from previous change history can:

- ❖ **Enhance Previous Change Success:** Establish what worked well previously so it can be used to enhance future change implementation success.

- ❖ **Mitigate Previous Change Weaknesses:** Establish what did not work well so the same mistakes are not repeated, mitigating previous implementation change weaknesses.

Enablers and Barriers

Enablers	Barriers
Analysing the reports from previous change programme's lessons learned processes and applying those insights.	Following the same approach to change and missing opportunities to become a learning organisation.
Planning the change history assessment© (CHA©) approach, crafting the e-mail text and the instructions to maximise the number and quality of responses.	Not properly communicating the CHA© purpose, its importance or including detailed instructions for completion.
Performing the CHA© to understand what worked well or less well during previous implementations.	Leaders preventing the CHA© being performed because it might demonstrate weaknesses in their previous change involvement.
Analysing the low scoring responses to obtain insights that might make this change more successful.	Sending out the CHA© but not allocating enough time and effort to understand the insights and feedback.
Comparing the CHA© results with previous changes or the results from other organisations.	Not allocating time and effort to compare the CHA© scores with other organisation's change results.
Using a data driven approach and stakeholder insights to make the next change better than the previous change.	Gambling with the organisation's finances by following the same change implementation approach that was previously unsuccessful.
Sharing the CHA© results and relevant insights or interventions with the impacted stakeholders.	Leaders not sharing the CHA© results, or worse still, screening the results of some elements or questions.
Using the CHA© results to make the change programme better than previous organisational changes.	Leaders not allocating time to perform a CHA© and therefore not improving the next change approach.

3.3.2 Case Study - Gambling with Organisation Finances

Your organisation's history in managing and delivering change should be one of your starting points when managing a new change. Past change could have a lasting effect on the organisation, and this may work against future change, making change management much more challenging.

One of my favourite quotes, supposedly from Albert Einstein, is his definition of insanity:

Insanity: doing the same thing over and over again and expecting different results.

I was leading a change and business improvement project with the objective of achieving better collaboration, planning, and governance between the client's assets, functions, and their third parties. Central to the project delivery process would be a week-long workshop, where the team would map out the existing work process and then develop an improved version, to ensure greater efficiency and better working collaboration.

Prior to the main one-week workshop, the charter and project plan were developed with the sponsor and signed off by a senior executive. One-to-one interviews were held with over twenty-five people, which included the workshop team members and a section of subject matter experts from across various functions to get qualitative data. If the right data is collected it can provide diagnostic analysis of previous implementation barriers and success patterns, resulting in strategies to improve future change implementation.

Before the workshop, each employee had to complete an online change history assessment© (CHA©) which provided qualitative data (specifically on change management). A wider comparison sample from employees in other organisations from similar industries would be used as a benchmark. The purpose of the assessment was to evaluate the previous change history of the workshop attendees, from both the client and the third party's organisation.

The assessment had ten elements:

1. People Involvement.
2. Change Readiness.
3. Organisation Structure.
4. Previous Change Success.
5. Communication.
6. Organisation Workload.
7. Sponsor Support.
8. Change Approach.
9. Change Resources.
10. Future Change Success.

All workshop attendees completed the assessment and the comparison group returned over 150 completed assessments from over twenty disciplines, countries, and companies. The results of the assessment were then shared during one of the first workshop sessions, and these insights would be used as the foundation for future change.

The workshop team scored lower than the comparison group in six elements. Of these, two had major gaps. These were **'previous change success'** and **'future change success'**.

'Previous change success' asks the employee questions such as, *"Has your organisation been good at previous changes and their implementation?"*

The workshop team scored **43 per cent** against the comparison group's 62 per cent.

'Future change success' asks the employee questions such as, *"Are you confident that future change implementation in your organisation will be a success?"*

The workshop team scored **46.2 per cent** against the comparison group's 78 per cent.

I am a strong advocate of performing a full CHA©. However, if the CHA© shows up critical elements of change weakness in the following three elements; **'previous change success'**, **'future change success'**, or **'sponsor support'**, you need to reflect on the chances of the organisation arriving at the future **'B'** state and achieving programme success.

Case Study - Insights:

- ❖ **Growth Mindset:** To achieve successful change, the organisation will need leaders with a growth mindset who have a clear understanding of how previous change has damaged the organisation. Leaders with a growth mindset embrace disruption and change and use it as an opportunity to learn and improve. The CHA© facilitates that learning, providing opportunities to improve the next change. Growth mindset leaders try new things, their motto is continuous and never-ending improvement (CANI).

- ❖ **Fixed Mindset:** Many leaders who have a Just-Do-It (JDI) approach and mentality tend to have a fixed mindset. They quickly dismiss the scores and insights from the CHA©, even when this is backed up with qualitative data and information. At their very worst, fixed mindset leaders will prevent true change. They consider themselves successful, they stick to what they know, and their approach has got them to where they are today so there is no need to change.

- ❖ **Roulette Wheel Odds:** The odds of landing on red or black on the roulette wheel are equal at **47.37 per cent** (**Figure 3.3.1**). If you ask your employees, *"Are you confident that future change implementation in your organisation will be a success?"* and the answer is **46.2 per cent**, then you will need to do some serious thinking as a leader. If the organisation has fixed mindset leaders with a JDI mentality, then you might be better off going to Vegas and putting the organisation's and the stakeholders' money on the black!

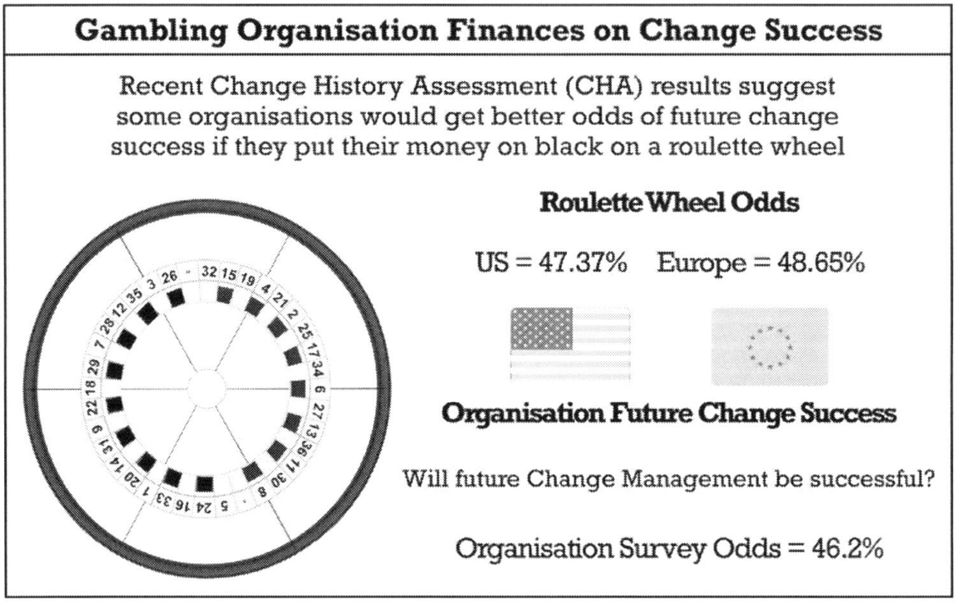

Gambling Organisation Finances on Change Success

Recent Change History Assessment (CHA) results suggest some organisations would get better odds of future change success if they put their money on black on a roulette wheel

Roulette Wheel Odds

US = 47.37%   Europe = 48.65%

Organisation Future Change Success

Will future Change Management be successful?

Organisation Survey Odds = 46.2%

Figure 3.3.1 Gambling Organisation Finances on Change

3.3.3 The Importance of Assessing Previous Change

The change history assessment© (CHA©) can be used to review the outcomes of previous change programmes and initiatives. It provides organisational insights that may increase the likelihood of successful implementation through the analysis of lessons learned, mitigating previous weaknesses and enhancing future success. Many large organisations use change impact and readiness assessments to establish organisational insights prior to change implementation. The CHA© provides a diagnostic analysis of previous change programmes to establish root causes (Ishikawa, 1990) that may have prevented a change from being more successful. The objective is to develop improved change management implementation plans using real data that will enhance future change success. This data driven approach can be used to establish internal organisational change management leading practices for future programmes. Previous change programmes can leave a lasting negative or positive effect, and it is important to learn from them by performing structured analysis.

3.3.4 Change and Learning Organisations

Central to the CHA© is organisational learning (Senge, 1990[1]). According to Senge, learning organisations are *"where people continually expand their capacity to create the results they truly desire, where new and expansive patterns of thinking are nurtured, where collective aspiration is set free, and where people are continually learning to see the whole together."* Organisational learning is an ongoing process which produces everlasting change. Organisational change is likely to be easier to implement into an organisation that understands the need for the change. Having employees with a growth mindset further improves the chances of successful change. The growth and fixed mindset concepts are developed further in **Section 3.7.10.**

3.3.5 Change History Assessment© - Elements

After having worked on change, transformation and improvement programmes over the last thirty years, it is easy to see consistent factors arising. The **Leadership of Change**® has defined ten key elements of the change history assessment© (CHA©). They are based on reviewing previous organisational change implementations, interviews with employees and lessons learned reviews. The recurrence of these factors may vary from organisation to organisation at any point in time, but they are data points that consistently surface when assessing the success of previous change implementations. The ten elements (**Figure 3.3.2**) are listed below, each outlined with their change principle and concept:

Element #1: Employee Involvement.

Change Principle: Are employees involved in the change?

The simple human truth is that people want (and like) to be involved in issues that affect them or resistance starts to grow.

Change Concept: *"People are never stronger than when they have thought up their own arguments for believing what they believe. They stand on their own two feet that way"* (Vonnegut, 1991).

Element #2: Change Readiness.

Change Principle: Was the organisation ready for the change?

Change experts have emphasised the importance of readiness: The three-stage theory of change is commonly referred to as 'Unfreeze, Change, and Freeze' (Lewin, 1997).

Change Concept: *"1. What is the present situation? 2. What are the dangers?*

3. and most importantly of all, what shall we do?" (Lewin, 1946).

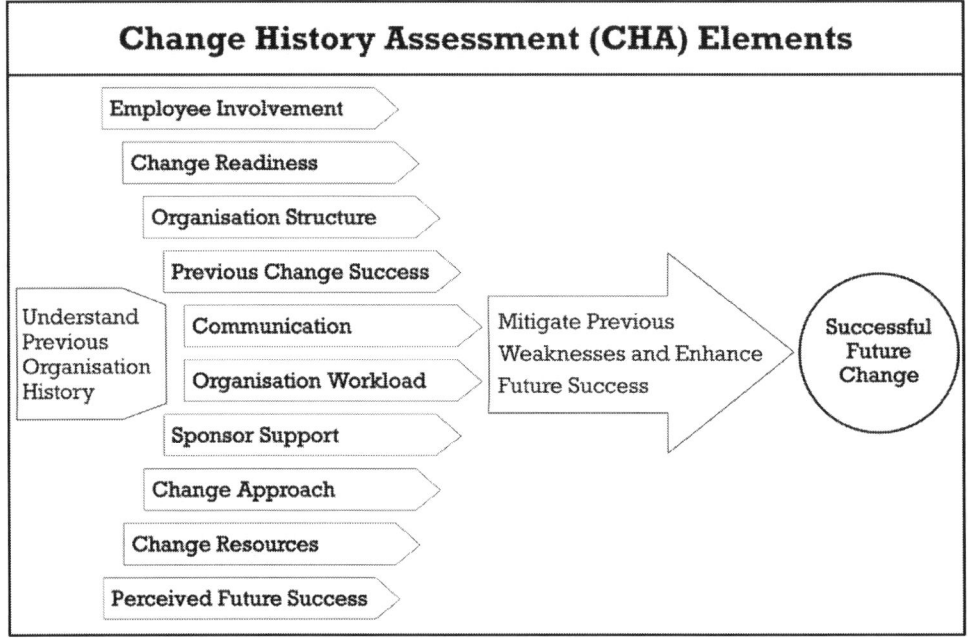

Figure 3.3.2 Change History Elements

Element #3: Organisation Structure.

Change Principle: Was the organisation structure in place to support the change?

Employee's role changes should be supported to ensure the change implementation is successful.

Change Concept: *"Error #5: Not Removing Obstacles to the New Vision. Sometimes the obstacle is the organisational structure"* (Kotter, 1999).

Element #4: Previous Change Success.

Change Principle: Was previous change in your organisation successful?

A good indication of future change success is to look back at what went well and repeat the success factors. Equally, change the factors that did not go well or were not successful.

Change Concept: *"If history repeats itself, and the unexpected always happens, how incapable must Man be of learning from experience"* ~ George Bernard Shaw (Simon, 2015).

Element #5: Communication.

Change Principle: Was previous change communicated clearly and repeatedly?

Communication is one of the biggest single success factors in change success. Communication of change is under communicated by a factor of ten (Kotter, 1999).

Change Concept: *"The single biggest problem in communication is the illusion that it has taken place"* ~ George Bernard Shaw (Shaw and Bentley, 1960).

Element #6: Organisation Workload.

Change Principle: Was employee workload considered during organisational change?

Workload and organisational change capacity should be a key consideration when changing technology, systems or processes.

Change Concept: *"Ideally, no one's workload should increase more than 10%. Go beyond that, and the initiative will probably run into trouble"* (Sirkin, et al., 2005).

Element #7: Sponsor Support.

Change Principle: Was there active sponsor support for organisational change?

Sponsorship is the single most important element in any change journey, without sponsorship the change is likely to fail.

Change Concept: *"Sponsorship is the single most important success factor in any change, transformation, or business improvement project"* (Gallagher, 2019[A])

Element #8: Change Approach.

Change Principle: Was the change approach a '**Sell**', with interventions and a resistance strategy?

Is the change about compliance or winning hearts and minds?

Change Concept: *"If it is about compliance, legislation or safety it will be a 'Tell'. If it is about winning hearts and minds it will be a 'Sell'"* (Gallagher, 2019[B]).

Element #9: Change Resources.

Change Principle: Were there enough change management resources as part of the change?

Success requires change agents and a change methodology to support the change transition.

Change Concept: *"An enormous responsibility falls upon the change team. They have not only to plan and oversee the change project, but also motivate others."* (Boddy and Buchannan, 1992).

Element #10: Perceive Future Success.

Change Principle: Will future change management be successful?

People will assess the likelihood of their organisation's future success based on previous change experience and knowledge.

Change Concept: *"The best predictor of future behaviour is past behaviour"* Mornell Maxim (Mornell, 2003).

3.3.6 Change History Assessment© - Guide

The change history assessment© (CHA©) is used by change teams to review the outcomes of previous change programmes within their organisation. It provides organisational insights that can increase the likelihood of successful implementation through the analysis of lessons learned, mitigating previous weaknesses and enhancing future success. It is important to learn from previous change by performing structured analysis to identify negative issues and to avoid repeating them on the next change. The insights from the CHA© will help to shape the change approach, planning and the resistance strategy.

Assessment 3.3.3 - Change History Assessment© (CHA©)

#	Assessment Questions	Strongly Agree	Agree	Neutral	Disagree	Strongly Disagree
1	**Employee Involvement:** Were you given the opportunity to be involved in the last organisational change?					
2	**Employee Involvement:** Did your organisation ask for your opinion during the last change?					
3	**Change Readiness:** Did your organisation prepare you for the last change it implemented?					
4	**Change Readiness:** Was the required training and skills development provided to get you ready for the change?					
5	**Organisation Structure:** During the last change, was the structure modified to make the change successful?					
6	**Organisation Structure:** Did the functions within your organisation work effectively to support change success?					
7	**Previous Change Success:** Has your organisation been good at previous changes and their implementation?					
8	**Previous Change Success:** Was the last major change essential to meet the organisation's strategy and objectives?					
9	**Communication:** Have the business case and reasons for change been well communicated?					
10	**Communication:** Was the progress of the change well communicated throughout the change process?					
11	**Organisation Workload:** Was your existing workload considered when previous changes were implemented?					
12	**Organisation Workload:** Does your current workload allow for extra work associated with a new change?					
13	**Sponsor Support:** Did the sponsor discuss the importance of the new behaviours to ensure change success?					
14	**Sponsor Support:** During the last change implementation, was the sponsor actively and visibly involved in the change?					
15	**Change Approach:** Does your organisation have consequence or intervention management to address change resistance?					
16	**Change Approach:** Did your organisation make interventions if there was change resistance from employees?					
17	**Change Resources:** Does your organisation use change agents to implement change?					
18	**Change Resources:** Does your organisation have its own change management methodology, models or process?					
19	**Perceived Future Success:** Are you confident that future change in your organisation will be a success?					
20	**Perceived Future Success:** Do you understand the key principles of change management?					

Assessment 3.3.3 Change History Assessment©

Previous change programmes can leave a lasting negative or positive effect on the employees of the organisation. A negative experience may make employees resentful and resistant to future change programmes. The CHA© should be performed early on in the change programme, right after the change team has been formed and before the detailed project change plan (PCP) is started.

Assessment Steps: The most effective and efficient way of performing the CHA© is to send out a mass company email with an anonymous intranet link to the assessment. The suggested process steps are:

1. Check if previous change programmes collected lessons learned when the last programme was closed.
2. With the change team, collate any previous lessons learned to establish trends or repeating change success or weaknesses.
3. Review the CHA© questions based on the above output and edit if necessary.
4. Recreate a draft outline of the **Assessment 3.3.3** to work on.
5. Develop and tailor the CHA© questions to align with the specific organisation.
6. Add free text boxes to capture open question responses (qualitative data) and other information such as role, function, business unit, location, etc.
7. Create the respondent list using the stakeholder analysis (**Assessment 3.1.9 Stakeholder Analysis**) created in **a2BCMF® Step 1 - Change Definition** and add other respondents if appropriate.
8. Carefully craft, review and approve all e-mail text that will be sent to assessment recipients.
9. Two to four weeks before the assessment is due to be sent out, send a communication e-mail to the identified stakeholders providing an overview on the assessment. Follow up with staged reminders.
10. Send out the assessment on the planned date and follow up with reminders.
11. After the assessment closes, compile the results for graphical analysis and share with the sponsor.
12. Modify the change approach if necessary.
13. Input the results into the detailed project change plan and communication plan.

14. Communicate the results to the stakeholders.

Change History Assessment© - Insights:

❖ No matter how negative the CHA© results may be, the change team and sponsor should see this as an opportunity to improve and become a learning organisation.

❖ Ignoring negative assessment results and moving to the next **a2BCMF®** step will reduce change implementation success and cause reputational damage to the change programme. Interventions and adjustments to the change approach should be defined and structured into the project change plan accordingly.

3.3.7 Assessment Results

Presenting Individual Element Results

Typical results for an individual CHA© question can be represented in a pie chart with commentary, as shown in **Figure 3.3.4**. The assessment results of this particular question indicate the change team and sponsor have some work to do in their approach to the next change. The change team have an opportunity to present the CHA© results back to the sponsor and the organisation's leadership team. This is both an opportunity to build on previous success and to close gaps in elements that did not score well.

Change History Assessment (CHA) Question Result

Element #4: Previous Change Success   **Results**

Question 7: *"Has your organisation been good at previous changes and their implementation?"*

- 20% Strongly Disagree
- 20% Agree
- 20% Disagree
- 40% Neither agree or disagree

Results:
❖ No employee scored this question as **'strongly agree'**

❖ This question scored the lowest of all ten question elements of the CHA

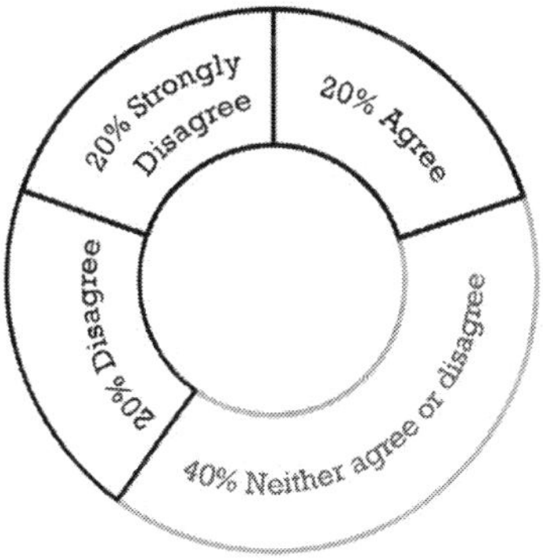

Figure 3.3.4 Change History Question Result

Change Interventions

Results from the **Element #4 - Question 7** should indicate to the change team that there are serious challenges in implementing change into this organisation. No employees have strongly agreed that the organisation has been good at previous change. In fact, 20 per cent of employees strongly disagree. Organisations that have such a low rating should perform an in-depth examination of the organisation's structure and its leadership. The change team is also likely to be dealing with a leadership team that does not engage employees, does not listen and could have a fixed mindset.

Any interventions or change to the implementation approach should feed into **a2BCMF® Step 4 - Develop Detailed Change Plan**. The project change plan (PCP) can then be developed using real data and insights from the CHA© to enhance future change success. Specific focus should be given to weaknesses highlighted within the ten elements of the assessment to improve the chances of adoption and benefits realisation. The change team should also revert to earlier **a2BCMF®** steps if the assessment identifies major weaknesses. For example, if the assessment provides data and insights which show that sponsorship has been a major barrier to success, the sponsorship approach should be reviewed and strongly considered during project change planning.

Change History Assessment© Comparisons

Results for the organisation's change history assessment© can be compared with a wider global composite in a line chart, as shown in **Figure 3.3.5**. Structured and detailed analysis of the CHA© data and feedback can provide powerful insights into change history, this can be used to improve future change success. Four typical insights are:

1. Obtain greater insights into each of the ten change elements to establish which elements are strong or weak.

2. Obtain greater insights into specific CHA© questions.

3. Compare results against another organisation.

4. Compare an organisation's change history over time.

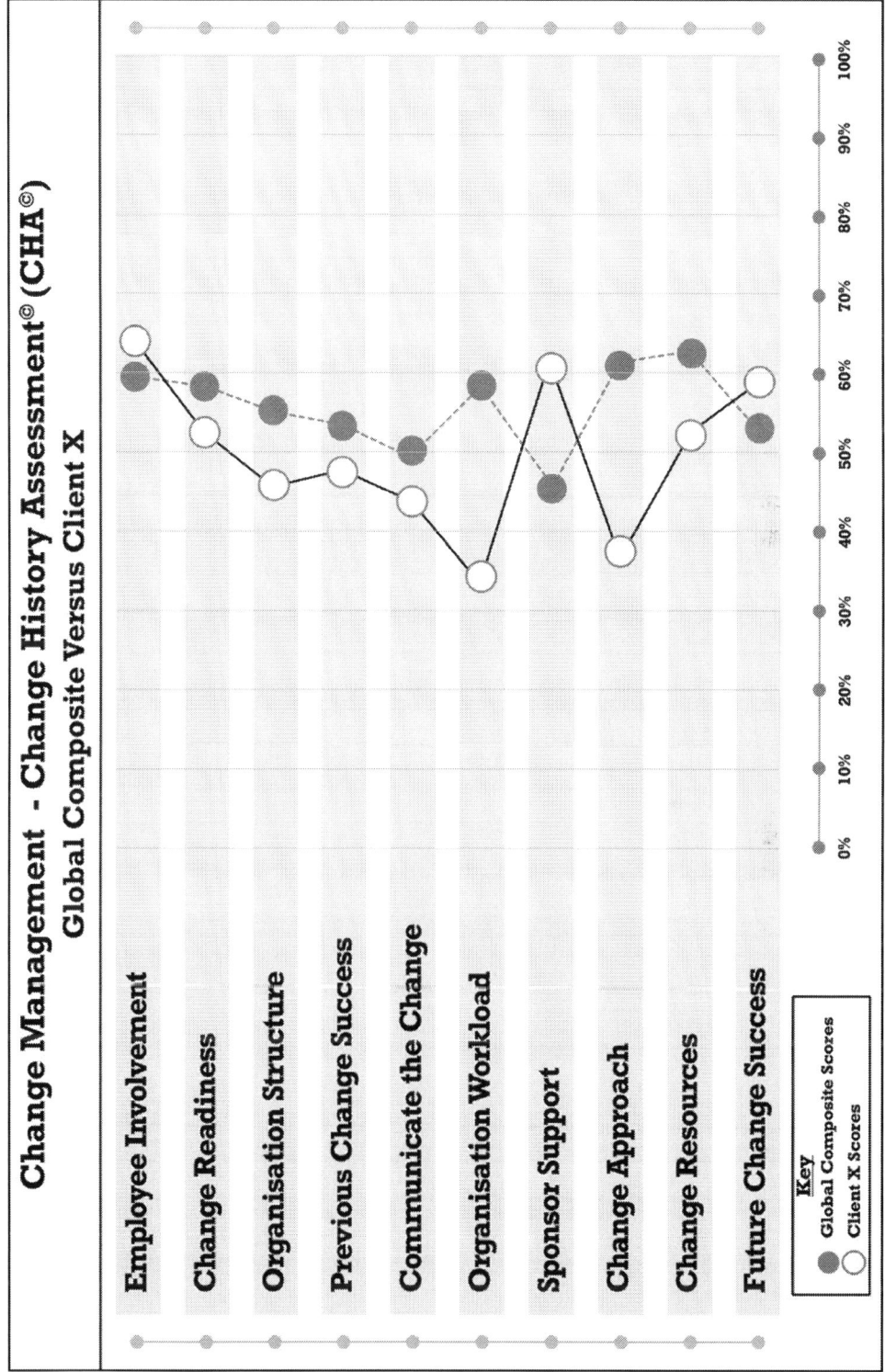

Figure 3.3.5 Change History Comparison

3.3.8 Review and Checklist

Previous Change: The process of assessing previous change for future success. This involves analysing previous organisation change history to mitigate previous weaknesses and enhance future success.

Enhance Future Success: The CHA© can provide invaluable organisational insights that will increase the likelihood of your change programme being more successful.

Planning and Instructions: Plan the CHA© approach, craft the e-mail text and the instructions to maximise the number and quality of responses.

Learning, Not Criticism: Try to prevent organisational leaders from avoiding the CHA©. Some leaders might try to avoid learning from their previous mistakes because it demonstrates a weakness in their leadership of change.

Benefits: The change team and sponsor should allocate reasonable focus and time to the change, as this effort can greatly benefit the programme.

Understanding Low Scores: Analyse the low scoring responses to obtain insights that might make this change more successful.

Organisation Comparison: Comparing the CHA© results with previous changes or the results from other organisations for further learning.

Data Driven Improvement: Using a data driven approach and stakeholder insights to make the next change better than the previous change.

Openly Sharing the Results: Sharing the CHA© results and relevant insights or interventions with the impacted stakeholders, both the good and the bad without sanitising painful facts.

Future Plans: The results from the CHA© should be entered into the other **a2BCMF®** steps. The results will improve the chances of future success, identify interventions, improve the change approach, the project change plan and change communication plan.

a2BCMF® Step 3 - Checklist

#	a2BCMF® Questions	Complete Yes/No
1	**Previous Steps:** Have the previous **a2BCMF®** steps been completed?	☐
2	**Lessons Learned:** Has the change team checked for lessons learned on previous change programmes?	☐
3	**CHA©:** Has the CHA©, along with the crafted text and instructions, been sent to the impacted stakeholders?	☐
4	**CHA© Question Analysis:** Have the CHA©'s ten elements been compared against another organisation or the organisation's change history over time?	☐
5	**CHA© Question Analysis:** Have the CHA© questions been analysed to obtain greater insights into their results, with a special focus on low scoring responses?	☐
6	**Share Results:** Have the CHA© results and relevant insights or interventions been shared with the impacted stakeholders?	☐
7	**Change Approach:** Are there any major concerns from the CHA© results that require change programme interventions?	☐
8	**Future Plans:** Will the CHA© results be fed into the detailed change project plan and change communication plan?	☐

Notes:

3.4 Develop Detailed Change Plan

Change management is a process that must be planned so it follows a structured approach, transiting the organisation from the current 'a' state to the future improved 'B' state, aligning employees, processes and systems to achieve adoption and benefits realisation.

3.4.1 Project Change Plan - Overview

Definition: This step is about producing a **project change plan** (PCP) which should reflect the overall complexity of the change effort and include all the **a2BCMF® steps**. It should identify all the key activities that are required to deliver the organisation's change objectives and strategy.

Business Benefits: The detailed PCP should be used to drive benefits realisation with a special focus on delivery, transition and sustainment. The plan should also drive all of the associated activities, milestones and interconnections to deliver adoption and successful change.

Key Stakeholders and Elements: All stakeholders should have access to the PCP and should provide input where possible. If there is a change to the plan it should be communicated to all stakeholders once it is formally approved.

Business Objective: The purpose of developing a detailed change plan is to produce a PCP by documenting the actions, timelines, milestones and resources needed to deliver the successful programme or project. The PCP can then be used to deliver the change.

Enablers and Barriers

Enablers	Barriers
Structuring and aligning the project change plan (PCP) to the ten-step **a2BCMF®**.	Only focusing on the people side of change and not having a structured, detailed PCP or activities.
Using the change roadmap as input into the PCP and further developing the activities for each of the **a2BCMF®** steps.	Not aligning the change roadmap with the PCP in terms of key dependencies, milestones and benefits delivery.
Using the change history assessment© (CHA©) data and insights as important input into the PCP development.	The PCP not having, as a minimum; activities, actionee(s), timelines, governance, milestones and dependencies.
Preparing supporting plans to mitigate against previous CHA© weaknesses, such as high employee resistance.	Ignoring the weaknesses of previous changes and not mitigating these by preparing supporting plans.
Getting input from selected stakeholders and socialising the PCP before final approval and release.	**Not** involving and sharing the PCP with key and impacted stakeholders, hoping that resistance will not surface.
PCP activities that support the main project deliverables and their work streams.	Letting the work streams operate as autonomous silos away from the development of change adoption activities.
Aligning the PCP with the wider master project plan and continually updating the plan.	The PCP **not** being aligned with the wider master project plan and activities.
Communicating the PCP updates to all stakeholders to keep them aware of critical change activities.	Lack of regular updates to the PCP and its inaccessibility to impacted stakeholders.

3.4.2 Case Study - Fail to Plan, Plan to Fail

I'd flown into Kuwait on Saturday evening as we needed to make an early start on Sunday morning, the first day of the working week. It was now past eight o'clock and I was waiting for Raheem to come to our session. As usual, he was late. I sighed. He had already failed one of project management's triple constraints (cost, scope and time) of project delivery - schedule adherence. The challenge was that Raheem lacked the relevant scheduling skills and had no sense of urgency, and I needed to ensure that the project management role was covered in the resource plan with someone with the appropriate skill set.

Raheem was part of our consulting team and was my project manager on the diagnostic - the current state assessment that we had spent the last two months working on. We had provided a detailed assessment of the finance function's current state in terms of their business operating model, key processes, and employee skills. We were asked back to draft a change transformation roadmap and project charter, which had been approved by the organisation's senior leadership team, and we were now back again to develop a detailed project change plan.

There was a knock on the door, followed by a short delay, and Raheem walked in.

"Peter, I'm sorry I am a few minutes late."

"You're here now, so let's start. We have just under an hour to prepare before the client team arrive."

Raheem sat down, opened his folder, and removed the A0 prints of the one-page charter and the change roadmap. We both looked at the project charter. There were nine sections on the approved standard document. It was a good draft and we needed to ensure that the content was reflected in the project change plan, which would be drafted and socialised over the next five days.

Raheem and I tided the room and sat waiting for the client team. We would shortly be joined by Farah and Amir. I looked at the prepared roadmap which was now on the wall adjacent to the charter. It outlined the change approach agreed with the sponsor, and would be documented in detail in the change management framework. The structure of the change management framework would be mirrored in the project change plan.

There was a soft knock at the door. I knew it was Farah. It was a great triumph to get her on the project. She had had a Western education, was intelligent, and had a personality to match. And, more importantly, she was respected by everyone in the organisation. Farah was deliberately twenty-four minutes late. For her, it was respectful to give the person you are visiting additional time to prepare, in case they were running late. Farah was forever the diplomat, and she would greatly enhance change adoption and benefits realisation. She was potentially the perfect change agent.

I stood up and made my way quickly across the room so I could open the door for Farah, as I knew she would wait for it to be opened before entering.

"Welcome, Farah. So good to see you again. Please come in."

"My dearest Peter, it is a great honour to see you again. Welcome back to my beautiful country."

Her greeting made up for her lateness, a cultural shortcoming. It was an unrushed, sincere welcome that made you feel special.

I walked into the room so she could greet Raheem. About fifteen minutes into their discussion there was another knock at the door. Immediately the door opened, and Amir walked in. Amir was also a local. I walked over to welcome him and shake his hand.

Raheem projected the charter on to the screen, stood beside a flip chart, and started to write down the agenda for the week. Day one and two were creating the draft change project plan, day three was socialising this plan with the finance leadership team, day four was developing cost estimates, and day five was presenting the detailed approach to the sponsor. At the end of each day we would be joined in the conference room by the sponsor, so we could provide him with an update on progress.

I asked Raheem to take Farah and Amir through the updates we'd completed earlier. I stressed the importance of aligning our change as much as possible with the organisation's strategy. This was for two main reasons. Firstly, the project would have a better chance of success if it was clear how it supported strategy execution. Secondly, there is only so much capacity in the organisation for change, and it was important to prioritise the importance of this project to get employee focus, energy, and time. Raheem took Farah and Amir through a very detailed review of the nine charter elements and they added their input with notes and stickies.

"OK, we're going to design the change management framework. This will feed into the project change plan, and both of these will define how this change project will be delivered over the next nine to twelve months. The two documents behind me will act as the input."

I grabbed the large yellow stickies and a red marker. "This is an easy one. Step one is 'Strategic Alignment'," and I wrote it on the sticky, attaching it to the flip chart's top left-hand corner. "It all starts with strategy, our first step." We had all worked together before and were pretty much aligned in how we would approach this change. However, I still needed their input and agreement.

"Is there any disagreement?"

There was a chorus of "No," so I grabbed my next yellow sticky and the same red pen.

"Another easy one. Step ten: 'Sustain and Close'."

They all nodded but Farah looked up, ready to say something. She spoke softly but with confidence.

"A natural last step for the framework. Easy to write, but oh, so difficult to complete." She paused. "Every change framework step must be given the chance to make it successful."

She was right.

We continued with the same format to develop the remaining eight steps. After several hours of rich conversation and debate, we had defined the ten-step change management framework.

After a late lunch, we went back to the conference room. I pointed at the first sticky and started the session off.

"It all starts with strategy, so let's ensure that we are aligned with the organisation's strategy. Raheem, can you log on to the home page and project this on to the screen? It is important that we can articulate how this project fits into the organisation's strategy if we are asked questions on this, and where to find the appropriate information."

We captured a few edits that needed to be applied and we all agreed that the project change charter was aligned with the organisation's strategy. The charter on this project would be a living document and would be continually updated and improved until the project was launched. We would now start to define the project governance and define potential KPIs, another important factor in project success.

"I am going to propose that the governance meeting should be monthly, unless otherwise advised by the sponsor."

They all nodded in agreement.

"Good. That was easy. Now the KPIs for the three key improvements." I moved to the charter and read out the KPI elements. Once I had done this, I turned to face the team.

"OK, they are defined. Our previous hard work has paid off. Does everyone agree?"

There were three yeses, but they were less vocal than earlier.

I quickly picked up two small blue stickies and wrote 'KPIs' at the top in red, attaching one to step one and the other to step four under project plan, as a reminder to add these activities into the plan later.

"Benefits tracking is also detailed in the charter. We agreed to it earlier, so I will add it too?"

I wrote it down on the blue sticky, along with a note for a 'Benefits Tracking Plan', which might be needed when the project moved to the execution phase. There was a knock at the door and in walked the sponsor, Rashid. He walked into the room grinning. This was his project, his baby, and he was happy it was progressing. He looked around at the work we had completed on the flip chart and the prints hanging from the wall. This would be an informal debrief, with the flip charts and wall prints as the script. I was comfortable with this. Rarely are you in a situation when you have no worries about a sponsor or about giving a team update. It was a nice position to be in.

a2BCMF® Step 4 - Develop Detailed Change Plan

The next morning, I arrived back in the office early. Raheem still arrived two minutes late, but he'd also worked late last night. Farah and Amir arrived a few minutes later, and I decided to kick things off by starting with a review of the work from the day before, collecting their reflections and then sharing the plan for today using the flip charts.

"Right, let us start this morning with 'sponsorship and resources'. I don't think we need to spend too much time on the sponsor. As you saw last night, he is totally on board."

They all nodded, so I moved to 'programme resources'.

"Rashid has committed that all four of us will be on the project if it gets approved. Of course, Raheem's and my availability are based on no other clients securing our services first. Right. What are the main roles? Can we join around the flip chart again?"

We continued to build a team structure, identifying either part-time or full-time roles for a communications coordinator, a communications lead, a project manager, a competency and behaviour lead, an engagement manager, a change management lead, and several junior consultants. These consultants would support administrative activities, schedule meetings, and deal with benefits tracking, etc. We would also need finance and business process improvement expertise for intermittent periods of time. To achieve change adoption, we planned to use change agents to reduce resistance and support adoption.

"Once the team mobilises, the change history assessment© should be done quickly, as soon as we know the key stakeholders."

Amir interrupted.

"But, Peter, can we move directly to the project change plan and miss out the change history assessment©? It would save a lot of time."

I reflected a little before answering his question.

"We start with the assessment to gain insights that will shape our approach to change, and these usually impact the project change plan. Specifically, these insights can both enhance future change success and mitigate previous change weaknesses. Why do you disagree?"

"Well, it uses critical time. A cultural survey could be launched earlier, and it would give us the same insights," was Amir's quick answer.

"Not really, Amir. The organisation's culture consists of the values, beliefs, attitudes, and behaviours that employees share and use on a daily basis in their work. We might still perform a cultural survey and it could help, but a change history assessment© can provide both qualitative and quantitative insights about previous change. For me it is critical."

We were making good progress, so I decided to move quickly to the plan. The project change plan would encompass all elements of the change management framework, but it would also detail how the three project deliverables would be scheduled, mostly within the 'project change plan' step. I picked up three blue stickies and created a title for each of the three deliverables: 'finance products/reports', 'finance process improvement', and 'skills academy improvement', before sticking them on to the flip chart. I turned to the group to get their attention.

"We have made great progress this morning, but we need to keep going. Let's start with 'skills academy improvement', as it is probably the most complex and touches heavily on step seven: 'develop the new skills and behaviours'."

We worked our way through the three deliverables, adding the high-level activities, milestones, dependencies, and responsible function to the plan.

I knew that Raheem would be very good at being the project deputy. He was highly professional and courteous in front of the client, and he was able to read the audience very well. This meant that I could trust his insights and opinions. The challenge with Raheem was that he was not a hard-nosed project manager, and this was what I needed. Not to be hard on the client, but to be hard on the plan and our core team so they would adhere to a structured approach and ensure that actions were executed, as per the estimated completion date. The project manager needed to be someone who would not be influenced by group norms.

I have been involved in too many business assessments, projects, or programmes where the main weakness is simple basic project management expertise. In terms of the project management triple constraint, I knew that Raheem would be strong in cost and quality but not in driving the schedule.

Raheem was the first one back in the room after a quick coffee break, and he advised me that Farah and Amir had gone back to their office to check emails. Now was my chance to have a word with Raheem in quiet.

"Raheem, you did a great job on the diagnostic. The current state assessment was an excellent client work product, delivered within cost and meeting the highest quality standard. We delivered on time, but I felt it was a challenge. So, for this change project, I am going to bring in someone more junior to manage the project activities. I think we need someone with project management skills, as well as experience, as this project has a much longer duration.

"I have not got a name in mind yet, but from across the region we should have a good pool to pick from, and they will report to me. This will free you up to focus on the client engagement side and lead project activities, rather than tracking them. For this change project we need an independent project manager, focused purely on pushing activities to ensure that milestones are adhered to. You will be the deputy engagement lead. Are you comfortable with my direction on this?"

Raheem smiled and replied,

"OK, I will take your steer on this."

"Great. And thank you, Raheem. I'll share that with Farah and Amir when they return."

Once Farah and Amir returned, I continued,

"The final things we need to add to this step are line items for other change support component plans.
1. Sponsorship and Resource Plan.
2. Stakeholder Engagement Plan.
3. Skills and Behaviours Learning Plan.
4. Resistance Strategy Plan.
5. Benefits Plan and Tracker.
6. Risk Management Plan.
7. Sustain and Close Plan.

"The need for these plans or documents will be considered after the project is approved. Input from the change history assessment© and from the sponsor will determine the need for these."

Moving straight into the next step, I raised my voice.

"In terms of importance, step 5, 'communicate the change' ranks alongside sponsorship. Change communication is like the blood that flows through our bodies. Amir, what would happen if your blood stopped flowing through your body?"

"It would stop, Peter."

"And so will our change programme if we don't communicate constantly with a feedback loop." They all smiled.

"Farah and Amir are going to lead this session. Please use the flip chart and stickies to create a draft communication plan."

Our experience, from performing the earlier diagnostic, indicated that this organisation welcomed open dialogue and would expect regular communication updates with an open feedback format. We had had mini communication sessions with the four separate finance teams and several plenary sessions, and they were, without a doubt, the most open and honest I had experienced outside Norway.

I told Farah and Amir that they had created a fantastic draft communication approach, with lots of face-to-face engagement, multiple media formats, and a feedback loop. All that was needed was to check the timeline to ensure that there were no conflicts with either national holidays or the leadership calendar. Raheem was standing beside the flip chart, waiting to continue.

"The change history assessment© looks back at survey data with the aim of enhancing future success and mitigating previous weaknesses. The change readiness assessment is similar, but it looks forward. It evaluates whether or not the key elements are in place to support change implementation. Finally, it assesses if there is a new desired organisational culture and behaviour to support the change. Change readiness is typically performed using a survey or structured interviews. The objective is to assess if the employees are ready and have the capacity for change. If the score is high, we proceed, and if it is low, we close the identified gaps."

I walked over to the flip chart. It was getting a lot more detailed.

"Now for resistance. My definition of resistance, 'Resistance is the reaction by the organisation, departments, or employees when they perceive that an organisational change coming their way could be a threat to them. Without further awareness and understanding, resistance will cause fear. It will trigger actions that negatively impact the pace of organisational change implementation, adoption of the new ways of working, and benefits delivery.' It will work against the change solution."

Sometimes a picture says a thousand words, so I drew a histogram using a black marker, then three vertical lines. I hatched the area on the left side of the histogram in red, the middle area with orange, and the right side in green. I add a title in red ink - 'People Involved in a Change' - to the top of the flip chart. Then under the red hatched area I wrote '**REBEL**', under the orange hatched section I wrote '**Observers**', and under the green hatched section I wrote '**Advocates**'. I paused to look back at the team.

"The '**Advocates**' will embrace and lead the change within the organisation. The '**Observers**' will monitor the '**Advocates**' and assess if the change actually benefits them. The '**Rebels**' will tend to resist change blindly, even if the change is to their benefit. As this is going to be a '**Sell**' as opposed to a '**Tell**', this project is about winning hearts and minds.

"OK, everyone, let's talk about the 'Skills Academy Improvement'." The 'Skills Academy Improvement' was the name given during the diagnostic to develop the skills of the finance team.

"First, we need more employees with globally recognised finance skills and qualifications. We have everyone's qualifications already, so we just need to compare them with an external benchmark."

"Yes, Peter, but I think we should ask the training department to lead this activity with our support."

"Agreed. Next, we need to develop finance training courses for each of the four functions, based on leading practice. The training has to improve the function's finance skills within the work environment. This is similar to the qualifications, and we will have to work with the training department."

Amir interrupted.

"Yes, but we will need to perform a TNA." His face lit up, as this was a topic he liked.

"Peter, the TNA will identify gaps in competency and skills. We can then design and deliver the training, create a test to verify the effectiveness, and arrange follow-up coaching to close remedial gaps."

"Amir, have you done this kind of thing before?"

"I have done a TNA with another organisation, and the process is usually similar."

I thought to myself, *it was great to have a keen resource for this*. I walked back to the flip chart.

"Amir, can you lead this activity and coordinate with the training department?" I looked back at his beaming face and he was nodding.

Moving on, I thought to myself, *I have not really explained the adoption concept in an open forum to this team, so what story should I tell?*

"Firstly, I am not sure how adoption fits into the Middle East and I will come back to that point. My technical definition is that change adoption is the way that the organisation and employees make the transition from the current '**a**' state to the improved future '**B**' state, leaving the old ways behind and adopting the new way of working and behaving. It is confirmation that they have fully accepted the change, both in their hearts and minds. It is an agreement that the new way of working is more efficient, that it benefits both the organisation and customers, and that it is part of the organisation's future DNA."

"Peter, in the Middle East most educated people understand the concept of adoption, so the word should not cause confusion. I suggest we use the concept, but I will take the action to check with the communication department on any unintended consequences."

"Farah, thank you for sharing your insights and taking that action." I looked around the room and assumed it was safe to progress. "I suggest we use the **AUILM® Model** throughout all ten-steps of the change management framework." Farah and Amir looked confused.

"Peter, they are not familiar with this model. We will have to explain."

"Apologies. Let me give you a quick overview. Firstly, this **AUILM® Employee Change Adoption Model** helps teams to understand how employees might react during a change transition, which they may perceive as a threat to them. Although individual employees will react to change differently, the model highlights some personal emotions that each person may be feeling. It provides a perspective on why there might be resistance. It also provides solutions that the change team could use to counter resistance along the change transition journey. Secondly, we will share the model and how we will take the employees through the change right from day one.

"The '**A**' stands for '**A**wareness', the '**U**' for '**U**nderstanding', the '**I**' for '**I**nvolvement', the '**L**' for '**L**earning', and finally, the '**M**' stands for '**M**otivation'. The model is all about supporting the employee through the change, so they know what the change is all about and resistance does not take hold or is minimised. The '**A**wareness' starts on day one and '**M**otivation' continues well beyond the point the change team exits the project, to ensure the sustainment of the change. I strongly propose we use it."

I stood up and walked to the flip chart.

"Sustain and close the change … Hmm. By this stage, the change team has usually moved on, either back to their old role or on to the next project without properly completing this stage. As a result, the benefits are not fully realised or sustained, and the project is not officially closed or handed over to the responsible parties.

"Let us create a plan for this step so that it can that can be accomplished successfully.

"So, what is 'Sustain'? It is a critical project activity if the organisation is to deliver value and achieve its strategic goals. For me, it is sustaining the change by adhering to the benefits plan and tracker, and aligning it with organisation and employee measures. These measures are the organisation's balanced scorecard and the individual performance plan. Each employee's individual performance plan is part of the '**M**' in the **AUILM® Employee Change Adoption Model**. 'Sustain' can be the biggest challenge in any change journey." I took a breath.

"Great. We are nearly finished. In my mind, 'Close' should involve an official approval within the project governance structure, and the transfer of ownership to the nominated party with documented acceptance. Before this happens, the benefits plan and tracker and the KPIs should be approved, and if we have all these in place, we do stand a strong chance of sustainable change.

"We also need two more activities: one for capturing lessons learned and one for knowledge transfer. Farah and Amir, this information, once added to the change history assessment©, will be invaluable for any subsequent change programmes or projects." They both agreed.

"Thanks, everybody. That's it for now, as the sponsor will be along soon for an update. Tomorrow morning, we will review the material and then Farah and I will meet the four finance leaders to socialise the presentation and plan with them to get their input and buy-in. While we are doing that, Raheem and Amir will start to estimate the internal resource hours and budget for communications, benchmarks, etc. On Wednesday, we will update the presentation and plan with the input from the leaders and finalise our approach. On Thursday morning, we will present this to the sponsor and brief the CEO after lunch."

Later that day, I reflected on a great, productive week. We had defined our change management framework, a detailed project change plan, and a supporting presentation to help articulate the value and the benefits of the change project. We had successfully presented it to the four finance leaders to get their input and had received their approval. The sponsor had engaged with us throughout the week and had put his handprint all over the approach. The CEO seemed to support the proposal and, if nothing else, it was on his mind and he was prepared to invest time in it so far. By all accounts, it was a positive week.

Case Study - Insights:

- ❖ **Change Team Involvement:** Too often the project change plan (PCP) is created in isolation by members of the change team. In many cases, not enough discussion, input and detail is given to the PCP. According to Benjamin Franklin, *"If you fail to plan, you plan to fail."* If the organisation is going to implement a change, improvement or transformation which will take up organisation capacity and compete against other initiatives, it needs to clearly articulate all of the planned activities. The activities need actionee(s) and timelines. Other PCP criteria includes programme governance, milestones and dependencies. Supporting change plans may be required, such as a resistance strategy plan (RSP), should high levels of resistance be anticipated from certain employee groups.

If the change team wants to ensure successful change, they must invest time and effort into creating a detailed high-quality plan that leads the organisation through the change, with consideration from strategic alignment though to sustaining the benefits. The hunch and launch syndrome have rarely delivered strategic change or sustainable benefits. To ensure change success, this plan should be collectively created with subject matter experts from both within the change team and more widely within the organisation. The sponsor should have active involvement in the process.

- **More than a Communication Plan:** Many organisations and leaders think that a communication plan is the same as a project change plan. While a communication plan is important, it is in no way enough. A communication plan does not include the other nine critically important elements of the **a2BCMF®**.

- **Master Project Plan Connection:** In many cases there is no connection between the project change plan and the wider master project plan and its key milestones. The master project plan will detail all non-change project activities, such coordinating the work of the other work streams. The project change plan needs to be aligned with these activities and milestones to coordinate the best time to launch communications etc.

3.4.3 The Importance of a Project Change Plan

The project change plan (PCP) is important because it helps to ensure the change programme is delivered as planned, achieving employee change adoption and benefits realisation for the organisation. Other benefits include:

- Organising the main activities of the change in a structured, logical format with prioritised actions, responsible parties, a timeline, milestones and interdependencies.

- Providing a shared vision and common understanding of what the change will accomplish.

- ❖ Being a very powerful communication mechanism, a reference for the team and the wider stakeholders to understand the key activities and progress.

- ❖ Clarifying the responsibilities of the change team members, leaders, other stakeholders, departments and employees in contributing to the goals of the project.

- ❖ Binding the change team together in completing the ten **a2BCMF®** steps and actions that will deliver successful change.

3.4.4 Project Change Plan - Key Elements

The project change plan (PCP) is structured around the ten-steps of the **a2BCMF®** and, at a minimum, should include the following:

- ❖ **Activities:** Identifiable and measurable tasks of the change programme scope.

- ❖ **Actionee(s):** The person responsible for delivering the specified activity.

- ❖ **Timelines:** The date the activity is due, sometimes referred to as the *target* date.

- ❖ **Governance:** The authority for decision-making, approving/rejecting the programme.

- ❖ **Milestones:** An important date, the start or end of significant work phases.

- ❖ **Dependencies:** The relationships between tasks.

- ❖ **Key Performance Indicators (KPIs):** The key metrics used to determine the organisation's progress in achieving its strategic change.

3.4.5 Project Change Plan - a2BCMF® Steps

The ten-steps of the **a2BCMF®** should be included in the plan to depict interdependencies and other programme delivery details:

1. **Change Definition:** This step should outline in detail the key elements of the '**Change Definition**'; case for change, benefits

a2BCMF® Step 4 - Develop Detailed Change Plan

realisation, stakeholder engagement, governance and the change roadmap.

2. **Secure Sponsorship and Resources:** This step involves identifying the sponsor and other change resources, such as the change agents and change team.

3. **Access Previous Change:** This step will shape the change approach. Insights from the change history assessment© will feed into **a2BCMF® - Steps 4 and 5**.

4. **Develop Detailed Change Plan:** This step is covered in this section.

5. **Communicate the Change:** This step details the change communication activities which require simplicity and repetition with a feedback loop.

6. **Assess Readiness:** This step assesses if the organisation and employees are ready for change implementation. If the organisation is not ready, a second assessment may be required.

7. **Manage Resistance:** This step helps to plan and manage inevitable resistance and the likely responses. If strong resistance is expected a resistance strategy plan (RSP) might be created during this step.

8. **Develop New Skills and Behaviours:** This step is about planning how the new skills and behaviours will be developed. This could include a training needs analysis (TNA), scheduled training time and reinforcement coaching. The plan should outline the employee behaviour change approach using the **a2B5R® Model**.

9. **Adoption:** This step is about getting the employees to adopt the new way of working. The plan should outline the employee adoption life cycle using the **AUILM® Model**: **A**wareness, **U**nderstanding, **I**nvolvement, **L**earning and **M**otivation.

10. **Sustain and Close:** This step is about ensuring the change is sustainable and there are processes in place to make this happen.

The close plan ensures processes are in place to officially hand the project over to operations and close all administrative activities.

3.4.6 Supporting Component Plans

Depending on the complexity or challenges of the change programme and organisation structure, there may be a need for further component plans to be included in the main PCP. These plans focus on specific **a2BCMF®** steps. A selection are listed below:

- **Sponsorship and Resource Plan (SRP):** Identifies the change sponsor and defines the strategy and actions to develop the required programme resources; change lead, communication lead, change agents, etc.

- **Stakeholder Engagement Plan (SEP):** Identifies the actions to engage groups, departments and individuals affected by the change and mitigate resistance by enlisting their support, adoption and ownership.

- **Skills and Behaviours Learning Plan (SBLP):** Identifies skills and behaviours that will be required for the employees to adapt to the new way of working. A training needs analysis (TNA) can be used to identify skill and behaviour gaps.

- **Resistance Strategy Plan (RSP):** This plan provides specific actions to understand and address resistance. This plan focuses on the change implementation strategy, is it a **'Tell'** or **'Sell'**?

- **Benefits Plan and Tracker (BPT):** This plan will document the activities necessary to achieve the benefits outlined in the **a2BCMF® Step 1 - Change Definition**.

- **Risk Management Plan (RMP):** This is the plan that supports and actively identifies, monitors, analyses, accepts, mitigates or avoids programme risks. The absence of a risk identification process is one of the reasons why many organisations often fail to manage their risks effectively (Loosemore, et al., 2006).

- **Sustain and Close Plan SCP):** The sustain part of the plan provides an approach to sustaining adoption and benefits realisation. The close plan will officially transfer ownership and close off the programme, ensuring administrative activities are completed as per the organisation's procedures.

3.4.7 Work Streams Change Support

The change management team will support many different types of organisational change and the many different reasons for change. The delivery of these organisational changes will vary greatly, but one typical format of delivering the change or improvement is to use work streams.

Work streams can be structured as discrete elements of the work scope or deliverables used to optimise the way work is organised. These work streams are usually led by one person and will collectively cover the most important elements of the work scope or deliverable. Whatever way they are arranged, the important thing is that the change team supports these work streams throughout the change, whatever their structure or deliverables. Typically, this change support, at the very least, should include communication and collaboration within each work stream and between the work streams. Work streams can be fully autonomous, independent groups that can all too often operate as silos. The change team and sponsor should prevent these from developing.

Whatever the change type or change delivery approach, it is important that the PCP should identify and outline the important change support activities.

3.4.8 Project Change Plan - Guide

The project change plan (PCP) is a formal and approved document, designed to guide the execution and control of the change programme. It is a key enabler to change success and one of the most important documents within the change programme. It should be fairly graphical and easy to understand, with the minimum of explanation.

The PCP will quickly help to structure the **a2BCMF®** ten-steps that will deliver high-level change activities. It will define how the change programme goals and benefits will be delivered. The PCP should be developed using input from the roadmap and the CHA©, and once approved it will become the key measure of change activity progress.

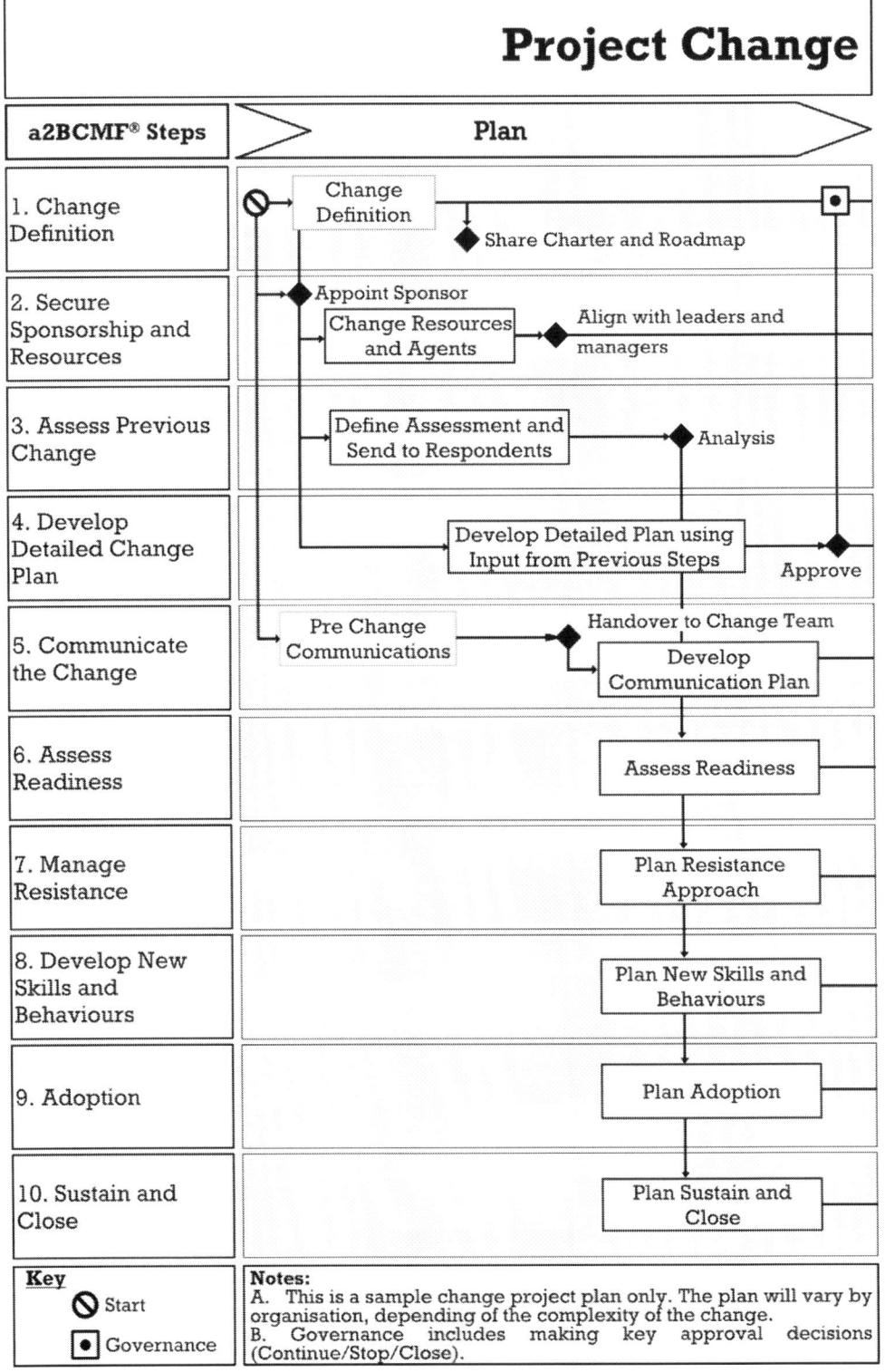

Plan 3.4.1 Project Change Plan

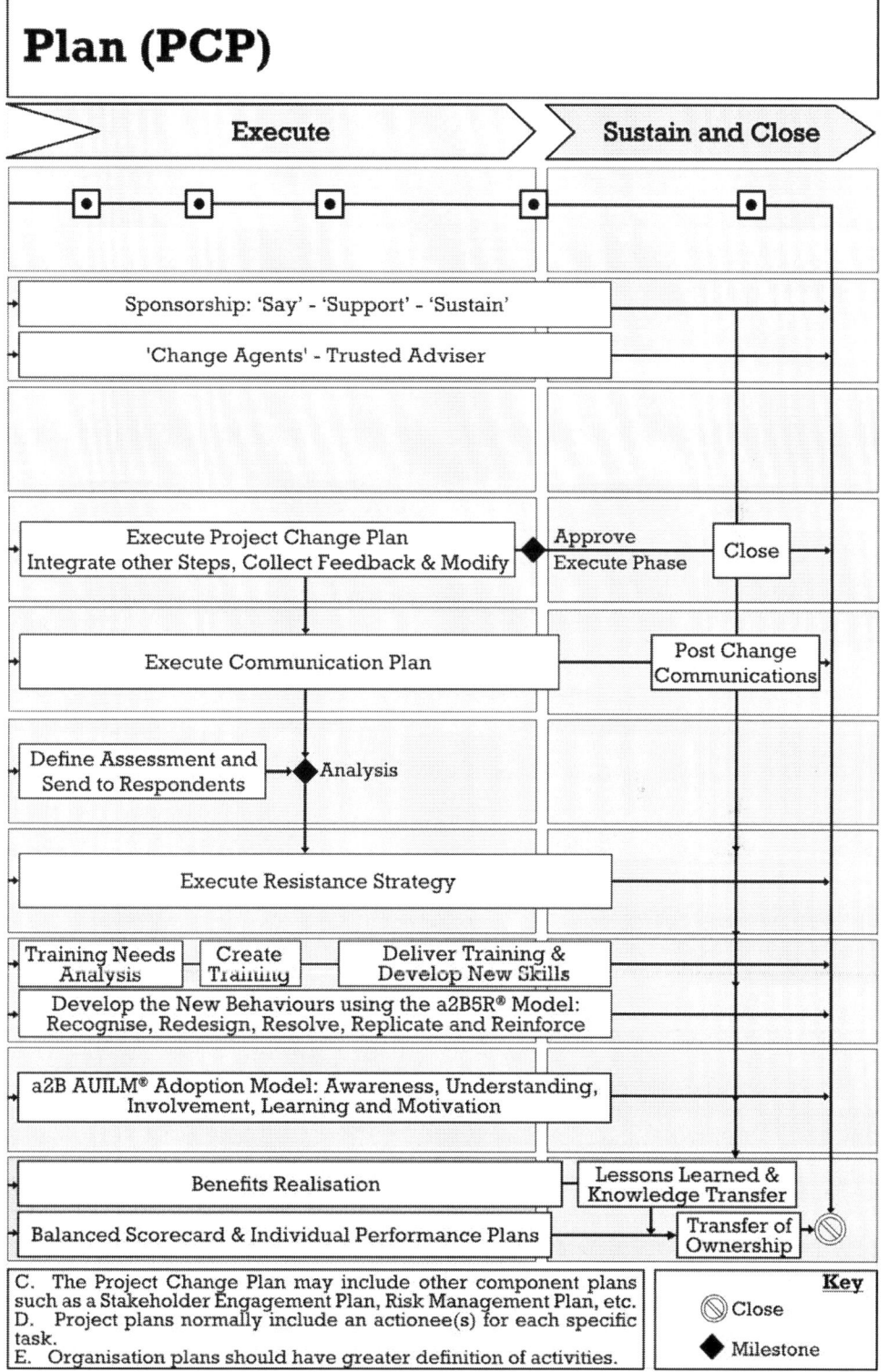

Creation Steps: The PCP (**Plan 3.4.1 Project Change Plan**) should not be created in isolation. When creating the PCP there should be project management expertise on the team. The relevant subject matter experts should be heavily involved in the process as they will have a critical role in change success. The suggested creation steps are:

1. Assemble the change team who have subject knowledge and experience of the ten **a2BCMF®** steps, include the master project plan team's input, as well as wider stakeholder representation.
2. Recreate a draft outline of the **Plan 3.4.1** as a template to work on.
3. Individually and sequentially brainstorm each of the ten **a2BCMF®** steps, capturing activities, actions and stakeholder support for each step.
4. For each of the ten **a2BCMF®** steps, prioritise the activities and actions in order of their importance to change success.
5. Start to populate the PCP with the above information and review the first draft.
6. Develop the timeline and key milestones for each of the steps and identify interdependencies. Ensure these milestones are aligned with the master project plan and there is a process to keep both plans aligned during the **Execute** phase.
7. Prepare draft two. Review and repeat process step five until the team is ready to socialise the PCP.
8. Ensure the PCP aligns with other high-level organisation project plans and then socialise the draft with selected stakeholders.
9. Collect feedback, update and gain approval.
10. Publish the PCP and use it as input into the communications change plan.
11. Add to the governance structure and ensure the PCP remains updated and accessible to the relevant stakeholders.

3.4.9 Master Project Plan Alignment

Good project managers will take a holistic approach to project management (Lock, 2013). They will integrate the key change management activities and milestones into the master project plan if this is how the organisational change is structured. Equally, good change management teams will be aware of how their change activities align with the master project plan and the other work streams.

Knowing how the master project will be delivered will require insights into project management methodologies or processes. The Project Management Institute (PMI, 2017) is the world's leading project management organisation with over half a million global members. Their guide to the Project Management Body of Knowledge (PMBOK® Guide) provides a best-practice approach to tackling project management challenges across the industry at all professional levels. The PMBOK® defines five general processes in every project and the PCP should be aligned with these:

Project Initiating Process: This is the foundation of the project and involves those processes performed to define a new project or a new phase of an existing project by obtaining authorisation to start the project or phase.

Project Planning: Once the project receives the green light, it needs a solid plan to guide the team, as well as keep them on time and on budget. A well-written project plan gives guidance for obtaining resources, acquiring financing and procuring the required materials. The project plan gives the team direction for producing quality outputs, handling risk, creating acceptance, communicating benefits to stakeholders and managing suppliers.

Execution Phase: A project deliverable is developed and completed, adhering to a mapped-out plan. A lot of tasks during this phase capture project metrics through status meetings and project status updates, other status reports, human resource needs and performance reports. This is an important phase as it will help you understand whether your project will be a success or failure.

Project Monitoring and Control Phase: This phase occurs at the same time as the execution phase. The main focus is on measuring project performance and progression in accordance to the master project plan.

Project Closure Phase: A project is formally closed. It includes a series of important tasks, such as delivering the product, relieving resources, reward and recognition to the team members and formal termination of contractors in case they were employed on the project.

3.4.10 Review and Checklist

Develop Detailed Change Plan: The process of developing the project change plan (PCP) is to document the actions, timelines, milestones and resources needed to deliver the change programme.

Roadmap Alignment: The roadmap should provide high-level input into the PCP in terms of the key dependencies, milestones and benefits delivery.

Change History Assessment© (CHA©): The CHA© insights should help to formulate the change approach to mitigate previous weaknesses and enhance future success.

a2BCMF® Steps: The PCP includes all **a2BCMF®** steps that are relevant to the organisation's change, it should also include activities, milestones, etc.

Supporting Plans: These plans should be considered, especially if the CHA© has identified previous weaknesses that will need focus. A change resistance plan (CRP) is a proactive way of preparing for anticipated resistance with planned mitigation actions.

Stakeholder Input and Socialisation: Selected stakeholder input and wider socialisation of the PCP will gain change buy-in and help to reduce resistance.

Support: The PCP should ensure there is change team support for the s and their main deliverables. The change team should ensure they do not operate as autonomous silos away from the development of news skills, behaviours and adoption plans.

Master Project Plan: The PCP should be aligned with the wider organisational master project plan to ensure there is communication within and between work streams.

Planned Communication: Ensuring the PCP updates are communicated regularly and it is easy to access helps with continued buy-in, as well as creating awareness about the progress of critical change activities.

a2BCMF® Step 4 - Checklist

#	a2BCMF® Questions	Complete Yes/No
1	**Previous Steps:** Have the previous **a2BCMF®** steps been completed?	
2	**Roadmap and CHA© Input:** Has the PCP been developed with the output of **a2BCMF®** steps one and three?	
3	**a2BCMF® Steps:** Does the PCP include all of the key **a2BCMF®** steps that are applicable to the change, including activities, milestones, supporting plans, etc?	
4	**Supporting Plan:** Have supporting plans been created to mitigate previous change implementation weaknesses that were identified in the CHA©?	
5	**Stakeholder Engagement:** Has the PCP been socialised with a sample of stakeholders and will it be openly communicated?	
6	**Change Success:** Do the key stakeholders have easy access to the PCP and do they know that it is a critical document, driving and tracking key activities?	
7	**Work Streams:** Does the PCP ensure there is change support for the work streams and their main deliverables, so they don't operate as autonomous silos?	
8	**Master Project Plan:** Is the PCP aligned with the master project plan and are there collaboration and communication links within and between work streams?	

Notes:

Section 3B: Execute - a2BCMF® Steps 5 - 8

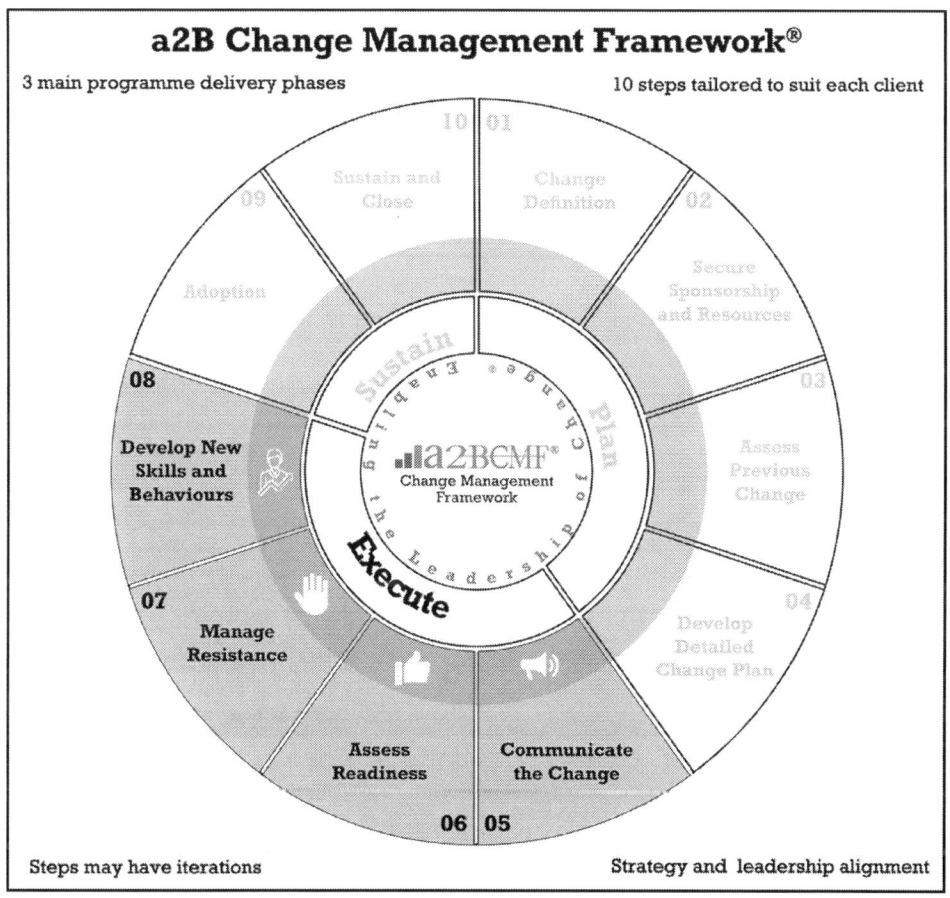

Execute: Implementing the change into the organisation.

3.5 Communicate the Change

Effective change communication is at the heart of successful change, it acts like the blood in our bodies, but instead of supplying vital oxygen and nutrients, communication supplies information and motivation to the impacted stakeholders.

3.5.1 Communicate the Change - Overview

Definition: This step is about **Change Communication**, the missing link between management and employees, and the drumbeat of successful change. Effective change communication is at the heart of successful change, it acts like the blood in our bodies, without it we would not be kept alive. Change is similar, without communication the change will fail.

Business Benefits: Without consistent and effective communication, change transition will not take place. A good communication strategy and plan will align the workforce, speed up adoption and support benefits delivery. It will support employee transition by building awareness and understanding, minimising resistance, and reducing rumours and fear.

Key Stakeholders and Elements: The impacted stakeholders should receive timely information and communication about the project. They should be involved in the change and be able to provide feedback that will be acted upon.

Business Objective: To develop and execute a good communication strategy and plan with a feedback loop that will minimise resistance, speed up adoption and support benefits delivery.

Enablers and Barriers

Enablers	Barriers
The relationship between change success and a very good communication plan cannot be overstated.	Leaders underestimating the importance of communication activities and the link to change failure.
Ensuring that when and where possible the 'WIIFM' is built into all communication channels and a2BCMF® steps.	Leaders thinking that a one-off change communication 'WIIFM' message will win over the impacted stakeholders.
Understanding stakeholder needs is critical in terms of the tailored message, the best channels to use and how to gather feedback.	Thinking that the communication needs of each impacted stakeholder group is the same, or trivialising specific needs.
Effective communication planning involves gathering stakeholder requirements such as key messages, channels, frequency, etc.	Planning communications without understanding the specific requirements of the various stakeholder groups.
Understanding the communication message components such as encoding, decoding, receiver, etc.	Thinking that a communication message sent by the receiver will be understood as intended.
Communicating 'why are we changing?', the business need, business case, change vision and the risks of not changing.	Leaders thinking that a one-off communication about the change business case and vision will suffice.
Creating a wide number of communication channels to engage and update the various stakeholder groups.	The change team and leaders not understanding the 'illusion of communication'.
Creating a meaningful and structured change communication plan to engage all stakeholders.	Not having a detailed or structured change communication plan, or worse, thinking it can replace a PCP.

3.5.2 Case Study - The Illusion of Communication

My first significant experience of the 'illusion of communication' came early on in my career. I was appointed as an operations team manager (OTM) as part of an organisational structure change. The new structure was part of the organisation's strategy to become more efficient and customer-focused. It would facilitate cellular manufacturing and would have a greater focus on customer quality, cost, and schedule targets, as well as focusing on better teamwork. The new structure was a critical strategic transformation, negotiated with the unions as part of a previous biannual pay agreement. The objective was to remove a layer of supervision from the organisation. One of the advantages of this new structure was that this would bring the managers closer to the operators, which would improve teamwork and communication.

The new working agreement was a contentious issue. Many supervisors would lose their jobs across the organisation and the supervisor role would no longer exist. Some production managers would also lose their jobs, but these would be fewer in number as they had the option of applying for the more senior OTM role.

Details of the new organisation structure were communicated repeatedly, so all employees understood the wider impact and the implications of the changes. Employees had the chance to vote for the new organisation structure with a secret ballot, linked to a two-year pay deal. It was accepted by the vast majority of employees and the change execution plans were therefore put in place. Job descriptions for the new roles were released and posted on the noticeboards, and anyone with the required experience and qualifications could apply.

After many months of recruitment, the new organisation structure was implemented. While there was some resistance from the more established supervisors and production managers, the new way of working seemed to be operating quite well. Communication was consistent from the initial announcement of the pay deal through to the implementation of the new structure. There was a feedback loop in the communication process that started with a '**Sell**' (winning hearts and minds) which changed quickly to a '**Tell**' (a mandatory change and the secret ballot acceptance). Weekly company-wide news briefs, which included tailored production division team briefs, provided implementation updates and an opportunity for feedback through a question and answer format. It was up to each OTM to hold a mandatory communication session once a week with their chargehands and operators.

Central to each OTM and its cellular manufacturing team was a team communication board. The boards were specially designed and built to stand out, as well as to host and communicate each team's performance. The boards stood two and a half metres high, were covered with blue felt and had castors to allow them to be moved about within the production area. They had three wide sides, clearly visible to anyone walking into the production area. One side was allocated to company-wide announcements and employee information, such as job vacancies. The other two sides covered four KPIs: team, quality, cost, and schedule information.

I chose to hold my weekly communication session on Fridays. I did this for several reasons. Firstly, it was an opportunity to share updates on the current week's performance, and to align the focus and targets for the following week. Secondly, it would motivate the team to complete all their tasks before finishing for the weekend.

The organisation manufactured carbon fibre aero structures, components that had a short material working life and had to be cured in an autoclave (a pressurised oven). The short material life meant that production schedules had to be adhered to, to avoid the material going out of date. Equally important was the schedule of the autoclaves, which were critical and ran like a bus timetable. If your team's parts were not ready at the autoclave at the right time, then one of the other teams would take your slot.

It was a Friday morning on the sixth week of this new way of working, and I was now focusing on ensuring our plans for the autoclave schedule could be adhered to. Everything was going well, and the team seemed to be on track to meet their weekly targets. I was going through the production schedule with two of my chargehands when, from the corner of my eye, I noticed the divisional director walk into the clean room. He headed to two of my operators, Davy and Jimmy, who were laying carbon fibre on the large metal tool as he started to chat with them. At that point in my early career, I had a little rule: Near the boss, near the exit door. However, I was confident that even though I'd recently been promoted, my schedule, cost, and quality KPIs were good and that I had no major people or team issues.

I completed my production planning discussion with the chargehands and looked towards the divisional director. He was a man I highly admired. He cared about the organisation and employees, and he wanted it to do well. He was positively involved in my promotion and I would always feel indebted to him and have the highest respect for him as a leader. Everything he did in work was aimed at delivering the strategy, company targets, and shareholder value, while developing the organisation to be even better, year on year.

He walked towards me, straight-faced.

"Hi, Peter. Could I have a word, please?" I replied,

"Certainly. What is this about?" He asked me,

"How is the new working structure going?"

"From what I can see and understand, the new structure is working well. In the first few weeks production dropped and the cost per aircraft set increased slightly, but we seem to be back on track."

"And change resistance? Are the operators working with us, and I mean really working with us? Have they bought into the new structure?"

I thought about my answer, not because I was unsure of my reply, but to show him that I'd reflected on his question before responding.

"In the first few weeks of implementation, there was natural resistance, if not trepidation. Some operators felt loyalty to the production manager who we replaced. I think most of that resistance was aimed at the chargehands, mainly because they were both giving instructions and working as a member of the team at the same time. This was a major change. It is easy to criticise a supervisor when he gives instructions and then walks off back to his office. It is much harder to do that when the chargehand gives an instruction you don't like, and you then have to work alongside them and say very little."

Again, he stood there, thinking about my answer.

"How are you handling that situation?"

"Softly, softly. I have instructed the chargehands to be patient, not to get frustrated, to show respect for their team … and over time we will gain their respect and support. For now, the change strategy is to win hearts and minds, and communication is our preferred tool to do this."

"Hmm." Obviously, I had said something to displease him. "But, Peter, are you communicating this message?"

"Yes," I said sternly. "Bill, you have just seen me reviewing and updating our plan for the rest of the day and the weekend." I was now speaking more quickly and more emphatically.

Bill's pause shortened only slightly, and only for effect. Like a good detective, he already had his questioning line laid out.

"Yes, I saw that. I commend you on holding the meeting in the work area among your team and not in your office. This is a principle of cellular manufacturing and teamworking." He paused, "But, Peter, are you communicating with the wider team?"

I paused, wondering where this conversation was going and remembered my strategy.

"Bill, I have over 120 people to manage and 20 per cent of the team is on night shift, so I don't speak to them all in groups or individually on a regular basis."

Bill held his poker face, but I could feel he was getting more frustrated. His response was immediate.

"Peter, are you holding a weekly briefing with the team around the team communication board?"

He had finally arrived at the pinnacle of his questioning and the reason he was talking to me. Just before Bill had entered the production area, I had completed my Friday team communication. I went through it quickly in my head, trying to get a sense of the balance between change communication and delivering normal day-to-day operations. Everything was going well, and the team seemed to be on track to meet their weekly targets. Bill had only seen me talking to the chargehands and had missed me giving the team brief.

I paused for a longer time and changed my facial expression from one of stress to one of slight relaxation.

"Yes, Bill. I held the weekly team brief just before you entered the room." Bill looked down at me.

"Are you sure, Peter?"

I give a slight smile, but Bill's eyes were glazed and empty, and I could feel him thinking that I was just another manager telling him mistruths.

"But Peter, I have just spoken with your two operators. I clearly asked them whether they have weekly team briefs and one assured me that not only did they not have a team brief this week, they have never been to one."

There was a tense silence. I looked confused and Bill nodded slightly, and I felt like he was about to read me my rights.

"OK, Bill, I am not sure why they told you that because they both attended the team brief. I am sure of that."

"Right. We should go over and clarify with them."

Bill nodded, probably in disbelief that a condemned man would want witnesses to verify his guilt. We walked through the clean room, towards Davy and Jimmy, who were focused on finishing their weekly task. There was always a fantastic buzz among the team on a Friday morning, with a strong focus on finishing any remaining tasks and discussing plans for the weekend. Normally Davy and Jimmy would have noticed the tension in the air between Bill and me, but not on a Friday morning, an hour before finishing the working week. They were sealing the carbon fibre material with the vacuum bagging over the tool but they stopped working as they saw us approaching.

"Excuse me, guys. I know you're trying to prepare this tool for the autoclave, but could I please have a few minutes of your time?" They stopped working and nodded, and we all stood around the large tool. I continued my conversation.

"You were talking to Bill earlier, and he asked you about the weekly team briefs, didn't he?"

Davy said,

"Yes." Jimmy returned his attention to the vacuum bag.

"Davy, you told Bill that you did not have a team brief this week, or ever. Is that right?" I could see Bill out of the corner of my eye. He had changed his demeanour for the sake of the operators and stood more relaxed.

"Yes, Peter, that's correct."

I could feel Bill's body tense up a little, but he said nothing.

"But Davy, we had a team meeting around the communication board less than an hour ago. You were there."

Davy looked at me blankly, so I pointed to the board. I could feel Bill's shoulders tense up. There were three different accounts of events and only one could be true. Bill had heard directly from the operator that he had never been to a team brief and the operator had confirmed that that was correct. Now I was stating that we'd just had the team brief. We all stood silently, looking at the large communication board five metres away from us. From this distance you could see two full sides of the board and even make out the KPI charts. At the top of each side there was a large laminated white paper frame with the words written in clear print, 'Boeing Cell Team Communication Board'.

After a long pause, Davy spoke.

"Ah, Peter. Was that the team brief? Nobody told me that's what they were."

The tension between Bill and me diminished. I thanked Davy for his time and waved at Jimmy, wishing them both a good weekend. Bill and I walked away and headed to the exit door. There was no exchange between us, although there was a realisation that this misunderstanding could have ended a respectful relationship, even between two aligned people. Once again, as change professionals we should all reflect on the words of George Bernard Shaw *"The single biggest problem in communication is the illusion that it has taken place"* (Shaw and Bentley, 1960).

Case Study - Insights:

❖ **The Illusion of Communication:** During times of change, no matter how well and how much we communicate there will always be gaps. The least likely complaint you will encounter during change execution is over-communication. Communication is a core part of the human experience, without it we feel isolated. This is the same for employees who receive insufficient communication during a change.

Every leader who has been involved in a successful change management effort will stress the need for communication. Yet, this is still one of the toughest issues for an organisation. Lack of communication is the most frequent complaint received from employees during organisational change. Even when we think we are communicating to the employee clearly, regularly and frequently there are still misunderstandings. *"When I find poor communication, I find problems, and when I find a problem, I tend to find poor communication"* (Gallagher, 2019[A]).

❖ **Frame of Reference:** A frame of reference is a complex set of assumptions and attitudes which we use to filter perceptions to create meaning. This will include our values, beliefs, culture, preferences, bias, understandings and judgement. Two employees can have the exact same experience but come up with different conclusions about it. When implementing change, we need to understand the employee's frame of reference before we can effectively communicate our message as part of achieving successful change.

3.5.3 The Importance of Communicating the Change

Effective communication is at the heart of successful business change, creating awareness and understanding about the change. Even in normal day-to-day operations many business problems encompass communication failure, equally communication failure causes business problems. All too often change managers do not give enough consideration towards the need for communication (Hayes, 2010).

Change programmes focus on the human side of change within the business and must incorporate a clear, focused and repetitive approach to communication, which is strongly linked to their engagement with stakeholders. The change communication plan (CCP) should be produced which shows how information will be distributed and received by all stakeholders involved in the change programme. It identifies the means, medium, messages and frequency of communication between different stakeholders. It is used to establish and manage ongoing communications throughout a programme. It is important that the communication is proactive and consistent to reinforce the key change messages and vision.

As mentioned in **Section 3.2.7**, cascading change and communication through the organisation is similar to a multi-level fountain. The water flows from the top, soaking each layer of the organisation until it reaches the pool at the bottom. The water is pumped back to the top to create a continuous loop, similar to how critical feedback should flow (Tourish and Robson, 2004). If you want successful organisational change and communication, emulate the multi-level fountain (**Figure 3.2.4**). When and where feasible, the 'WIIFM' message should be built into as many communication channels and **a2BCMF®** steps as possible. Over communication is a rare complaint.

The change programme team should be highly skilled in communicating the change vision consistently and constantly at all levels within the organisation, and the way recipients could interpret the message and the effects of the message should be carefully considered before communicating. A good CCP will minimise resistance, align the workforce, speed up adoption and support benefits delivery. The objectives of this plan are:

❖ Support employee transition by building awareness and understanding.
❖ Minimise resistance, reducing rumours and fear.

* Provide support and assurance to gain employee involvement.
* Create an informed, involved and committed workforce.
* Help to maintain productivity and ensure the retention of individuals throughout the change.
* Gain business ownership of the solution prior to, during and after the change.

3.5.4 Communicate the Stakeholder Needs

Authors Dow and Taylor (2010) write in their Project Management Communications Bible that;

"Communication is the key to keeping team members, managers and stakeholders informed and on track to pursue the project objectives."

They believe that the lack of a communication plan is probably the biggest mistake on projects. In fact, they believe that communication is the main cause of unsatisfactory projects 90 per cent of the time. Again, if this is important in general project management, think how much more important it is in a change project which focuses primarily on the people side of change.

Communication planning is the process of determining the information and communication needs of the change programme's stakeholders. Purposeful stakeholder communication needs to be planned. The change team needs to know precisely what they are seeking to achieve when communicating with the stakeholders. Each change programme has different objectives, therefore so does the communication with the stakeholder. The change team should define what they want the stakeholder to start doing, what needs to be done differently and what they should stop doing. It should answer the following questions (**Figure 3.5.1**):

* Who is the audience?
* What is the message?
* What are the best channels to use?
* How do we gather feedback?

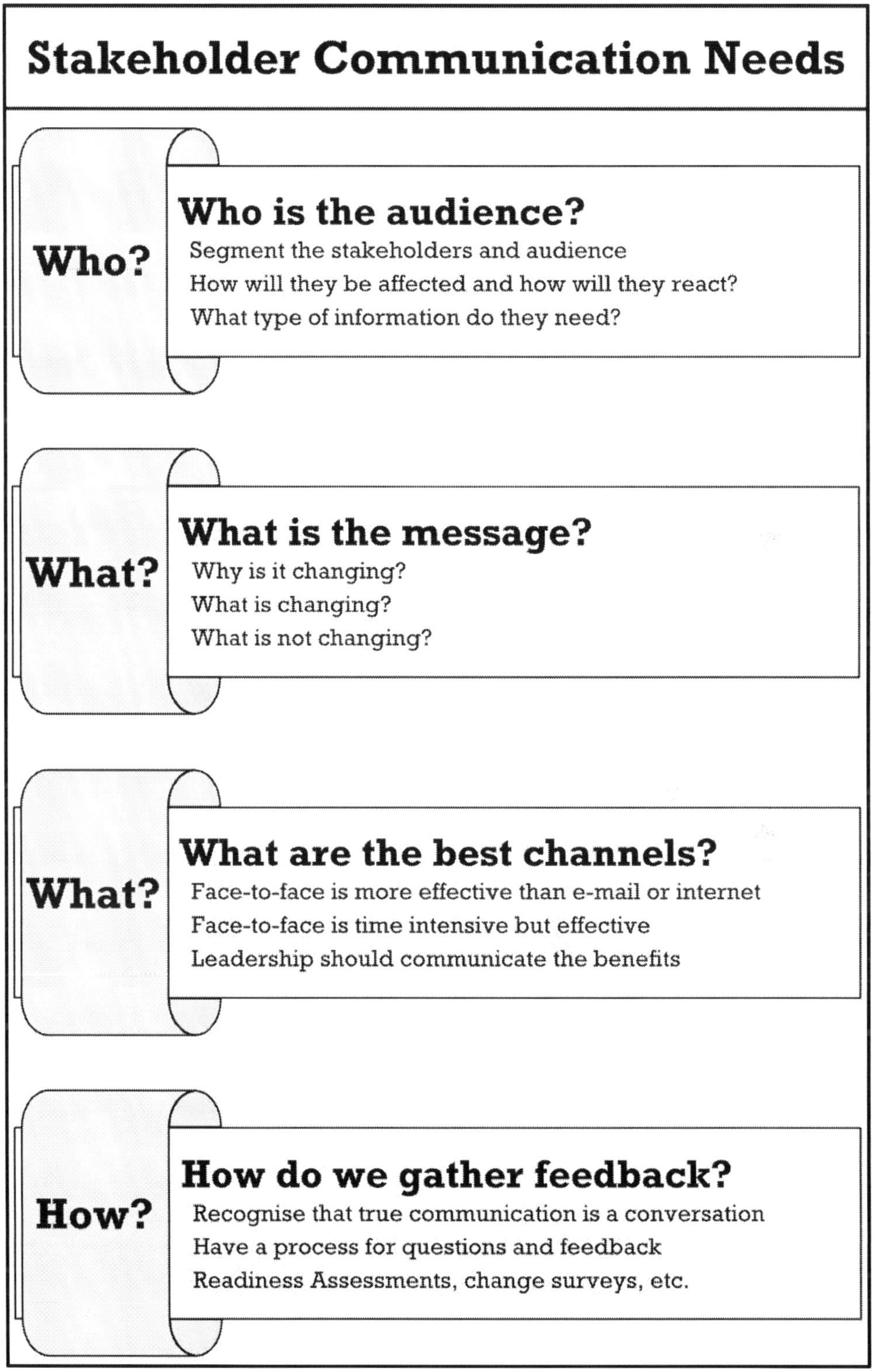

Stakeholder Communication Needs

Who?

Who is the audience?
Segment the stakeholders and audience
How will they be affected and how will they react?
What type of information do they need?

What?

What is the message?
Why is it changing?
What is changing?
What is not changing?

What?

What are the best channels?
Face-to-face is more effective than e-mail or internet
Face-to-face is time intensive but effective
Leadership should communicate the benefits

How?

How do we gather feedback?
Recognise that true communication is a conversation
Have a process for questions and feedback
Readiness Assessments, change surveys, etc.

Figure 3.5.1 Stakeholder Communication Needs

Template 3.5.2 Communication Planning

#	Stakeholder Information		Communication Requirements						
	Name	Role	Key Message	Assumptions	Frequency	Channels	Feedback Loop	Actionee Responsible	Comments
1									
2									
3									
4									
5									
6									
7									
8									
9									
10									
11									
12									
13									
14									
15									
16									
17									
18									
19									
20									

Template 3.5.2 Communication Planning

3.5.5 Communication Planning - Guide

The communication planning process defines the communication strategy and the best methods to deliver timely and useful information to various impacted stakeholders. The communication plan is an important part of every company's change management toolkit. It should cover the following:

- Who do we want to communicate with?
- What is the communication message?
- How do we want to communicate with them?
- What is the frequency of communication?
- What is the feedback loop?

A good change communication strategy and plan will align the workforce, speed up change adoption and support benefits delivery. It supplies critical change programme information and motivation to the impacted stakeholders.

Communication planning should start as soon as the organisation announces the change. This plan should build upon the elevator speech (**Tool 3.1.8**) and the stakeholder analysis (**Assessment 3.1.9**).

Creation Steps: The creation of the communication plan (**Template 3.5.2 Communication Planning**) should not be performed in isolation. The suggested steps are:

1. Assemble a diverse team with relevant experience and knowledge of the organisation and the impacted stakeholders. Include someone with communications expertise.
2. Recreate a draft outline of **Template 3.5.2** to work on.
3. Brainstorm what communication planning success would look like and list the key success factors.
4. Brainstorm the key messages for the change programme and select the most effective options. Consider 'why are we changing?' (**Template 3.5.4**).
5. For each of the key stakeholders ('name' and 'role'), brainstorm their communication needs ('key message' and 'assumptions'). Consider the 'What's In It For Me' (WIIFM).
6. For each stakeholder or grouping, record the following; 'frequency', 'channels', 'feedback loop', 'actionee responsible' and any relevant 'comments.'

7. Review the completed document to ensure consistency.
8. Share with the sponsor and test with selected stakeholders for applicability.
9. Use the output from this tool as input into the communication change plan (**Plan 3.5.5**).

3.5.6 Communication Message Components

Communication can be described as the process of exchanging verbal and nonverbal messages from a sender to a receiver in an understandable manner. The importance of effective communication is immeasurable during change implementation and every effort should be made to understand, plan and execute the process. The main components of the communication process are as follows (**Figure 3.5.3**):

- ❖ **Sender:** The person who initiates the communication and is initially responsible for the success of the message. The sender's experience, attitude, knowledge, skill, perceptions and culture will influence the message.

- ❖ **Encode:** This is about creating the message. It is the process of turning the change message into verbal and nonverbal formats. The sender encodes the information in terms the receiver will understand.

- ❖ **Message:** The ideas and feelings that make up the content of communication.

- ❖ **Decode:** The process of obtaining, absorbing, understanding, and using the change information. The receiver has to decode or decipher the information sent. The degree to which the decoder understands the message is dependent upon various factors, such as knowledge of change and their responsiveness to the message.

- ❖ **Receiver:** The person who is the target of the communication. It is the receiver who tries to understand the message, trying to interpret it as it was intended so the desired action or objectives are achieved. This is why the trusted advisor equation is so important: **Credibility** - *"I trust what you say about the change improvement!"*

- ❖ **Channel:** The medium or means used to exchange or transmit the message (see **3.5.8 Communication Channels**).

- ❖ **Noise:** This is any interference with encoding and decoding the message. This prevents the change message from being heard or understood.
- ❖ **Feedback:** Open and honest feedback from the impacted stakeholders during change implementation is critical if the change is to be successful. It should be seen as constructive and welcomed as a positive opportunity to learn and improve. Just as important is negative feedback, according to Churchill (1931), *"the temptation to tell a chief in a great position the things he most likes to hear is one of the commonest explanations of mistaken policy."*

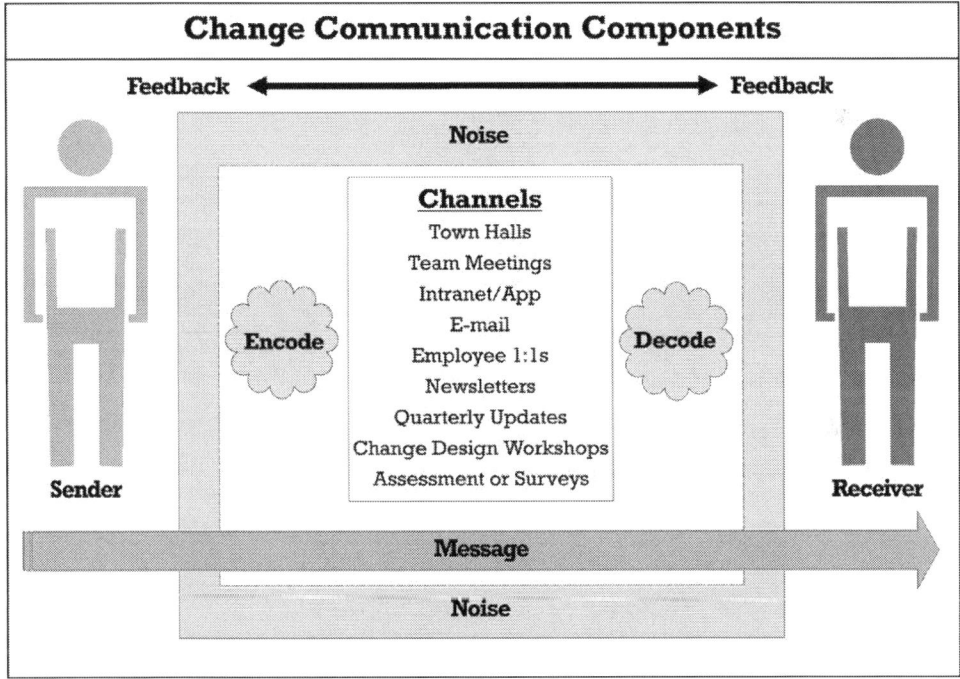

Figure 3.5.3 Communicate Message Components

3.5.7 Why Are We Changing? - Guide

The 'why are we changing?' concept addresses the typical questions the impacted stakeholders ask when they become involved in an organisational change. It helps to create key communication text that answers these questions in a concise and consistent way. It should be used in communication strategy planning and feed into the communication change plan.

Creation Steps: The 'why are we changing?' template (**Template 3.5.4 Why Are We Changing?**) should not be created in isolation. A selection of impacted stakeholders should be involved in this process. The suggested creation steps are:

1. Assemble the change team and brainstorm each of the four elements.
2. Recreate a draft outline of **Template 3.5.4** to work on.
3. Draft a few sentences for each element 'Why is there a business need?', 'What is the business case?', 'What is the vision for change?' and 'What is the risk of not changing?'
4. Test with selected stakeholders, modify as required.
5. Check the text is aligned with the organisation's strategic intent and change vision.
6. Share with the sponsor and gain approval.
7. Use in all communications and as input into the change communication plan (CCP) (**Plan 3.5.5**).

Template 3.5.4 Why Are We Changing?	
	Why is there a business need?
1	The business needs to change because …...
	What is the business case?
2	The business case for change is …...
	What is the vision for change?
3	The vision for change is …..
	What is the risk of not changing?
4	The risk of not changing is …..

Template 3.5.4 Why Are We Changing?

3.5.8 Communication Channels

Communication channels identify the specific ways that information is distributed to and received back from targeted stakeholder audiences. The channels should be selected based on their potential effectiveness in reaching each target audience and this will vary from organisation to organisation. The communication plan should include elements that facilitate delivering the right messages to the right audience, by using the right communication vehicles repeatedly throughout the change programme with a feedback loop. The feedback should gather the reactions to both the content of the change, and how the change is being implemented. Communicate consistently about the change, do this frequently by using multiple channels, including speaking, writing, video, training, focus groups, bulletin boards, intranets, etc. Suggested communication channels could be:

Town Halls: Town hall meetings, whether physical or virtual, are a great way to communicate with employees and stakeholders, engaging them directly about the change. They are an opportunity for the leaders to announce change programmes face-to-face with large groups. It encourages dialogue and employees can make their voices heard, as well as giving leaders the chance to answer questions directly and reduce potential growing resistance. Periodic town halls also ensure that stakeholders are not forgotten in the midst of the business changes. Other advantages include:

- ❖ Updates are shared first-hand.
- ❖ Visible sponsorship and leadership.
- ❖ Employees feel engaged.
- ❖ Unfiltered raw feedback.

Team Meetings: These already structured meetings can be used as a vehicle by the change team to communicate with the organisation's teams directly or through the team manager. They allow employees to discuss the change, share ideas, and provide input or feedback to the change team. The effectiveness and efficiency of using these meetings to engage employees should not be overlooked by the change team.

Intranet and Apps: The advantages of the intranet are that it has rapid and broad reach to communicate and share change management news and resources. The number of hits and clicks to other links, as well as time spent reading, can provide invaluable analysis to the change team on engagement and what interests the stakeholders. The change team can also use the intranet to encourage discussions and gather feedback. The disadvantages are few, although proprietary information must be secured and not everyone feels comfortable with this media type, etc.

Communication apps are becoming more and more popular, providing a way to centralise change programme information and enable the change team to quickly share information with the stakeholders. Almost every stakeholder will have a smartphone, this provides a weighty argument as to why the change team should focus on mobile technology. The big advantage is that you can engage your stakeholders wherever they are, at any time.

E-mail: It is all too easy to send out a general e-mail message with a detailed attachment providing information about the change (e.g. a thirty-page presentation), rather than using any of the other channels. Sending an instruction to stakeholders from the isolation of a keyboard is not as effective as discussing the issue with them face-to-face. The e-mail has low engagement impact and does not convey empathy to concerned employees, thus is not a great change management engagement channel.

Employee 1:1s: While face-to-face communication can be one of the most powerful channels (if used right), it does require a lot of effort and time. However, it does allow the change team to get messages out quickly and with empathy. Face-to-face communication also provides the opportunity to build in two-way communication and get real reactions to the change. The message can also be tailored to each audience, conveying their personal WIIFM. The disadvantage is that these meetings can be hard to control so they require much more preparation and insights about each individual.

Hardcopy Newsletters: This type of media is becoming less popular than electronic forms of communication, for obvious reasons. Printed copies incur additional costs for material and logistics, as well as recycling. However, it can be nice to have a colour print to catch stakeholder attention, especially at face-to-face events or discussions.

Quarterly Half Day Updates: These can be of a similar format to the town halls with visible leadership directly engaging the stakeholder and employees. They keep the drum beat of change communication and engagement going, allowing the sponsor and change team to engage a large group of employees face-to-face. They can also be suitable to host change design workshops.

Change Design Workshops: The objective of these workshops is to co-design and test the change solutions with selected stakeholders and employees. There are many different ways of structuring these workshops, but a typical approach is for the change team or change agent to facilitate the event to support the work stream lead(s). The work stream lead and members of their team present their draft solutions or deliverables to obtain design input, gauge acceptance and avoid potential resistance. This concept is very much aligned with the **I**nvolvement step in the **AUILM® Employee Change Adoption Model (See Section 3.9.5)**. The change team may also hold these events for **a2BCMF® Step 8 - Develop New Skills and Behaviours**.

Assessments and Surveys: With current technology and new innovative media, the opportunities to perform assessments and surveys has never been easier. Anonymous stakeholder assessments such as change history and change readiness assessments should, by default, be part of the communication and change plan. There are also other opportunities for assessment and surveys, some can be performed during large group meetings, providing instant insights and feedback on live events and questions can be put to the audience to get real-time feedback. They can also be sent out after events or meetings to get feedback on what the stakeholders thought. These assessments or surveys are powerful tools to learn and improve change management communication and engagement.

Other Methods: We are in the middle of 4IR and a new media technology comes on the market nearly every day. They bring new innovative ways for the change message to be communicated and, if proven, can bring both refreshment and excitement to the message.

Execution Considerations:
- ❖ **Frequency:** Defines the number of times that key messages will be communicated using the selected channel.
- ❖ **Timing:** Defines the schedule for communication activities and the interconnected dependencies.

- ❖ **Costs and Resources:** Identifies the resources and associated costs needed to produce and distribute the communication. While face-to-face communication is more effective, it costs more as it takes people away from their work, rooms need to be reserved, refreshments provided, etc.
- ❖ **Review and Approval:** Identifies the governance process and the individuals that are needed to review and approve the plan.

3.5.9 Communication for Adoption

The adoption process is discussed specifically in **a2BCMF® Step 9 - Adoption** and should have been be considered in **a2BCMF® Step 1 - Change Definition**. However, communication should be driving and supporting change adoption. Communication will play an important role in supporting the adoption life cycle using the **AUILM® Employee Change Adoption Model:**

- ❖ **Awareness:** What early communication does the employee need at the start of the programme? Does the change team understand the importance and urgency of issuing the change elevator speech (**See Section 3.1.10**) early in the change programme?
- ❖ **Understanding:** What communication does the employee need so they get a greater understanding of the change? What are the best channels to convey this message?
- ❖ **Involvement:** What communication channels and messages does the employee need to get them involved in the change?
- ❖ **Learning:** What communication channels and messages does the employee need to develop the new skills and behaviours?
- ❖ **Motivation:** What communication channels and messages does the employee need to keep them motivated to fully adopt and sustain the change?

Similar consideration should be given to behaviour change which is discussed specifically in **a2BCMF® Step 8 - Develop New Skills and Behaviours.** Behaviours will also have been considered during **a2BCMF® Step 1 - Change Definition.** If the CCP is aligned with the PCP then activities to deliver behaviour change and adoption should have been identified.

3.5.10 Change Communication Plan - Guide

The change communication plan (CCP) is a formal and approved document designed to guide the execution and to control the change communication programme. It is a key enabler to change success and one of the most important documents within the change programme. It will help to structure what, how and when the change communication will be executed. It is one of the most effective plans in delivering successful organisation change.

Creation Steps: The CCP (**Plan 3.5.5 Change Communication Plan**) should not be created in isolation and there should be someone with communication expertise on the team. The suggested creation steps are:

1. Assemble the change team who have subject knowledge and experience of the ten **a2BCMF®** steps.
2. Recreate a draft outline of the **Plan 3.5.5** as a template to work on.
3. Individually and sequentially brainstorm each of the communication channels. Ask what has worked in the past, what works best now and what innovative techniques could be explored. Define and include what communications are necessary to support behaviour change and change adoption.
4. For each of the communication channels, decide the milestones, interdependencies, timing and frequency.
5. Start to populate the CCP with the above information and review the first draft.
6. Prepare draft two. Review and repeat process step four until the team is ready to socialise the CCP.
7. Ensure the CCP aligns with the PCP then socialise the draft with selected stakeholders.
8. Collect feedback, update the CCP and gain approval.
9. Publish the CCP, ensuring it is accessible to all stakeholders.
10. Add to the governance structure and ensure the CCP remains updated.

Change Communication Plan - Insights:
- ❖ Ensure the CCP uses the project change plan (PCP) as input, and both plans stay aligned throughout the change programme.
- ❖ The change team should modify the communication channels and approach if the original channels are not effective.

Leadership of Change® Volume 3 - Change Management Handbook

Change Communication

Communication Channels	Plan
1. Town Halls	Official Launch
2. Team Meetings	Leadership Briefing — Team Briefing
3. Intranet or Apps	
4. E-mail	
5. Employee 1:1s	
6. Newsletters	
7. Quarterly Half Day Updates	
8. Change Design Workshops	
9. Assessments or Surveys	
Linked to Governance and Project Change Plan (PCP)	

Key
◯ Start
▣ Governance

Notes:
1. Sample plan for discussion and learning only.
2. The Communication Plan should be accompanied with a detailed document outlining stakeholder groups, target audience, frequency, key messages, etc.

Plan 3.5.5 Change Communication Plan

Plan (CCP)

Execute → Sustain and Close

3. The Change Communication Plan should be aligned and be a component of the Project Change Plan (PCP) developed in a2BCMF® - Step 4.
4. Some organisations may include change programme status report distribution as part of communications.

Key
- ⊘ Close
- ↕ Governance Link and Feedback

3.5.11 Review and Checklist

Communicate the Change: Communication is the process of getting information to the impacted stakeholders about the change. It requires simplicity and repetition with a feedback loop.

Importance of Communication: Effective change communication is at the heart of successful change, it acts like the blood in our bodies, but instead of supplying vital oxygen and nutrients, communication supplies information and motivation to the impacted stakeholders.

Communicate the Stakeholder Needs: If you don't communicate with the impacted stakeholders, the change will fail.

Communication Planning: Planning is the process that defines the strategy and the best methods to deliver timely and useful information to various impacted stakeholders.

Communication Message Components: Within every communication there is; sender, encode, message, noise, decode, receiver and feedback loop.

'Why Are We Changing?' Message: The 'why are we changing?' message should be communicated throughout the change implementation. It should include the business need, business case, change vision and the risks of not changing.

Communication Channels: Using a wide variety of media channels such as e-mail, intranet, apps, town halls and workshops improves the chances of communication success.

Change Communication Plan: The CCP is a formal and approved document designed to guide execution and control the change communication programme. It is an important part of every organisation's change management toolkit.

a2BCMF® Communication Input: The CCP should connect across all a2BCMF® steps, it is not an isolated or one-off activity.

Communication Complaints: One of the few complaints you will get as a change team, sponsor or leadership team, is 'over communication'!

a2BCMF® Step 5 - Checklist

#	a2BCMF® Questions	Complete Yes/No
1	**Previous Steps:** Have the previous **a2BCMF®** steps been completed?	☐
2	**Communication Importance:** Does the team understand the importance of communication and that without it the change will fail?	☐
3	**Stakeholder Needs:** Is there an understanding of stakeholder needs: The audience, the message, the best channels and how to gather feedback?	☐
4	**Communication Planning:** Have the requirements been gathered in terms of: Key messages, assumptions, frequency, channels, feedback loop, etc.?	☐
5	**Message Components:** Is there an understanding of message components: Sender, encode, message, decode, receiver and feedback loop?	☐
6	**'Why are we Changing?':** Has the 'why are we changing?' been defined: Business need, business case, change vision and the risk of not changing?	☐
7	**Communication Channels:** Are there a wide variety of channels, providing different media formats, to communicate and engage the impacted stakeholders?	☐
8	**Change Communication Plan:** Has a meaningful and structured CCP been created that sets out communication channels, timing, frequency, etc.?	☐

Notes:

3.6 Assess Readiness

Readiness is about ensuring the sponsor and leadership team get the organisation and its employees ready so that resistance is limited, and adoption is maximised.

3.6.1 Assess Readiness - Overview

Definition: Assess Readiness is the process of assessing the organisation and its employees prior to change implementation, ensuring that they are ready to start adopting the change.

Business Benefits: Assessing readiness can provide data and insights into potential gaps so corrective actions can be executed to close them. Closing gaps supports change implementation success, improving adoption and benefits realisation.

Key Stakeholders and Elements: Assessing readiness involves all impacted stakeholders. The assessment provides the change team with invaluable data and insights that can be used to modify or improve the change approach and implementation plan.

Business Objective: To ensure the organisation and the employees have the capacity to start adopting the new change:

- ❖ **Identify Potential Change Implementation Gaps:** The assessment will provide data and insights that will identify gaps which need to be addressed.

- ❖ **Execute Corrective Actions to Improve Readiness:** Corrective actions and intervention plans should be prepared and executed to close any identified gaps.

Enablers and Barriers

Enablers	Barriers
Balancing normal day-to-day operations or workload with the implementation of legislative and strategic change.	Not actively engaging and checking with the employees to ensure they have capacity on top of their existing workload.
Preparing to develop the new skills and behaviours to match the change, prior to performing the change readiness assessment (CRA).	Not starting to reinforce the required behaviours that support the change until the CRA is executed.
Tailoring the CRA and crafting suitable accompanying text to engage and motivate the respondents to complete the assessment.	Sending out an untailored CRA, not related to the organisation's specific change.
Giving employees adequate time to complete the assessment and sending out staged reminders.	Too short or too long a response time to complete the CRA without reminders or prompts.
Full and proper analysis of the CRA results (quantitative and qualitative data) that can identify change programme improvements.	The sponsor and leadership team not openly accepting the CRA results, or worse still, sanitising those aspects that might embarrass leaders.
Governance ensures the programme has appropriate oversight and the change implementation (Go/No Go) decision is approved.	Leaders not intervening when employee resistance surfaces, this slows down change implementation.
Using poor scores and insights from the CRA as an opportunity to learn and improve.	The sponsor and the leadership team thinking that gaps in readiness can be closed during implementation.
Using the CRA results to improve readiness by developing interventions and corrective actions to close any identified gaps.	Not focusing on the two critical **a2BCMF®** steps (sponsorship and communication) before the other key elements.

3.6.2 Case Study - Preparation Generates Readiness

The aerospace industry is highly competitive, and as a supplier to Boeing, Airbus, Rolls-Royce and GE, the company was under constant pressure to improve its cost, quality, and scheduling performance. Initiatives were always being sought to deliver improved performance, and the implementation of a new ERP system would achieve this. The ERP management information system introduced new software to improve the manufacturing, planning, purchasing, inventory, and finance processes. It was launched as a strategic initiative to support and achieve customer cost reduction targets and improve schedule adherence.

An external consultant was leading the implementation of the new ERP system. Their engagement scope covered the hardware, software, change management, training, and post go-live coaching. The hardware and software were installed and signed off by the leadership team ahead of schedule, without any major issues. The training was rolled out, communications were constant and consistent, and a change readiness assessment was performed as part of the change management programme. The readiness assessment had highlighted some issues, but corrections had been made and the go-live date was to remain the same.

The go-live seemed to happen without any major problems, and the new system successfully uploaded the old system's data. A team worked over the weekend to ensure that any technical issues or bugs would be sorted for the start of the following week. Over the next six weeks, there were stock audits of the stores and work in progress (WIP) on the processing site to ensure that the data processed by the new system was accurate. For the first few weeks it was at almost 99 per cent, but then it slowly started to drop. By about the fifth week the figures were still showing a downward trend and unauthorised aircraft sub-assemblies started to appear throughout the processing site. Senior management started to be concerned that the new ERP system was not delivering what had been promised. The store and stock accuracy audit results had never been lower, and the factory WIP continued to increase. More completed aircraft wing sub-assemblies were discovered at the end of the production line.

All flight components used in commercial aircraft must have full traceability in terms of the approved manufacturer or distributor, the part or material to a lot, the batch, the treatment number, etc. Thankfully, the new wing kits had the full manufacturing processing record documents. The first question was: how were the components that were part of the sub-assembly released from the store? Who authorised the manufacturing order number?

The order cards for the unauthorised completed aircraft wing sub-assemblies were analysed. There were twenty different completed aircraft wing sub-assemblies with one thing in common: they all had handwritten production cards. You might have assumed that this would have been easy to spot and that surely someone would have picked up on it. However, from time to time the printers would go offline and the production cards would then have to be handwritten by production planning, so these cards had not been questioned.

So, someone had created the production cards that permitted the sub-assemblies to enter the production process, but how did the parts leave the store? It seemed impossible. A store person was highly unlikely to bypass the authorised process. The component parts of a sub-assembly were released to a holding store that required access through two secure doors, and the store was only accessible to staff with an authorised security pass. The store perimeter wall was three metres high with an additional two-metre-high wire fence, and it was highly unlikely it could be breached.

It was a highly contentious decision, but the on-site management team had no option but to fit hidden surveillance cameras directed at the store. They were fitted by a private contractor on a Saturday night when no one was on the premises except the security guards. No one outside security, senior management, and HR was aware that a live feed to monitor the store was in place. We all waited for the unlikely breach of the store.

We did not have to wait long. On Monday night the surveillance camera recorded someone place three ladders up against the perimeter, climb up, and enter the store by jumping on to the upper mezzanine floor. The employee then proceeded down to the printer area and removed a preprinted manufacturing processing record document and an order card. For the next twenty minutes he loaded a trolley with a full set of components, including the very large outer aircraft skin panel. He then exited the store through the double doors.

It was very clear who had climbed over the fence and made an unauthorised withdrawal from the store. It was not an unscrupulous employee with an ulterior motive. Instead, it was Gary, a loyal, trusted, and highly respected employee with fifty years' experience.

The first question was to ask Gary whether he had been working alone and how he had not been seen entering the store over a five-metre fence. The ingenious part was his ability to connect together three ladders using a set of quick release brackets that he seemed to have made specifically for this manoeuvre. After senior management reviewed the videos, Gary was asked to the HR office for a 'chat'.

Gary admitted what he had done right away, without the need to review the video evidence. He confessed that he knew it was wrong, but only from the point of creating a new order card with a legitimate production order number once the handwritten card and sub-assembly had been detected. His main priority was to keep the operators busy and to keep them producing sub-assemblies, as this is what they were getting paid for. That was his measure of production and output. He struggled to understand the just-in-time concept.

I bumped into Gary as he came back from the HR interview and he shared the full details with me about what had happened.

"Did Norman (Gary's supervisor) not ask whether you were you ready for the new system to go-live?"

"He did, and I told him we were not ready. I tried to explain that with all the teams on rotating shift patterns we were not all briefed or trained." He paused to control his frustration.

"I also told him that I'd be on holiday during the go-live, but he said that he was not going to the production manager to ask him to tell the ERP consultant team that he was not ready. He basically told me to just get on with it."

I had to ask him,

"Where did you get the ladders from?"

"Peter, they were old ladders the painter left twenty years ago at the back of the hangar. I always kept them for emergencies and kept them hidden. The quick release brackets were something I made one night on night shift when I was bored."

I moved back to the new systems.

"Gary, did you attend the training at all?"

"No. During the interview I was asked about the communications briefing before the new ERP systems went live, and the system training and the ongoing coaching since the system went live. I told them I had been to a couple of briefing sessions but had missed the training due to more important unplanned operational issues that popped up as I was on my way to the training."

"But, Gary, how were these shortcomings not picked up by the consultant during the change readiness assessment?" I waited for Gary's answer as a smile came over his face.

"Peter, I heard the results indicated that the go-live should be postponed. But Norman told the consultant he disagreed, and it was his call to proceed. I heard him promise to close the gaps before the go-live."

The consultants were called back in to establish the root cause of the new system implementation failure, as it was not providing the results expected. The major focus was on why the store inventory accuracy had dropped and what the failings were before and after go-live. The consultants would focus on the four weeks before go-live and the six weeks afterwards. They then spent the next two weeks interviewing the key stakeholders and a random selection of the operators, and their report was presented to the leadership team.

The report confirmed that all the hardware and software had been successfully installed and were working fully with no connection or system bugs. The communication briefs had been completed on the scheduled dates, but there was no record of how many people attended and there was a poor collection of questions from the operators. Seven system training sessions were completed prior to go-live but the take-up of these was never more than 72 per cent. Three follow-up sessions were rescheduled to catch employees who had missed the initial training, but the take-up on these was only 20 per cent. The final consultant report observed that the communication and training records had been poorly managed and not given the proper focus required. The process lacked a means of structured feedback and allocated ownership.

The readiness assessment had been handled much more professionally, but the stark results were ignored. Three major gaps had been identified, which should have been closed before the go-live. These results were disappointing, and below the external benchmark comparison from other organisations.

The first major gap was the business case and vision for the new ERP system. The expected benefits were not articulated in a meaningful way for the employees, supervisors, and stakeholder groups across the organisation. The second major gap was the sponsorship element. There was a lack of effective and proactive sponsorship, which is one of the most important elements in change programme success. The sponsor took Norman's advice at face value: that everything was either already in place or that any gaps would be closed before go-live. They did not go into the workplace and ask either the operators or the rest of the change team. The final gap was not developing the new skills and behaviours to ensure that all impacted employees had the ability and the right attitude to perform their new role. The TNA, a gap identification, and a subsequent training programme would have enabled the employees to operate the new system, but not enough employees attended the training.

The report clearly articulated that the go-live should have been delayed until the assessment gaps were closed and should only have been given the all-clear after a second change readiness assessment had been completed. It did recommend that the ERP implementation should continue, but with immediate improvements in articulating the system's business case, sponsorship coaching, and the training processes that also had a focus on behavioural change. Ultimately, it was felt that the credibility of the change implementation had been damaged, and it would be a risk to continue without some staff changes.

Case Study - Insights:

❖ **Don't Ignore Change Readiness Assessment Results:** If the CRA results are poor, do not proceed with change implementation. Some leaders think that they will be able to close readiness gaps while simultaneously implementing the change, but in reality, this is very unlikely. *Ignoring any negative assessment results and moving to implementation* will reduce change implementation success and potentially cause reputational damage to the change programme.

❖ **Opportunity to Learn and Improve Negative Results:** Similar to the change history assessment© (CHA©), negative results are a great opportunity to learn and improve. The CRA results can provide great insights into the ten key readiness elements and, when corrective actions are put in place, these improvements can greatly enhance the chances of change success.

3.6.3 The Importance of Assessing Readiness

A change history assessment© (CHA©) looks back at assessment data with the aim of enhancing future success and mitigating previous weaknesses. The CRA looks forward and evaluates if the key elements are in place to support change implementation. An organisation ready for change would be one that has a shared psychological state in which employees feel committed to implementing a change and confident in their collective abilities to do so (Weiner, 2009). The ten key elements are typical enablers to support change implementation, by reducing resistance and maximising adoption. They start with ensuring that employees understand the business case and vision for the change. Finally, they assess if there is a new desired organisational culture to support the change.

Change readiness is typically performed using an assessment, but in some cases structured interviews may be used. The CRA will, firstly, provide data and insights that might identify potential change implementation gaps. Secondly, analysis can then be used to create corrective actions to close gaps in the applicable readiness elements (**Figure 3.6.1**). Finally, corrective actions can then be implemented to close the identified gaps improving change readiness for the organisation and its employees.

There is often the risk that some of the organisation's managers will ignore the assessment results or launch corrective actions, hoping the gaps will be closed in parallel. This approach tends to be counterproductive and usually slows both implementation and employee adoption. The objectives of the CRA are:

- ❖ Assess if the organisation and the employees are ready for change implementation.
- ❖ Assess the effectiveness to date of two critical **a2BCMF®** steps:
  - ➤ **Sponsorship:** Has this been effective and proactive?
  - ➤ **Communication:** Is this effective and has it been flowing through all parts of the organisation?
- ❖ Assess the success of the earlier **a2BCMF®** steps:
  - ➤ **Change Definition:**
    - o **Business Case and Vision:** Have these been clearly articulated?
    - o **Organisation Workload:** Does the organisation and its employees have the capacity for this change?

- **Governance:** Does the change programme have proper oversight and decision-making capacity?
- **Leadership:** Are the leaders modelling the new behaviours and intervening when required?
- **Organisation:** Does the organisation's structure facilitate the new change?

❖ Assess the effectiveness of the **a2BCMF® Execute Phase**:
- **New Skills and Behaviours:** Has the development of new skills and behaviours started?
- **Involvement and Motivation:** Have the employees been involved in the change and are they motivated to adopt the new way of working?

3.6.4 Change Readiness Elements

The **Leadership of Change®** has defined ten key elements of the CRA (**Figure 3.6.1**). These elements and their assessment questions are related to concepts within the **a2BCMF®** steps and are considered important elements of change implementation. So far, we have covered most of these elements in earlier sections, the remainder are mentioned in subsequent sections.

During the **Execute Phase**, **a2BCMF®** steps five to eight should happen in parallel and be interlinked. The remaining elements of the CRA are:

❖ **New Skills and Behaviours:** The **a2BDNS© Model** and the **a2B5R® Behaviour Change Model** are used to develop the new skills and behaviours respectively. These concepts are discussed in more detail in **a2BCMF® Step 8 - Develop New Skills and Behaviours**.

❖ **Involvement and Motivation:** This is part of the **AUILM® Employee Change Adoption Model** and this concept is discussed in more detail in **a2BCMF® Step 9 - Adoption**.

❖ **Culture:** Each organisation has their own culture and the way this enables or acts a barrier to change will vary greatly. The impact of culture is a key consideration of the **a2B5R® Model**. Culture is discussed in more detail in **Section 3.9.7**.

Change Readiness

Assessment Element	Element Details
1. Business Case and Vision	The actionable business case for the change programme supports the organisation's vision and clearly articulates its expected benefits in a meaningful way for employees and stakeholder groups of the organisation.
2. Sponsorship	Effective and proactive sponsorship is one of the most important elements in change programme success. Without effective and proactive sponsorship the programme will eventually fail.
3. Governance	Programme governance establishes the processes and procedures for maintaining programme oversight and decision making. It will provide authorisation, approval, rejection, monitoring and adjusting activities of change and risk management plans.
4. Leadership	Successful organisational change is dependant on leaders, they must constantly communicate the business case and vision, role model the new behaviours and intervene when resistance surfaces.
5. Communication	Effective business communication and feedback is at the heart of successful organisational change. It acts like the blood in our bodies, but instead of supplying vital oxygen and nutrients, communication supplies information and motivation about the change.

Figure 3.6.1 Change Readiness Elements

Assessment (CRA) Elements

Element Details	Assessment Element
Change saturation occurs when the number of changes exceeds the capacity of an organisation to absorb them. Employees are exhausted and stressed from their efforts to distinguish which change is the most important.	6. Organisation Workload
Modifications to the organisational structure, processes and systems to align and support the change sends a clear tangible message to all employees that this change is happening and this will be the future state 'B'.	7. Organisation Structure
The development of new skills and behaviours ensures all impacted employees have the ability and right attitude to perform their new role. This is a critical stage to inspire personal confidence, reduce resistance and ensure adoption.	8. New Skills and Behaviours
An organisation change will only be successful if it has motivated employees to support the change. The sponsor, change team and leaders must facilitate an environment for employees to be involved in shaping the change.	9. Involvement and Motivation
Organisation culture is a system of shared values, assumptions, beliefs and norms that unite the employees of an organisation and reflect the views of its employees. Culture is critical to business success but is often missed as a strong enabler of change.	10. Culture

3.6.5 Change Readiness Assessment - Guide

The purpose of a change readiness assessment is to analyse the level of preparedness of the organisation prior to the change implementation. It assesses the key elements that should have been completed for the change to be successful.

The assessment is used by the change team to assess the employee's readiness to implement the change. Key elements check that each employee has the capacity to take on the change and establish whether they have been trained for their new role. The assessment should be completed just before the change is implemented. If the results indicate the organisation is not ready, then corrective actions should be put in place before the assessment is repeated.

Assessment Steps: The most effective and efficient way of performing the CRA is to send out a mass company email with an anonymous intranet link to the assessment. The suggested process steps are:

1. With the change team, create the respondent list using the stakeholder analysis (**Assessment 3.1.9**) created in **a2BCMF® Step 1 - Definition** and add other respondents if appropriate.
2. Recreate an outline of **Assessment 3.6.2** as a template to work on.
3. Add free text boxes to capture open question responses (qualitative data) and other information, such as role, function, business unit, location, etc.
4. Two to four weeks before the assessment is due to be sent out, send a communication e-mail to the identified stakeholders providing an overview on the assessment and follow up with staged reminders.
5. Send out the assessment on the planned date and follow up with staged reminders.
6. After the assessment closes, compile the results for graphical analysis and share with the sponsor.
7. Widely communicate the results.
8. If the results indicate that the employees and the organisation are not ready for change, interventions should be implemented.
9. On verifying that the interventions are supporting readiness, repeat steps-two through six.
10. If subsequent assessment results provide evidence that the organisation is ready for change, start implementing the change as per the project change plan (PCP).

Assessment 3.6.2 - Change Readiness Assessment (CRA)

#	Assessment Questions	Strongly Agree	Agree	Neutral	Disagree	Strongly Disagree
1	**Business Case and Vision:** Do I fully understand the organisation's strategy and why this change is important?					
2	**Business Case and Vision:** Do I feel the change vision has been clearly articulated and do I understand what we are trying to achieve?					
3	**Sponsorship:** Do I know who the sponsor is, and have they engaged my work area face-to-face?					
4	**Sponsorship:** Has the sponsor communicated the business case and vision for change?					
5	**Governance:** Am I aware that there is change management governance providing oversight of the change team and sponsor?					
6	**Governance:** Am I aware that governance will make the change implementation decision based on the results of this assessment?					
7	**Leadership:** Do I feel the leadership team have repeated the change message communicated by the sponsor?					
8	**Leadership:** Do I feel the leadership team are modelling the new behaviours required to fit the culture the organisation is aspiring to?					
9	**Communication:** Do I feel satisfied with the communication I have received throughout the change so far?					
10	**Communication:** Does communication have a feedback loop that allows me to ask the change team questions about the change?					
11	**Organisation Workload:** Do I understand how the change will impact my current workload?					
12	**Organisation Workload:** Do I feel confident that changes to my workload will enable me to work on the new change?					
13	**Organisation Structure:** Have modifications been made to the organisation structure to align and support the change?					
14	**Organisation Structure:** Do I understand the new processes and procedures in place to support the change?					
15	**New Skills and Behaviours:** Do I have the new skills to perform my new role and am I ready for implementation?					
16	**New Skills and Behaviours:** Have I understood the new required behaviours that I need to exhibit to make this change a success?					
17	**Involvement:** Do I feel the change team and sponsor have involved me in the change by asking for my input?					
18	**Involvement:** Do I feel the change team have used employee input to design the new change?					
19	**Culture:** Do I understand how the new required behaviours fit with the culture the organisation is aspiring to?					
20	**Culture:** Do I understand how the current culture needs to change to make our organisation more competitive and successful?					

Assessment 3.6.2 Change Readiness Assessment

Change Readiness Assessment - Insights:

- ❖ **Bad Results:** No matter how bad the results, these should be seen by the organisation as an opportunity to learn and improve.
- ❖ **Intervention:** If the results indicate that there are weaknesses within any of the ten key elements of the assessment, change implementation should be delayed and interventions should be put in place.

3.6.6 Change Readiness Assessment - Results

The CRA is used by the change team to gauge the organisation and the employee's readiness to implement the change. Typically, the results can be displayed on a radar plot, similar to **Figure 3.6.3**, which represents the scores for each of the ten CRA elements.

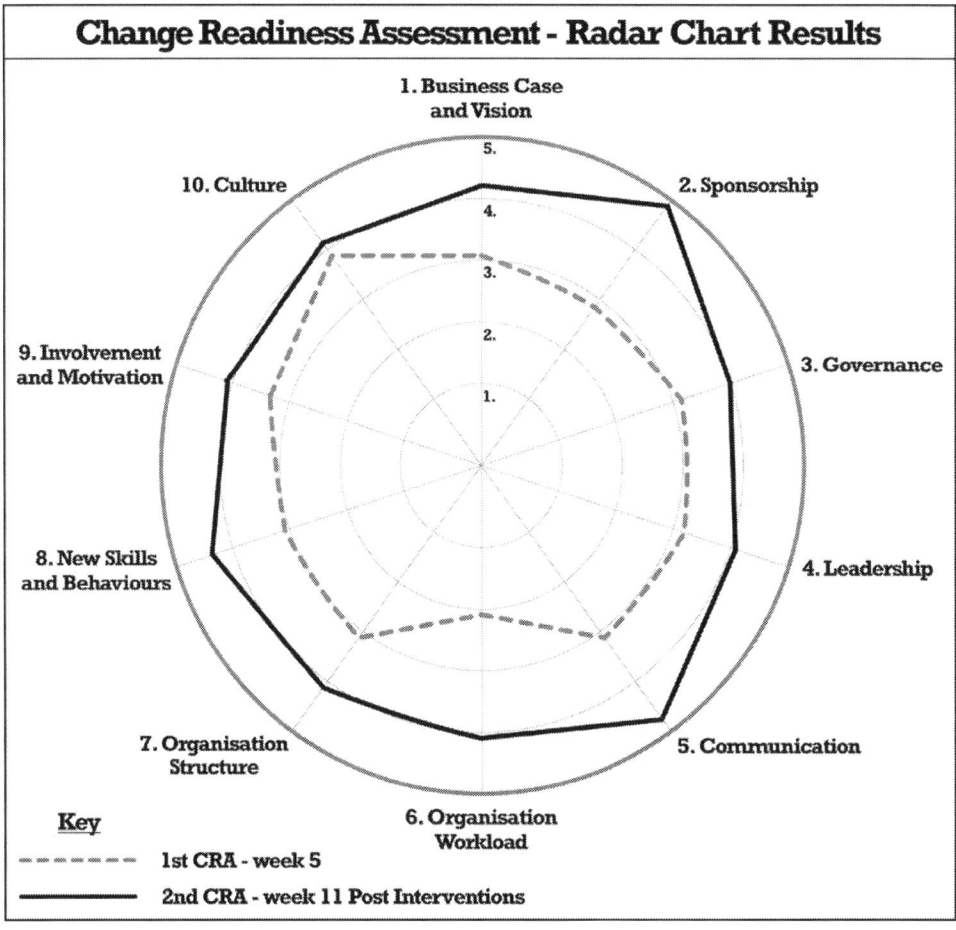

Figure 3.6.3 Change Readiness Assessment Results

3.6.7 Change Readiness Assessment - Interventions

If the results indicate that there are weaknesses within the any of ten key elements of the assessment, change implementation should be delayed and interventions should be executed. The results of each organisation's assessment will be different, but the result from the '1st CRA - week 5' (**Figure 3.6.3**) will be explored as an example. The CRA indicates that all ten elements score below four and intervention and actions will be required for all ten elements. The sponsorship element is developed below to demonstrate typical analysis and interventions:

CRA Analysis:

- ❖ **Sponsorship:** Without effective and proactive project sponsorship, the change programme will eventually fail, it is the single most important element in change success. It is concerning that the sponsorship element scored low, however it would also explain why the other elements did not score well.
  - ➢ **CRA Questions:** The CRA questions focus on if the sponsor is engaging the employees face to face and has the sponsor communicated the business case and vision for change.
  - ➢ **Analysis:** Before any analysis is performed it should be noted that if the **a2BCMF® Step 2 - Secure Sponsorship and Resources** was adhered to then this element would not score negatively.
  - ➢ **Intervention:** The change team should first check if the sponsor assessment was performed as outlined in **Section 3.2.5**. Even if the assessment was performed it should still be performed again as it will identify interventions and actions to close gaps.

2nd CRA - Week 11 Post Interventions: Once the intervention actions have had time to make an improvement, the CRA should be performed again. A reasonable amount of time will be required for the improvement to take place. **Figure 3.6.3** shows the results six week after the intervention, '2nd CRA - week 11'. It shows improvements have been made in all ten elements, each scoring above four. This indicates that the organisation and its employees are ready for change implementation. A word of caution, it is possible that not all the elements improve after intervention have taken place, and another CRA may have to be performed. Equally, the change team should proceed with caution because if the change was being successfully implemented up to this point the CRA would not have been this negative.

3.6.8 Review and Checklist

Assess Readiness: Change readiness is the process of assessing the readiness of the organisation and its employees prior to change implementation, ensuring that they are ready to adopt the change.

Change Readiness Assessment: The CRA results can provide data and insights into potential readiness gaps so corrective actions and interventions can be executed to close gaps and start the implementation.

CRA Design: Has the assessment been tailored to suit the organisation? Have the invitation text and instructions been crafted and tested?

Assessment Completion Time: The respondents should be given adequate time to complete the assessment. An early announcement about the CRA and follow-up reminders to complete the assessment will increase the number of responses.

Results: The results (quantitative and qualitative data) should be properly analysed, independently verified, approved and communicated to the impacted stakeholders.

Low Scoring Results: Poor CRA results should be seen as a great opportunity to learn and to close gaps that could prevent successful change implementation. They are also a very strong business signal to delay the change implementation.

Implementation Go/No Go: Based on the results from the CRA, the decision can be made to implement or delay the change. This decision is best taken by the programme's governance team who will ensure independent oversight. The final decision should be communicated widely and outline the next steps.

Case Study: Consideration should be given to the case study insights; unintended consequences should be considered if the decision to implement the change is taken when the CRA results suggest otherwise.

Interventions: If the first CRA produces low scores, interventions and corrective actions should be developed to close the identified gaps. Time should be allowed for these actions to close the gaps before another CRA is launched.

a2BCMF® Step 6 - Checklist

#	a2BCMF® Questions	Complete Yes/No
1	**Previous Steps:** Have the previous **a2BCMF®** steps been completed?	☐
2	**CRA Design:** Has the assessment been tailored to suit the organisation? Have the invitation text and instructions been crafted and tested?	☐
3	**CRA:** Have communications announced the CRA process, purpose, etc.? Has the CRA been sent to the impacted stakeholders?	☐
4	**Time to Complete Assessment:** Have the respondents been given adequate time and reminders to respond?	☐
5	**Results:** Have the results (quantitative and qualitative) been properly analysed, independently verified, approved and communicated to the impacted stakeholders?	☐
6	**Implementation Go/No Go:** Have the results been independently verified, approved and communicated?	☐
7	**Case Study:** Have the case study insights been shared? Was implementation delayed if there were low scores in the CRA?	☐
8	**Interventions:** Has the CRA been analysed using both quantitative and qualitative data to develop interventions to close the identified gaps?	☐

Notes:

3.7 Manage Resistance

Nothing negates organisation performance quicker than employees who resist change and believe that the way they work today is the way they will work tomorrow.

3.7.1 Change Resistance - Overview

Definition: Resistance is the reaction by the organisation, departments or individuals when they perceive that an organisational change coming their way could be a threat to them. Without further awareness and understanding, this resistance will cause fear. It will trigger actions that negatively impact the pace of organisational change implementation, adoption of the new ways of working and benefits delivery.

Business Benefits: Change resistance can be a major obstacle in achieving change adoption and benefits realisation. The change team must understand this and have tactics to address resistance.

Key Stakeholders and Elements: All impacted stakeholders; organisations, departments and employees are involved. There are three typical individual standpoints that stakeholders are inclined to embrace in any change management journey. The standpoint each stakeholder takes will require a different approach to manage their resistance.

Business Objective: To prevent resistance developing by following the previous **a2BCMF®** steps, as well as ensuring employee **A**wareness, **U**nderstanding, **I**nvolvement, **L**earning and **M**otivation (**AUILM®**) to minimise resistance.

Enablers and Barriers

Enablers	Barriers
Adhering to previous **a2BCMF®** steps should ensure minimal change resistance.	The leadership team, sponsor and change team thinking that change resistance can be tackled when it arises during change implementation.
The change team understanding change resistance and the potential impact it can have if they are not prepared to address it throughout the change programme.	Lack of change implementation understanding by the sponsor and the leadership team, and the negative impact resistance could have on change success.
Understanding the three key employee resistance standpoints: **'Rebels'**, **'Observers'** or **'Advocates'**.	Thinking that everyone will react to the change in the same way, and because the change has strategic importance it will be accepted positively.
The change team understanding the reasons for change resistance and having tactics to deal with it.	Hoping any change resistance will be logical and easy to manage.
The change team understanding the importance of the **'Tipping Point'** and having a strategy to entice the **'Observers'** to become **'Advocates'**.	The leadership team thinking that the employees will see the importance of the change and that they will follow instructions and adopt the change as directed.
Defining whether the change approach is compliance (**'Tell'**) or winning hearts and minds (**'Sell'**).	The leadership team not understanding the pros and cons of implementation speed (**'Tell'** versus **'Sell'**).
Proactive planning and preparation for resistance, with mitigation and actions to manage it.	Lack of change resistance planning by the leadership team and thinking a reactive resistance strategy will suffice.
Identification of growth mindset employees who can create a powerful coalition with the change agents.	The leadership team thinking that all employees will embrace change because it is in their best interests.

3.7.2 Case Study - Employees with Different Agendas

After losing more than $200M (out of a revenue of $5.5B), a global technology company appointed a new CEO. One of the CEO's first tasks was to complete a comprehensive benchmarking exercise. This would provide data and information to support the tough decision to re-engineer the infrastructure of the organisation for better efficiency.

The new CEO's strategy started to show promise, although there were challenges in the maintenance contract capture rate of ATMs, as well as cost reduction measures. Two strategic projects were announced. The first project was on grouping and discounting service contracts with ATM sales. The second was to understand why the company was winning fewer services contracts than their competitors and to establish if their competitors were getting spare parts at a lower cost.

I was selected by the sponsor to be the project manager for the second strategic initiative. At the time, I was working for the global procurement team based in Europe and reporting into the corporate office in Dayton, Ohio, in the US, supporting the procurement process and the commodity directors. The commodity directors worked under the leadership of the sponsor, John.

John and I were given access to company resources, systems, sites, and staff, and we were able to pick a global team of key leaders for the project team. John was the head of manufacturing procurement and it was agreed that we would report monthly to the CEO, the SVP of the financial solutions division, and the SVP of the worldwide customer services division.

The first team meeting took place at corporate headquarters in Dayton, US. There were two objectives. Firstly, form the team and scope. Secondly, to meet with the CEO, share the approach, and get his direction and steer.

At the meeting the team deduced that our competitors could only be winning service business and making sustainable profits if they were getting the parts more cheaply than they cost us to design, manufacture, store, and distribute globally.

I asked each team member the following question in turn:

"Are you aware of, or do you have knowledge of, any critical parts leaving the organisation and getting into the hands of our service competitors by any non-authorised approved vendor process?"

Everyone answered with a clear, unequivocal 'No'.

Experience has taught me that change resistance is always there, you just have to find it. Would it be any different in this project?

On Friday morning, we had our first meeting with the CEO, Martin. He selected John as the project lead and asked to be provided with monthly face-to-face updates on progress.

In the meantime, the project team agreed and set up global weekly conference calls to keep the team connected. The plan was to investigate globally if any of our manufactured parts were on open sale in the market, and if so, to establish the source and how much they were being sold for. My main task was to attend global electronics trade exhibitions and establish if our parts were on general sale.

The second monthly team meeting was in Ireland. I provided a detailed update on my findings from the global trade exhibitions, with no evidence of spare parts sales. Several team members suggested I should check the European logistics centre and the global manufacturing sites for part leakage.

The weekly conference calls continued to progress actions and I prioritised my visit to the European global part distribution centre. I performed a site inspection, plus a random detailed analysis of selected orders and the order book, which proved the integrity of the distribution centre's processes and procedures.

The next key action for the month was to understand if there was any leakage from the manufacturing plants. John told us that he would be joining each commodity director on a least one supplier visit over the next three months.

We flew into corporate headquarters for the third team meeting and to prepare for the next CEO presentation. So far there'd been no evidence of leakage and he was disappointed in the progress we had made so far.

"I would have expected more progress by now" said Martin. "So, you're telling me that you can't find any part leakage from this organisation, but by all accounts, including the people I speak with, our competitors are getting our parts for less than it costs us. How?" His voice was raised but controlled.

I decided to intervene.

"Martin, thank you for hearing our presentation and giving your feedback. It is a real honour to work on this strategic project for you. Thank you for trusting our team so far. This morning we've presented all key activities completed over the last month and what we will be focusing on over the next four weeks. I understand the financials have not changed enough for you. However, is there anything new you think we should also be focusing on?"

After what seemed like ages, Martin gave a half-smile and adopted the growth mindset approach.

"Right." He paused. "Keep on doing what you are doing and give me an update next month."

Over the next two weeks, I focused my efforts on working with the global procurement team members connected with the manufacturing sites. A week before the next meeting we received an email through a third party, which showed photographs of our ATM parts for sale on the open market. The photos displayed not only the spare parts themselves but also the packaging with the manufacturing site label, an address, and a barcode. We were not only able to identify which manufacturing site the parts came from, but we could also get the complete history of the order using the barcode. A major leak had been found in the US!

The leak was associated with a member of our team and, when challenged with the evidence that had been found, their denial was weak and very unconvincing. "Guys, this is very disappointing. Four months into the project and we've eventually found the critical spare parts that are being bought by our competitors from the service division. Worse still, they are being sold at 10 cents to the dollar. Our service competitors are getting them at 10 per cent of the cost."

"Remember the team activity we completed at the first meeting back in Dayton?" John paused for effect. "Peter asked everyone around the table, one by one." He paused again. "He asked if you were aware of any critical parts getting into the hands of our service competitors by any non-authorised routes." A long pause. "You all answered 'No.'" There were a few seconds of silence before anyone spoke up.

Garth, who represented the services division, was first to speak.

"We didn't know about that. We thought that all the controls were in place. We found out who was involved, and it has been dealt with. It won't happen again." John looked at him sternly.

"It shouldn't have happened at all."

At the next CEO update, Martin listened intently to John's presentation with no change in his body language. In my notes, I wrote down that he definitely knew about the leak and had seen the photographs. I was sure that he'd been well briefed. John gave a detailed explanation on how more controls needed to be put in place to prevent this from happening again.

The next logical step was to visit the most critical spare part suppliers. Analysis identified that this was in the UK, which was natural. Historically most of the suppliers were located near the ATM design and engineering centre. Over the next few weeks I visited nearly twenty key suppliers. I was able to verify that there were no obvious sales of our spare parts to the open market. Based on this evidence, our supply base was in good order.

We had just over a week before giving the next update to the CEO, but intuition told John and me that something was not quite right. Right from the project kick-off, I'd had a feeling that some key and senior employees had an agenda that was in conflict with the project's objective. You should always be aware of people's personal motivations when implementing change. Initially trust no one!

I shared my concerns and John agreed that we needed to do one final audit before the next CEO update. We had not audited an office connected to one of the main manufacturing sites as we were assured by the senior VP that it would never sell parts to competitors. If I was to gain access to the office it would have to be an unplanned visit, when the senior leaders and the VP were off-site or otherwise engaged. Late afternoon on a Friday looked to be a good time to do the visit of the suspected office and store.

I arrived outside the manufacturing plant at just before 15:20 and asked to see Hamish. I introduced myself, described the project in detail, and explained that I was there to visit the premises. As expected, Hamish told me that he was not authorised to give me access, but he would go and call his boss. I advised him the project was for the CEO and that I had his authority.

"Right, Hamish. Could you please switch on the computer, log on to the order system, and project it onto the screen? Can we go to the completed purchase orders and could you refresh the screen to show the newest orders first?" Hamish refreshed his screen and I could now see the order details horizontally across the large screen. For each order, I could see the dispatch date, the customer, their address, the part numbers, the part description, the quantity, the monetary value, and the total order value.

I scanned the list. After having worked on the project for five months, I knew who was an approved services partner and who was a direct service competitor. The fifth order on the list was not an approved service partner. They were an aggressive competitor and we were supplying them with critical parts at a discount price. Finally, I had found the major UK source of leakage in our own backyard. Our intuition had been right. I took out my phone and took several photographs of the projected image.

The project team had been together for nearly six months and there was a feeling that this would be the last major update to the CEO. There was also a realisation that the financial landscape of the organisation was improving slowly, in terms of cost control and efficiency.

During the meeting, the manufacturing site leakage was talked through, and John mentioned that the photographs and details were in the appendix. He continued,

"You can see by the line chart, showing ten years of data, how the number of ATMs not sold with services contracts is directly inverse to the decrease in the services business."

The resulting actions that came out of the meeting were twofold. Firstly, the two SVPs and their divisions had to work together strategically to promote the strategy of selling ATMs with the bundled service contract as part of the sale. Secondly, employee resistance to the above strategy had to be addressed aggressively. This was a **'Tell'** rather than a **'Sell'**. It was not an approach to win hearts and minds.

At the end of the presentation, the CEO thanked the team for all our hard work and quickly left with the two SVPs in tow. The leaks had been found and stopped, and the change had passed the resistance stage. Our role in the project had now come to an end.

Case Study - Insights:

- ❖ **There will always be Resistance:** It does not matter if the change programme or project is an important organisation initiative and its success is an enabler to future profits. It does not matter if the project is directly sponsored by CEO and they have personally articulated the business case for change. It does not matter if the project team are hand-picked by senior leaders because of their knowledge of the organisation and subject matter expertise. It does not matter if a team member is working with you in different countries, late into the night, eating and socialising with you and other team members. It does not matter if you ask team members about resistance in front of the team, *"Are you aware of, or do you have knowledge of, any critical parts leaving the organisation and getting into the hands of our service competitors by any non-authorised approved vendor process?"* Even when everyone answers with a clear, unequivocal 'No', it does not matter because there will always be resistance against change within an organisation. It would be pure folly to expect otherwise.

- ❖ **Personal Motivations:** Sometimes employees have personal motivations for resistance to change, and they see their own interests as more important than the profits of the organisation. These employees could be at any level in the organisation. The next time you are working on a change programme and you ask the employees, "Is there any resistance against this change?" and they answer "No", just remember one thing, there will always be resistance no matter what you see and hear!

3.7.3 The Importance of Change Resistance

One of the most baffling problems that C-suites and leadership teams face is employee resistance to change. For them the change is not optional, the organisation has to implement the change to remain competitive, profitable or to even survive. "Why do our employees not understand this?", they ask. Simply put, whether the change is good or bad for the organisation there will be change resistance. Organisational leaders cannot control the world changing around them, but they should try to understand and manage their employee's change resistance.

Resistance can take many forms. It can be overt or covert, it could be direct defiance or affect the whole organisation, just some departments or individual employees. However, organisations and change teams should expect the greatest resistance from those with the most to lose. The sponsor and change team should be prepared for change resistance and the impact and challenge it brings to change implementation, adoption and benefits delivery.

Not all resistance should be viewed negatively. Resistance has an important psychological function as it guards against things that cause too much fear or anxiety and might otherwise damage the change programme. Remember, if it were not for resistance, bad change programmes would be initiated and implemented along with good change programmes. Finally, be warned, if you are not encountering resistance then you are probably not achieving the change. Impacted stakeholders do not usually nod and accept any new change in full. Change resistance is inevitable, ignore it at your peril.

3.7.4 Resistance Standpoints

Organisations should treat resistance as an integral part of delivering the change. The stakeholder analysis (**Assessment 3.1.9**) performed during **a2BCMF® Step 1 - Change Definition** will have categorised the stakeholders into three simple groups: '**Rebels**', '**Observers**' and '**Advocates**' (**Figure 3.7.1**). The "rebels" (**Template 3.1.10**) will have mapped these stakeholder's current and desired levels of influence and cooperation. The change team and sponsor will then manage these three groups in every **a2BCMF®** step from '**Change Definition**' through to '**Sustain and Close**'. The template should feed into other key change plans and activities, in particular the change communication plan (CCP) and change resistance plan (CRP).

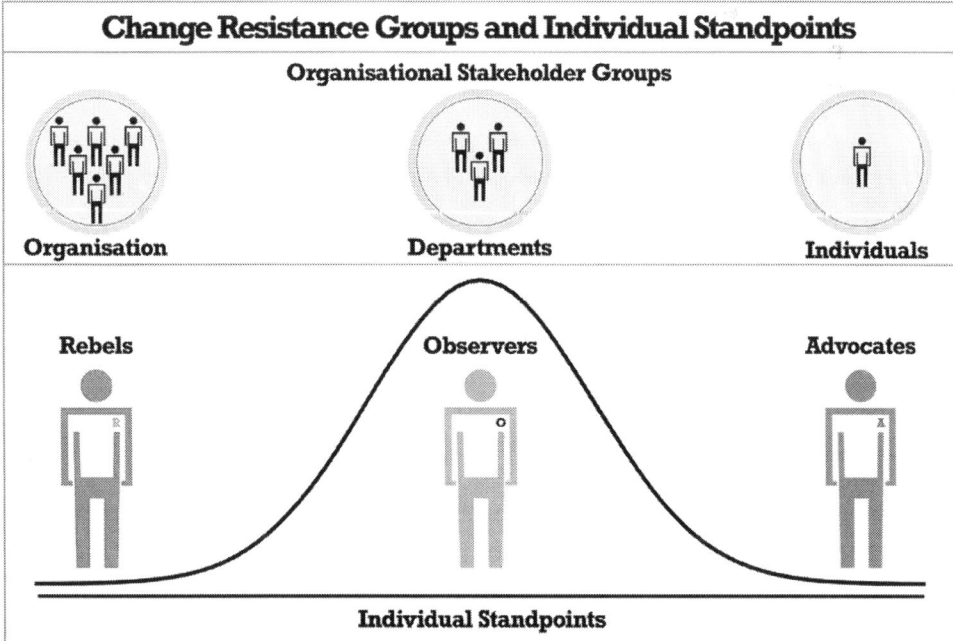

Figure 3.7.1 Change Resistance Standpoints

Stakeholder Groups and Reasons for Resistance

The **Leadership of Change**® defines three organisational stakeholder groups that should be considered as part of resistance planning. If high resistance is anticipated, they should be considered as part of the stakeholder engagement plan, the change communication plan (CCP) and the change resistance plan (CRP).

Organisation: In today's world of change disruption and fast-moving technology, change is accelerating, and organisations find it difficult to keep up, actively resisting change. Typical reasons for resistance are:

❖ Previous change history weaknesses and consequent lack of confidence in future change success.
❖ The change is not in the interests of the organisation.
❖ Lack of resources to support the change.

Departments: Department or individual teams are one of the most important groups, without them the organisation will not function properly. Typical reasons for resistance are:

❖ Changes in group or team status and power.
❖ Team or individuals become redundant.
❖ Group norms may be impacted if there is a loss of team members.
❖ Reduction in team cohesiveness or social interaction.

Individuals: Resistance to change is part of basic human nature. Individuals want to know, "Is my job secure and will this impact me and my family life?" Typical reasons and fears of resistance are:

❖ Economic factors impacting personal and family finances.
❖ Psychological factors, such as wellbeing and emotional work factors (feelings, worries, etc).
❖ Social needs, like friendship and the sense of belonging.

Individual Resistance Standpoints

In addition to the three main organisational stakeholder groups, there are three typical individual standpoints that employees are inclined to embrace in any change management journey. Each group will react differently to organisational change and will have different levels of resistance:

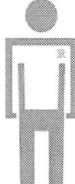

Rebels: Tend to resist change blindly, sometimes this can be a natural reaction even if the change is to their benefit. The default reaction is that change is a bad thing and will put them at a disadvantage.

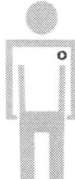

Observers: Monitor the '**Advocates**' and assess if the change is benefiting them. If this appears positive, they will tend to move towards being receptive to the change.

Advocates: Similar to the change agents with their positivity towards change. Their energy should be captured as they can play an effective role in leading and rolling out the change. The coalition of change agents and '**Advocates**' can work together to lower resistance in the other groups.

3.7.5 Individual Reasons for Resistance

Expecting resistance to change and planning for it during **a2BCMF® Step 1 - Change Definition** will greatly help to minimise resistance right from the start of the change programme. The change team should also be aware of the most common reasons people resist change and what might be typical in their organisation. Resistance, for whatever reason, will negatively impact change implementation and adoption speed. Defining and being prepared for any of the typical reasons for change resistance will enhance the efficiency and effectiveness of the change process.

Ten typical employee reasons for resistance are listed below. This list is not exhaustive and will vary from organisation to organisation.

1. **Lack of Change Awareness:** Many organisations tend to follow the traditional project management approach when implementing change, thinking that general project announcements and pre-

implementation training activities will suffice. Unfortunately, this falls a long way short of answering the key questions a worried employee will have. Without change awareness the employees will fill in the missing gaps themselves. The less they know about the change and its impact on them, the more fearful they will become, and rumours will propagate which will add fuel to growing resistance.

2. **Lack of Change Understanding:** Not understanding the business context of the change or the urgency for the organisation to make changes. In business, change is a constant, organisations are always adapting to meet market demand, changing technology, etc. While this may be clear to the business leaders constantly looking at the balance sheet and dwindling profits, it is not a perspective that a typical employee is familiar with or understands.

3. **Job Security:** Employees tend to resist any change that threatens their job security, as this will have both emotional and financial implications. For the employee, the word 'change' can have the same negative connotations as the words 'downsizing', 'restructuring', 'automation', etc. These words will be associated with the elimination of jobs, becoming redundant or their role no longer being essential after the change.

4. **Fear of the Unknown:** The first thing any employee thinks when they hear there will be an organisational change is how it will impact them and their family. Apart from family tragedies, there are probably very few other events that can impact the financial security and living pattern of a family. The less the organisation's employees know about the change and its impact on them, the more fearful they will become. Fear of change is likely to convince employees that the change is bad for them and their resistance will heighten the more the change is negatively perceived.

5. **Low Trust:** If employees have low trust in the organisation and its leaders, they are unlikely to support the change. The more distrust, the more resistance. Meaningful organisational change does not occur in a climate of mistrust, and low trust will doom an otherwise well-conceived change initiative to failure. Regaining trust can be a long and arduous process for the existing leaders.

6. **Lack of Communication:** The importance of communication in any organisational change cannot be overestimated. The **Leadership of Change®** advocates that *"effective change communication is at the heart of successful change, it acts like the blood in our bodies, but instead of supplying vital oxygen and nutrients, communication supplies information and motivation to the impacted stakeholders."* Without vital oxygen and nutrients your body would not continue to work for very long, and the same can be said with nearly any change programme. Without constant and consistent communication, rumours will fill any voids and resistance will grow exponentially, damaging the change programme and successful implementation.

7. **Lack of Competence:** This resistance comes from the fear of not having the competence or skills to perform the new role. It is a fear that many employees don't freely or quickly admit. Thus, this type of resistance can be perceived as illogical or emotional, with the true root cause difficult to identify. Employees may feel that they won't be able to make the transition to the new role and will reject the change based on survival instincts.

8. **Fixed Mindset:** Employees with a fixed mindset will, by default, reject and resist disruption and change. In their minds, change will nearly always have a negative impact on work and their private life. Resistance is the reaction to change which they perceive as a threat to them. They are comfortable with the status quo and they stick to what they know, connected to the old way. In the past they may have been receptive to change, but after a bad change experience they now resist all change.

9. **Loss of Power:** Resistance can come at any level in the organisation, even from the senior leadership team, and this can be more difficult to uncover. Leaders and managers will resist change if they perceive it will decrease their power, authority or reputation within the organisation. The change team and sponsor should be prepared for covert resistance and, in some cases, spurious verbal attacks on the change team's performance aimed at damaging their credibility. These leaders and managers might even create a strong coalition working diligently in the background against the change.

10. **Increasing Workload:** Leadership of Change® highlights how all of a sudden there is a change explosion that disrupts normal day-to-day operations and results. Thus, the leadership and organisation paradox: *"implementing change versus delivering day-to-day operations."* Leaders and employees will resist change as all their energy and focus is on current operations and they perceive change as increasing their workload. Essentially, they are not really against the change, it is more to do with having no extra capacity for anything else.

3.7.6 Actions to Reduce Resistance

Most resistance to change can be avoided by effectively following all the **a2BCMF®** steps, which help to mitigate change resistance right from programme initiation. The change history assessment© (CHA©) and the change readiness assessment (CRA) will also provide invaluable insights in how to prevent resistance. The advice to any change team is to expect and treat resistance as an integral part of delivering the change programme.

Effective resistance management is about uncovering change resistance and establishing the root causes to understand the reasons for resistance. In nearly all cases, these need to be acknowledged and the stakeholder's emotions validated. Knowing how to overcome resistance to change is a vital part of any change management programme journey. Direct engagement with the stakeholder is often the best way and understanding their concerns is fundamental, showing respect and care. The sponsor and change team should be patient and demonstrate the ability to understand concerns from the stakeholder's frame of reference.

Ten typical tactics to reduce resistance are listed below. The list is not exhaustive and will vary from organisation to organisation.

1. **Constant and Continuous Communication:** No matter how much you think you are communicating, the old consultant rule is to communicate ten times more than you think you are. The change programme elevator speech developed in **a2BCMF® Step 1 - Change Definition** should have been aligned and linked to all change communication as early as possible in the change programme. **a2BCMF® Step 5 - Communicate the Change** defines in detail the comprehensive change communication plan. Defined feedback loops in the plan should ensure that any key

stakeholders would have had the chance to get their specific questions or concerns answered. If these have been adhered to, change resistance and negative reactions should have been minimised and potentially damaging rumours stifled.

2. **Change Awareness:** This action refers specifically to employee awareness about the change and focuses on ensuring the employee is aware that a new change is coming. Change awareness is about being transparent, answering any concerns the employee may have about the change. This should take care of any emotional, financial, job security or competency fears they may personally have. Awareness answers the basic questions we all have when change is introduced; why is it changing? what is changing? what is not changing? WIIFM? This is very much aligned with the first stage of the **AUILM® Employee Adoption Model**.

3. **What's In It For Me? (WIIFM):** One of the first questions an employee will want to know is what is WIIFM? These questions should be treated in a positive way and should be perceived by the change team as willingness to change. The impacted stakeholder wants to know how the change will affect them, what they will gain, what they will lose, and more importantly will they still have a job? The change team should have crafted a tailored answer for this as part of the stakeholder communication needs covered in **a2BCMF® Step 5 - Communicate the Change (Figure 3.5.1)**. The response needs to answer the WIIFM question because the stakeholders will use this information to consider whether the change is better for them or if it makes things worse. If answered well, it can start to reduce change resistance early and gain buy-in.

4. **Change Understanding:** This builds on change awareness by continuing employee engagement to help them understand why the business needs to change. The change elevator speech is a great way of communicating the 'What', 'Why' and 'Benefits' of the change programme. It is a powerful tool for helping employees to understand the strategic need for change. This topic should have been covered in **a2BCMF® Step 1 - Change Definition (Section 3.1.10)** and change understanding is very much aligned with the second stage of the **AUILM® Employee Adoption Model**.

5. **Sponsorship:** Without effective and proactive sponsorship, change programmes will eventually fail. The sponsor's role will be to reduce resistance in what they '**Say**', as well as '**Support**' and '**Sustain**' the change. Activities will include articulating the strategy, explaining the change business case and how this aligns to the organisation's vision and the employee perspective in terms of the 'WIIFM' factor. The sponsor should be visible and accessible to all stakeholders and engage employees face-to-face to answer questions that will impede resistance. This topic should have been covered in **a2BCMF® Step 2 - Secure Sponsorship and Resources (Section 3.2.4)**.

6. **Balance Employee Workload:** Employees who complete the change history assessment© (CHA©) consistently score 'workload' very low. Results across many organisations, sectors and countries indicate that the employee's workload is not considered when their organisation is implementing change. Further analysis indicates that what is perceived as resistance to change is, in fact, just not having capacity to take on further workload. **Section 3.1.6** refers to organisation change capacity and the need to strongly consider this when approving the change programme within the strategic portfolio. Part of this should include the employee's capacity for change when they have to balance day-to-day operations versus implementing change. The sponsor, change team, leaders and managers need to create employee change capacity. Extra capacity is required for learning new software, technology, systems, taking on more responsibilities, learning new methods or adjusting to new processes. This topic should have been covered in **a2BCMF® Step 1 - Change Definition (Section 3.1.6)**.

7. **Employee Involvement:** The direct involvement of employees in any organisational change is critical to success implementation. It gives employees the opportunity to shape the change, moving them from a position of 'change is done unto them' to a happier position where they are involved and are influencing the change. The organisation is indicating that they trust the employee's input. This is a win-win scenario, not only reducing resistance but gaining buy-in. This is very much aligned with the third stage of the **AUILM® Employee Adoption Model**.

8. **Training and Competency Development:** If the change will require learning new software, technology, systems, methods or processes then it is imperative the change team quickly communicates that employees will be fully supported with training and coaching. This type of resistance comes from the fear of not having the competence or skills to perform the new role and it is a fear many employees don't freely or quickly admit. Thus, this type of resistance can be perceived as illogical or emotional with the true root cause being difficult to identify. Employees may feel that they won't be able to make the transition to the new role and will therefore reject the change based on 'survival instincts'. Workload capacity will have to be considered so the employees are able to learn new skills, as well as behaviours. A structured training needs analysis (TNA) should be performed to identify skills and behaviour gaps so that coaching and training plans can be scheduled to align with the change programme. This topic will be covered in **a2BCMF® Step 8 - Developing New Skills and Behaviours (Section 3.8)**.

9. **Motivation to Change:** To ensure resistance does not build after the training and coaching has taken place, the employee's individual performance plan (IPP) should be linked to the change. The IPP can be a powerful vehicle to support strategy implementation by aligning employee performance to the change and benefits realisation. It should define the skills and behaviours expected so that the employee can adopt the change. The IPP should be linked directly to the balanced scorecard (BSC) to show the employee how their individual performance supports the change programme. It can also directly link each individual's performance to their bonus and recognition rewards. This is very much aligned with the fifth stage of the **AUILM® Employee Adoption Model**. This topic is covered in **a2BCMF® Step 10 - Sustain and Close**.

10. **Change Agents:** Change agents can play an important role in organisational change, especially in supporting the sponsor and change team to communicate the change message to employee groups involved in the change journey. Each organisation will have a different way of selecting, using and naming their change agents. However, change agents who are representatives from business lines who work with the stakeholders on a day-to-day basis can play

a pivotal role in the change programme. By engaging the various groups, they can articulate and communicate the business case for change. By working with the '**Advocates**' they can form a powerful coalition to entice the '**Observers**' to become '**Advocates**', and by engaging the '**Rebels**' they can lower resistance, moving them towards the tipping point to become '**Observers**'.

3.7.7 Finding the Tipping Point

A typical question asked by the organisation's C-Suite and leadership team is, "How long will the change take before we start to see the benefits?" The project change plan (PCP) and the benefits tracking plan (BTP), if accurate and up to date, should provide a very good indication. The next question is usually, "Is there anything else we could be doing to speed up adoption and benefits delivery?" If all the **a2BCMF®** steps are being adhered to, then the simple answer is, "Yes, by reducing or removing resistance to the change." The best way of doing this is to work with the three groups with the support of the change agents to find the '**Tipping Point**' (**Figure 3.7.2**).

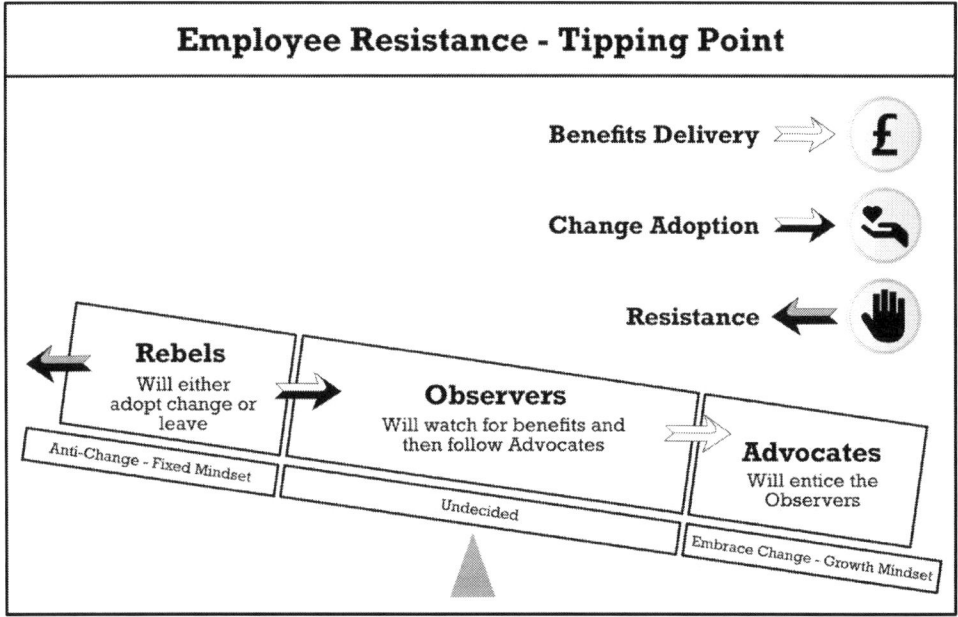

Figure 3.7.2 Employee Resistance

Once the tipping point is reached, an amazing phenomenon takes place, whereby more and more people start adopting the new way of working as well as embracing the change at an accelerated pace. There is no greater delight than to see a '**Rebel**' accept the organisational change willingly and even becoming an '**Advocate**'.

Advocates: Tend to embrace and lead change within the organisation as they are more comfortable with it. They have a positive and growth mindset and see this as an opportunity to grow and improve. The coalition of change agents and '**Advocates**' can have a massive impact in the organisation, positively enticing the other groups to adopt the change.

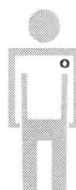

Observers: The change agents and '**Advocates**' should work together to create employee desire to move the '**Observers**' towards the '**Tipping Point**'. Communication, direct engagement, targeted messaging and events, such as socialising the future state, will help the '**Observers**' to adopt the change at a faster rate.

Rebels: The change agent can help greatly in this area by directly engaging the '**Rebels**' face-to-face. The change agent should listen with empathy to understand their concerns whilst communicating the organisation's change business case. A typical question that comes up is about how much effort you spend on this group. The answer varies from organisation to organisation, with cultures and local laws all having an input and impact on the approach. Another complication is whether the change is about compliance or winning hearts and minds. However, as long as you have tried to understand the root cause of '**Rebel**' resistance, you have respectfully engaged them and offered solutions by trying all the key tactics to reduce resistance. There might come a time when a difficult decision has to be made, that some of the '**Rebels**' can no longer be a part of the future '**B**' state.

3.7.8 Change Implementation Approaches

The change implementation approach depends on the type of change. If the change is about compliance, legislation or safety it will be a '**Tell**'. If it is about winning hearts and minds it will be a '**Sell**'. Both approaches have advantages and disadvantages, and both approaches will encounter some level of resistance (**Figure 3.7.3**).

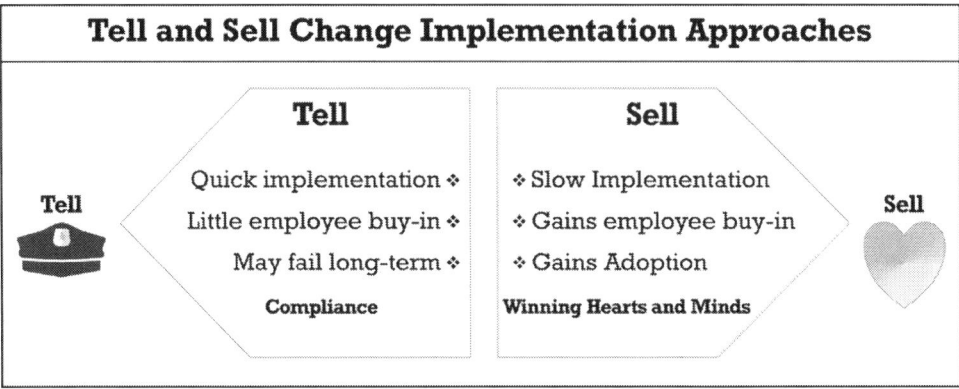

Figure 3.7.3 Tell and Sell Change Approaches

Tell

Advantages: Speed is the nature of this type of change implementation. The organisation enforces the implementation decision, with consequences for those who do not obey.

Disadvantages: Changes like this are implemented quickly with no time for staff consultation. As a result, people will feel that this change is 'done unto them' and it will take longer to achieve buy-in and acceptance.

Sell

Advantages: This type of change allows the organisation to communicate the change in advance, take feedback and gain staff buy-in, winning hearts and minds.

Disadvantages: The process of communicating, involving lots of people and receiving feedback, takes time. This type of change approach takes a lot longer than the '**Tell**' approach and much more organisational effort.

"Without employee resistance, you will not achieve organisational change."

3.7.9 Change Resistance Planning - Guide

A lot of resistance to change can be avoided by following all of the **a2BCMF®** steps. However, performing change resistance planning (CRP) is a proactive way of preparing for resistance, so the change team has planned mitigations and actions to manage it. The change team might decide at the '**Change Definition**' step that strong change resistance may be encountered, or it could become more apparent as the change is implemented. Either way, it is prudent to plan for resistance so it can be handled quickly in a structured and logical way. Change resistance can be a major barrier to successfully delivering a change programme, preventing change adoption and benefits realisation.

A CRP can be used to establish the cause of resistance, where or when it is most likely to occur and the impact to the programme, so that mitigations and corrective actions can be executed.

Other benefits of a CRP include:

- ❖ Effective change resistance planning to help minimise resistance.
- ❖ Preparing mitigation responses and actions to manage stakeholder resistance from the CRP outputs.
- ❖ Building insights and knowledge from the stakeholder assessment and mapping exercises.
- ❖ Supporting speedy change implementation, adoption and benefits realisation.

Although change resistance planning is outlined in this section, it is recommended that this is performed in **a2BCMF® Step 1 - Change Definition** or as soon as the change team becomes aware of surfacing resistance that could be a barrier to change implementation and success.

Creation Steps: The CRP (**Template 3.7.4 Change Resistance Planning**) should not be created in isolation and should have input from outside the change team. The suggested creation steps are:

1. Identify a team with relevant knowledge of the organisation and stakeholders.
2. Schedule a change resistance planning (CRP) session.
3. Recreate a draft outline of **Template 3.7.4** to work on.

Template 3.7.4 Change Resistance Planning

#	Resistance Details					Actions and Status			
	Cause of Resistance	a2BCMF® Step #	Change Impact	Organisation, Departments or Individual(s)	Resistance Description	Occurrence Date	Mitigation and Actions	Person Responsible	Status
1									
2									
3									
4									
5									
6									
7									
8									
9									
10									

Template 3.7.4 Change Resistance Planning

4. Appoint a facilitator and prepare for the meeting.
5. Use the stakeholder analysis (**Assessment 3.1.9**) as input.
6. Document and record the following information:
   a. 'Cause of Resistance' (**see Section 3.7.5**)
   b. '**a2BCMF® Step #**'.
   c. 'Change Impact' (low, medium or high).
   d. 'Organisation, Department or Individuals(s)'.
   e. 'Resistance Description'.
   f. 'Occurrence Date'.
   g. 'Mitigation and Actions' (**see Section 3.7.6**).
   h. 'Person Responsible'.
   i. 'Status' (open, in-progress, action required or closed).
7. Once approved, the output of this template should be shared with the sponsor and should provide input into the following documents:
   a. Change communication plan (CCP).
   b. Project change plan (PCP).
   c. Programme governance.

Change Resistance Planning - Insights:

❖ **Contentious Information:** The output of this exercise should be treated as confidential as it can tarnish or be used to tarnish selected stakeholders.

❖ **Factual Data:** All of the analysis, assumptions, data and actions should remain factual, without any bias. The objective is to successfully deliver the change programme by using appropriate mitigation and actions to address resistance.

❖ **Tread with caution:** Similar to stakeholder analysis and mapping, all change team members should tread with caution when engaging powerful or narcissistic leaders!

3.7.10 The Fixed Versus Growth Mindset

Change disruption has become the order of the day and with the rapid introduction of new technology the pace of change will increase.

However, even with various approaches to driving change initiatives, we are constantly reminded that 70 per cent of change or transformation programmes fail to provide the benefits initially defined. Some of the key challenges when implementing change are employee resistance and not learning or applying the new skills, as well as adopting the new behaviours. These traits can be described as aspects of a fixed mindset, when successful change implementation really requires a growth mindset (**Figure 3.7.5**).

Fixed Mindset: Change by default is nearly always bad and will have a negative impact on my work life. We are comfortable with the current state and stick to what we know.

Change resistance is the reaction to the organisation and the change team when change is being implemented. Resistance does not have to be vocal or overt, we can just nod our heads and pretend to go along with the change. A negative environment can be further compounded by a Theory X (McGregor, 1960) hard management approach, which minimises workforce cooperation, causes resentment towards management and resistance towards change. If you do not change an employee's mindset and behaviour, you will not get organisational change.

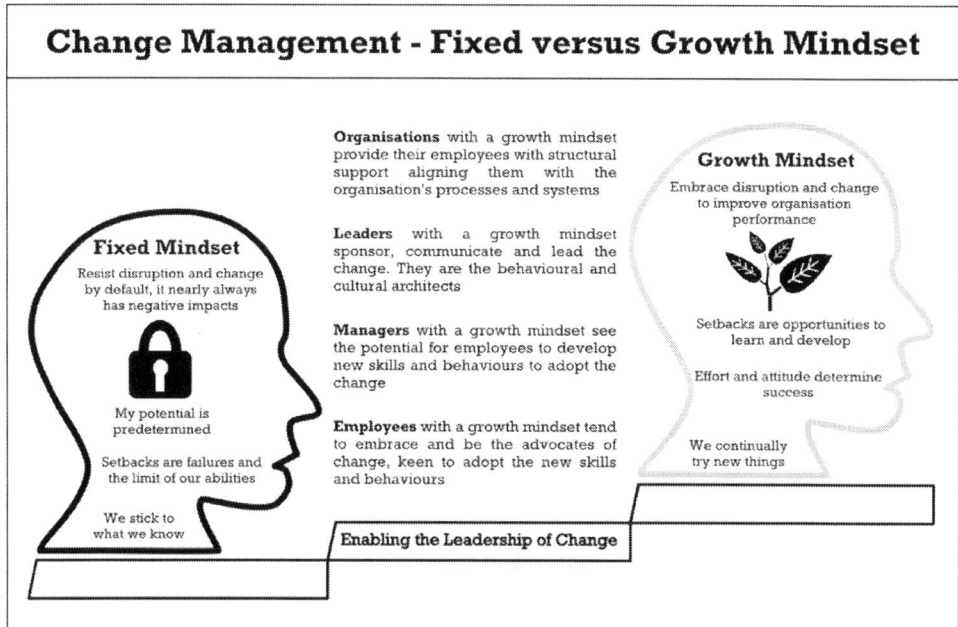

Figure 3.7.5 Fixed versus Growth Mindset

Growth Mindset: Employees with a growth mindset embrace change disruption by default, they understand the change will improve organisation performance and there will be an opportunity to develop and gain new skills. Mistakes will be made, but this adds to the learning and will create more opportunities in the future.

3.7.11 Change Resistance Costs

When an organisation does not address resistance, it will grow and become unmanageable. Implementation of the new way of working may stop or, even worse, the employees will revert back to the old way of working. The main benefits of using change management are to deliver successful change and meet targets. However, if the change sponsor, the leaders and the change team ignore resistance and the change is not delivered, then those benefits will be lost:

- **Time:** The project milestones will slip, or in the worst-case scenario, they will never be achieved.
- **Budget:** There will be cost overruns as more resources and effort will be required and expended on addressing change resistance.
- **Scope:** The full scope of the project will not be achieved and therefore neither will the benefits.
- **Change Adoption:** Change adoption relies on employees accepting the change, but this is unlikely if there is high change resistance.
- **Improved Business Performance:** If the change and related improvements are not implemented, the improved business performance will not be realised. Business performance may even drop because of change disruption.

Other Lasting Impacts: More important are the medium and long-term impacts for the organisation:

- Decrease in confidence to deliver future change successfully.
- Decrease in leadership confidence.
- Decrease in morale, especially with those who supported the change.
- Further increase in resistance to change.
- Future changes are more likely to fail.

3.7.12 Review and Checklist

Manage Resistance: The process of managing inevitable resistance, the negative reaction by the organisation or individual when they perceive that a change coming their way could be a threat to them.

Change Resistance Importance: There will always be resistance and the change team should be prepared for the impact and challenges this brings to change implementation, adoption and benefits delivery.

Case Study: Expect direct defiance and resistance even if your change programme has high strategic importance, its success is critical for organisation profits or it is proactively sponsored by the CEO. Do not be surprised that there are senior executives on the change team, sitting with you at meetings, socialising with you, but covertly working against you, protecting their own interests as opposed to the greater needs of the organisation, its stakeholders and shareholders.

Rebels, Observers and Advocates: The three typical employee standpoints, as defined by the Leadership of Change® when implementing change.

Reasons and Actions to Reduce Resistance: There are many reasons for resistance. Once identified and understood, there are actions that can be taken to reduce resistance.

Tipping Point: The coalition of change agents and '**Advocates**' can have a massive impact on the '**Observers**' and '**Rebels**'. They can entice the '**Observers**' to become '**Advocates**' and reduce '**Rebel**' resistance.

Change Approach: The change implementation approach depends on the type of change. A '**Tell**' is about compliance whereas a '**Sell**' is about winning hearts and minds. The latter takes longer.

Fixed Versus Growth Mindset: Employees with a growth mindset will embrace change and can become powerful advocates for organisational change, as opposed to those individuals with a fixed mindset who want to stick with the old way.

a2BCMF® Step 7 - Checklist

#	a2BCMF® Questions	Complete Yes/No
1	**Previous Steps:** Have the previous **a2BCMF®** steps been completed?	☐
2	**Change Resistance:** Does the change team understand the potential impact of resistance? Have they prepared for and addressed resistance throughout the change programme?	☐
3	**Resistance Standpoints:** Has the change team identified the main standpoints of the key stakeholders? Are they '**Rebels**', '**Observers**' or '**Advocates**'?	☐
4	**Reasons and Tactics to Reduce Resistance:** Has the change team assessed the potential reasons for resistance and tactics to engage relevant stakeholders?	☐
5	**Tipping Point:** Are the change agents working with the '**Advocates**' to entice the '**Observers**' to accept the change, as well as reduce '**Rebel**' resistance?	☐
6	**'Tell' or 'Sell':** Has the change implementation approach been defined and communicated? Is it about compliance or winning hearts and minds?	☐
7	**Change Resistance Planning (CRP):** Has there been proactive planning and preparation for resistance with mitigation actions to manage it?	☐
8	**Growth Mindset:** Have growth mindset employees been identified to create a powerful coalition with the change agents?	☐

Notes:

3.8 Develop New Skills and Behaviours

If you do not change employee behaviour, you will not get organisational change and performance improvement.

3.8.1 Develop New Skills and Behaviours - Overview

Definition: This step is about **Developing New Skills and Behaviours** by performing a gap analysis of existing skills and behaviours at the current state 'a'. Training can then be provided to close gaps for employees, to ensure adoption of the change and alignment with the new way of working at the future state 'B'.

Business Benefits: Most change requires improved skills and/or behaviours, so employees and the organisation can operate at the new level of working to ensure adoption, improved performance and benefits realisation.

Key Stakeholders and Elements: The key stakeholders are those who will deliver the service or product, or the stakeholders who receive these services and will therefore be the most impacted. Not closing gaps that are created by the change will leave a gap in the employee's skills and behaviours.

Business Objective: To evaluate existing skills and behaviours, identify skill and behaviour gaps, select available courses or design new courses to ensure employees operate effectively and efficiently in the new way of working. For your organisation to deliver a good service or manufacture good products, the employees must have the right skills and behaviours.

Enablers and Barriers

Enablers	Barriers
Adhering to the previous **a2BCMF®** steps to ensure that employees understand the change and are ready for skills and behaviour development.	The leadership team thinking that all employees will have a growth mindset, embracing the opportunity to develop new skills and behaviours.
Understanding that developing the new skills and behaviours is a critical step in ensuring the employees will be prepared for new way of working.	The leadership team thinking that employees will adapt their current skills to align with the news skills that the change will bring.
Protecting the skills and development budget against cost, schedule or scope overruns from earlier **a2BCMF®** steps.	Thinking that cuts to the skill and behaviour development budget, due to previous cost overruns, will not impact adoption.
Using the **a2BDNS© Model** to develop the new skills: **D**efine, **I**dentify, **E**valuate, **A**ssess, **D**eliver, **C**oach and **A**ppraise.	Developing the new skills without using a structured process or conducting a proper training gap analysis.
Understanding the difficulty in changing workplace behaviours if employees don't/can't even change their behaviour towards health.	Leaders thinking that because an employee is told, or knows that a behaviour is not acceptable, they won't behave in that way.
Using the **a2B5R® Model** and a structured process to: **R**ecognise, **R**edesign, **R**esolve, **R**eplicate and **R**einforce the new behaviours.	Developing the new behaviours without using a structured process, this starts with recognising there is an organisational challenge.
Using coaching to close gaps in skills and behaviours that might have been missed during the initial training.	Thinking that a one-time training session will close skills and behaviour gaps.
Leaders modelling the new behaviours and intervening directly to reinforce behaviours when they are not being exhibited by employees.	Narcissistic and deluded leaders thinking that employees will develop the new skills and behaviours on their say so.

3.8.2 Case Study - No Behaviour Change, No Change

A global energy organisation was having serious challenges in improving its health and safety record. The organisation was reporting high numbers of employee and contractor fatalities while performing global operations and was getting international bad press as a consequence. Throughout this period, the organisation had focused on improving safety, by developing extensive in-depth health and safety training modules. Completing these training modules was made compulsory for almost every manager and leader. Safety was prioritised and it was highlighted on all meeting agendas, and health and safety root cause workshops were held to gain learning on previous safety incidents.

The press continued to report that the organisation had a safety record that was worse than other operators. Given that this was around the same time a similar-sized competitor killed fifteen people in a single preventable refinery explosion (the Texas City Refinery explosion on March 23, 2005), the international press did not let up. A few years later, a whistle-blower accused the organisation of having a management culture that gave a higher priority to production than to the safety of its employees. A few months after this, the organisation announced profits of nearly $US30B, with one national newspaper branding the profits as 'obscene'.

The year after the national press had called the global energy organisation's profits 'obscene', operational fatalities moved back above the mid-twenties and one highly respected global broadsheet reported that the organisation had higher deaths than any other Western oil organisation. This was the catalyst to change their approach to safety and the CEO announced a new global life-saving rules (LSR) programme. I was asked to be the change lead for the UK upstream roll-out. Right from the start, it was clear this was going to be a change that had to match the scale of the challenge, and successful implementation was of the utmost importance.

At a high level, there are two options to approach most change implementations. The first is **'Sell'**: winning the hearts and minds of the employees. The advantages are that it allows the organisation to communicate the change in advance, take feedback, and gain staff buy-in. The disadvantages are that the process of communicating involves lots of people, and receiving feedback takes time. While this approach may suit an organisation with a consensus culture, it is not an approach the CEO can afford after more than a hundred deaths during his tenure, and not one he can sell to shareholders and other important stakeholders.

The second option is **'Tell'**, and this was the most appropriate to this challenge as it suits compliance, legislation, and safety issues. The advantages are achieving compliance quickly if the organisation enforces implementation, with consequences for those who do not conform. The disadvantages are that decisions like these are implemented rapidly with no time for staff consultation, and this may go against the organisation's culture (as it did in this case). As a result, employees tend to feel that the change is done unto them, and it will take longer to gain employee buy-in or to win their hearts and minds. It should be noted that some type of resistance is likely to be encountered when using either option.

The LSR were a set of simple and clear dos and don'ts, covering activities with the highest potential safety risk. Most energy organisations have implemented similar LSR but changed the number and category of their particular rules to best suit their own requirements. These rules were created from industry lessons and put in place to ensure that consistent behaviours were followed to prevent the kind of incidents that could result in a serious injury or fatality. None of the LSR were new concepts, and most people already complied through previous legal and internal regulations, but they were now being presented in a simple format for every employee to follow.

The rules gave employees and contractors a quick checklist of how to maintain safety in the organisation, and a list of mandatory rules that had to be adhered to when performing their daily jobs. These rules covered work activities such as having a permit to work (PTW), which refers to the management systems used to ensure that work is done safely and efficiently. These PTWs are used in hazardous industries and involve procedures to request, review, authorise, and document, but most importantly to deconflict tasks to be carried out by front-line workers. Other rules included safety elements such as wearing seat belts when in a moving vehicle, not driving or working under the effect of drugs or alcohol, verifying electrical equipment isolation before beginning work and using the specified life protecting equipment.

The objective of communication is to provide a clear message to the target audience and stakeholders over a defined timeline. Communication of the LSR was clear, concise and consistent throughout the implementation, with explicit consequences for non-adherence: *If you choose to break the rules, you choose not to work for our organisation.* The typical cultural consensus of debate and optionality was not a possibility for this critical initiative. It was now about consequence management. The change implementation approach was a '**Tell**', and resistance to following the rules was therefore not an option if you wanted to continue employment with the organisation. This initiative was about preventing employee and contractor deaths at work and ensuring that everyone would be able to go home safe and well at the end of the working day to their family.

The LSR implementation timeline was rolled out over a five-month period by the corporate communications team and was shared over all the organisation's media outlets. It started with the CEO sending a message to the senior leaders to introduce the programme, followed by an executive note sent to country chairs and senior leaders with further details. Briefing notes were sent to key leadership teams and all management and contractors, followed by links to the LSR internal websites. In just under five months from the CEO's announcement, the LSR went live and became the new way of working and behaving in the organisation.

During the year the LSR initiative was launched there were twenty fatalities. However, within eighteen months of the LSR going live, the fatalities had nearly reduced by 50 per cent. The next full year saw an even greater reduction, to a new low of six. When compared with previous years, there was a clear downward trend in the number of fatalities. There were, of course, some failures by employees and contractors to adhere to the new rules. These breaches resulted in either injury or death, and all incidents were examined by independent country and regional investigation teams.

A corporate team continued to ensure that the LSR became part of the organisation's DNA, breaches were dealt with consistently, and incidents of non-conformance and ultimately lessons learned were effectively communicated across the organisation. To date, the company still continues with its zero-target goal, and although an incremental improvement was made in safety by focusing on the new LSR behaviours, it is difficult to consider the initiative entirely successful if one employee or contractor does not return home from work to their family after a working day.

Case Study - Insights:

❖ **Skills Provide Competence, Behaviour Provides Change:** To improve organisational safety, comprehensive and compulsory training modules were introduced. Safety was prioritised and highlighted on all meeting agendas, and health and safety root cause workshops were held to gain learning on previous safety incidents. Still the company's safety record did not improve, and global negative news press followed. The organisation made two key changes:

> ➢ **Behaviour Change:** The CEO announced a new global life-saving rules (LSR) programme. These were a set of simple, clear dos and don'ts, focusing on behaviour change.

> ➢ **Compliance:** A 'Tell' implementation approach was decided with explicit consequences for non-adherence: *If you choose to break the rules, you choose not to work for our organisation.*

Within eighteen months of the LSR going live, fatalities had reduced by nearly 50 per cent. While training provides the new skills and knowledge to potentially operate at the new way of working, it does not always guarantee change success. Exhibiting the right behaviours in work can sometimes be more important than having the right skills and knowledge. To achieve successful change, there needs to be a reinforcement policy that matches the importance of the change and drives the right behaviours.

3.8.3 The Importance of New Skills and Behaviours

There was a time when employees stayed at the same company in the same role for many years. Although there were major technology changes in the past, such as moving from a typewriter to word-processing, the technology revolution is now moving far faster and is impacting employee roles more frequently. This means that learning new skills is now part of the employee's role.

The importance of employee behaviours on the organisation's change success cannot be underestimated. There is little purpose in learning new skills if you continue to behave in the old way. As a change leader you should be very aware:

"If you do not change employee behaviour, you will not get organisational change."

Developing effective skills and behaviours to deliver the new change is critical to support new processes, systems, technology, products, services, etc. When done properly, training facilitates change adoption and sustainable benefits. The employees will become confident, happy and more efficient. The organisation will also benefit, with improvements in efficiency, increased revenue and profits while decreasing costs, waste and inefficiencies. However, done badly, the opposite can happen. You can buy the best home computer system and software but without the right training to develop skills and competencies you might be more effective with the old computer.

"When desperate people seek easy solutions without doing the hard work of fundamental learning and change, resilience is undermined and real growth and learning fade" (Ulrich, D. et al., 2010). To realise the inherent value of the new change, skills or competencies have to be developed so the organisation and employees can perform effectively and efficiently at the new way of working. This does not always happen. Too many leaders do not see the importance of training and development and too few organisations genuinely fully close the skills, competence and behaviour gaps. Firstly, there may be budget overruns in the early **a2BCMF®** steps caused by cost, schedule or scope and as a result the training budget suffers. While this is highly counterproductive and prevents the organisation from achieving their ROI, the default reaction of organisational leaders, especially on technology projects, is to cut the training budget. Secondly, the development of the new skills does not always follow a structured and disciplined process.

3.8.4 Employee Training

Training helps employees learn specific skills and behaviours to prepare them to perform effectively and efficiently in their new role. Employee training is essential for an organisation's change success. Skills *training* aims to improve employee's work skills and behaviours, whereas *development* aims to increase future abilities in relation to potential promotion.

- ❖ **Skills Development:** Developing the skills, abilities and knowledge needed by the employee to perform specific tasks and activities within the organisation, its process and systems using the **Developing New Skills Model (a2BDNS© Model)**.
- ❖ **Behaviour Development:** Developing the organisation and employee behaviours required to support change adoption. It involves defining the critical few new behaviours, designing and delivering the training and applying the **a2B5R® Model**.
- ❖ **Training Benefits:** As well as preparing the employee for the new way of working and operating, training will also enhance change adoption and success. Other benefits include:
  - ➢ **Confidence:** Equipping the employee with the confidence to perform their new role.
  - ➢ **Motivation:** Increasing employee motivation and drive.
  - ➢ **Efficiency:** Increasing efficiencies in operating the new processes and systems.
  - ➢ **Safety:** Improving employee work safety.

3.8.5 Developing the New Skills

An organisation's survival depends on its ability to learn at the same pace as, or faster than, change in its environment (Burnes, 2009). It is a collective process and in change programmes it needs to involve the employees, leaders and also the change team. In business management, a learning organisation is a company that facilitates the learning of its employees and continuously transforms itself (Pedlar, et al., 1997). Senge (1990[1]) explains that a learning organisation develops as a result of the pressures facing modern organisations and this enables them to remain competitive in the business environment. Senge argues (1990[2]), *"the leader's new work"* is about building the learning organisation in terms of three roles: designer, teacher, and steward.

Equally, the change team should be developing their skills so they can effectively navigate and facilitate change implementation. These skills include change management, communications and associated skills such as interviewing, coaching and project management. If the change implementation involves working in new cultural environments then the leaders, managers and change team can become more effective with cultural skills training (Steers, et al., 2013). This concept is discussed further in **Section 3.9.7 - Culture and Change**.

3.8.6 a2BDNS© Developing the New Skills Model

The six-step process for developing the new skills and behaviours is outlined in **Figure 3.8.1**. The change management team should work with the human resources department (HRD) and the organisation's training department throughout this process. The objective is to facilitate the creation of corporate training that delivers the change objectives by providing the employees with the skills and behaviours to deliver the new way of working. A training needs analysis (TNA) can be used in this process. A TNA typically identifies gaps at the organisational level, the group level and the individual level. The six process steps for developing the new skills are listed below:

1. **Define:** Define the new skills and behavioural training objectives and align them with the change programme.
   - These training objectives are statements that define the expected goals of the training courses and coaching in terms of demonstrable skills, knowledge and behaviour for the employee to perform their new work activities. Learning objectives are clearly written, specific statements of observable learner behaviour or actions that can be measured upon completion of the development activities.

2. **Identify:** Identify the new skills and behaviour objectives.
   - **Skills:** From the skills that were defined in step one, assess how these align with the organisation's current competency framework and competency dictionary. Organisations have many different approaches to this topic and the change team should align their approach with internal processes. However, the focus of this step is to identify if the skills defined in step one already exist within the organisation.

- **Behaviours:** Inherent or specific behaviours, such as process safety, customer service or product quality can impact certain groups, functions or departments within the change programme.

   Note: The above behaviours are aligned with a specific role in the organisation and the skills associated with it. These role specific behaviours are additional to the wider change behaviours outlined in **Section 3.8.8**.

3. **Evaluate:** Evaluate the existing skills and behaviour traits for the impacted employees using structured analysis to establish gaps.
   - **Establish Gaps:** A structured analysis should be performed to evaluate the current skills and behaviours.
   - **Questions to consider:**
      a. Is the current skills and behaviour training meeting the needs at an organisational, group and individual level?
      b. If there is a gap in training, where is it and how wide is the gap?
      c. Can the training be modified or improved to address the new skills and behaviours required?
      d. What training needs to be redesigned?
      e. Can this training be aligned to the change strategy and vision?

4. **Assess:** Assess available courses or design new courses to close gaps in skill levels and behaviours.
   - **Available Internal Training:** What existing training can be used on the change programme in its current state?
   - **Modify Internal Training:** What existing training can be modified and used on the change programme?
   - **Design or Procure New Training:** What are the advantages and disadvantages of designing new training versus procuring external training? What are the costs versus the benefits? What is the total cost of ownership now and going forward, etc?

5. **Deliver and Coach:** Deliver the skills training programme to close the identified gaps and follow up with coaching.
   - **Deliver Training:** Many considerations will be required for this step. If the change impacts many employees across the

organisation it may involve the external supply chain. There will be initial capacity and capability challenges. Taking employees away from their normal day-to-day operations tends to cause organisation friction and an additional challenge is being able to develop trainer and employee capability quickly enough. A detailed training plan can greatly help this process, especially if it is transparent and easily assessible.

- **Coaching:** Coaching is a method of helping people to develop their skills and behaviours to improve their job performance. It is about unlocking an employee's potential to maximize their own performance (Whitmore, 2002) and is an extremely important part of developing new skills and behaviours. During change implementation, coaches can be brought in to support the change team and then the task can be transferred to the manager's day-to-day responsibility once the change team has dissolved.

- **Learning Styles:** *"Learning is the process whereby knowledge is created through the transformation of experience"* (Kolb, 1984). Kolb's Experiential Learning Cycle (ELC) is a well-known theory which argues that we learn from our experiences of life. The ELC is typically represented by a four-stage learning cycle. First, immediate and concrete experiences serve as a basis for observation. Second, the employee reflects on these observations and begins to build a general theory of what this information might mean. In the third step, the learner forms abstract concepts and generalisations based on their hypothesis. Finally, the learner tests the implications of these concepts in new situations.

6. **Appraise:** Appraise the new skills to establish the effectiveness of the training and coaching that prepares the employees to operate at the future state '**B**'.

- **Analysing and Evaluating Results:** Training appraisal enables an organisation to validate that their employees have the right skills and behaviours to perform their new role. The Kirkpatrick Model (Kirkpatrick, 2006) is one of the best known models for analysing and evaluating the results of training. The model can be implemented before, throughout, and following training to demonstrate the value to the business. The four main levels are:

a. **Level 1 Reaction:** Measures how participants react to the training.

b. **Level 2 Learning:** Analyses the training to establish if it was understood.

c. **Level 3 Behaviour:** Assesses if the employees are utilising what they learned at work.

d. **Level 4 Results:** Concludes whether the training content has had a positive impact on the organisation and supported the change.

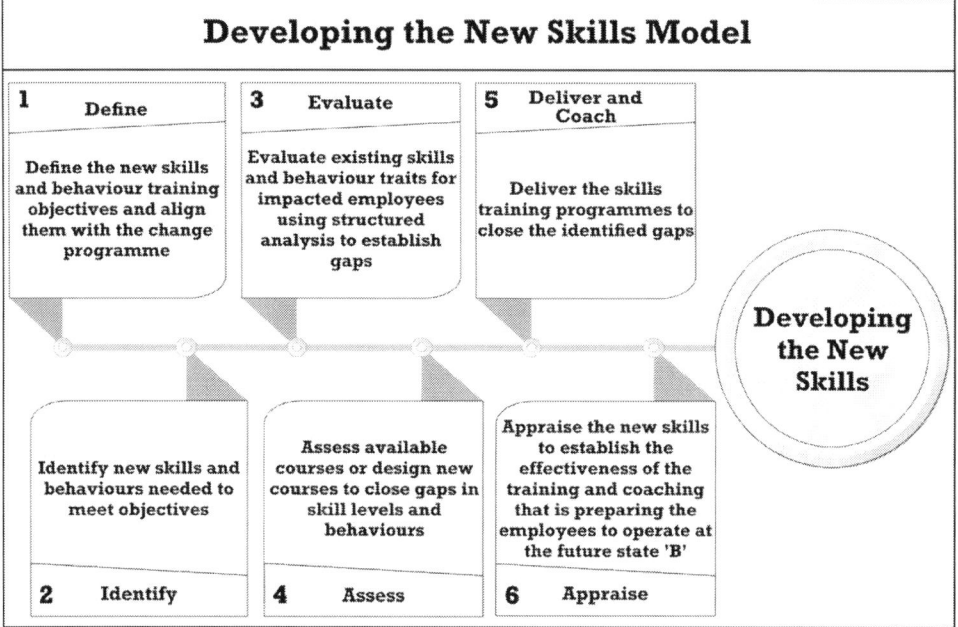

Figure 3.8.1 Developing the New Skills

3.8.7 The Behaviour Change Challenge

The term *employee behaviour* refers to the way in which employees respond to specific circumstances or changes in the workplace. While many elements determine an individual's behaviour in the workplace, employees are shaped by the organisation's culture. This behaviour is a key determinant of successful change and adoption of the new ways of working. Even with behaviour training, only a small percentage is thought to be transferred back into the workplace and an even smaller percentage of organisations believe that the coaching taking place in their business is effective.

Dr. Miller stated that. *"If you look at people after coronary-artery bypass grafting two years later, 90% of them have not changed their lifestyle"* (Deutschman, 2007). *"And that's been studied over and over and over again. And so we're missing some link in there. Even though they know they have a very bad disease and they know they should change their lifestyle, for whatever reason, they can't."* These men and women were given a choice to either change their behaviour or risk premature death and they chose **not to change**.

Putting this in the context of trying to change employee behaviours in work, it should highlight to all change management professionals and organisational leaders how massive the task is. Many change, improvement or transformation programmes are heavily reliant on changing employee behaviours but the effort or approach often fails. Having a '**Tell**' compliance change approach with consequences can help but it is not always the right solution. To change employee behaviours, we need to bring in the psychological and emotional dimensions that are so often ignored. The health industry has learnt that support sessions led by a psychologist have helped patients change their lifestyles long-term.

3.8.8 Developing the Behaviours

One of the most challenging aspects of any change programme is the way in which employee behaviours are addressed. In many cases, organisations miss this opportunity. Delivering the ROI relies on changing the employee's behaviour, and improving their performance is a critical part of the change management process in order to ensure sustainable change. Old behaviours may act as a major barrier to change adoption. In order to eliminate the old behaviours, the change team need to create the new required behaviours.

A Nudge in the Right Direction

Getting employees to change their behaviour is a big challenge, but what if we could give them a nudge in the right direction? Nudging is a part of choice architecture. Thaler and Sunstein (2008) define a nudge as, *"any aspect of the choice architecture that alters people's behaviour in a predictable way without forbidding any options or significantly changing their economic incentives."* We see examples of this in everyday life, e.g. green footprints painted on the footpath leading pedestrians towards different types of recycling bins, radically reducing the litter on our streets. In work, organisations offer 'opt out' pension schemes rather than 'opt in'. In the canteen, healthy food is put at eye level in bright packaging. This means placing unhealthy foods further away, but it works, and the concept could help to achieve the required behavioural change.

3.8.9 a2B5R® Employee Behaviour Change Model

Behaviours should be considered in **a2BCMF® Step 1 - Change Definition**. Serious thought should be given to this step if change adoption is highly dependent on behavioural change, i.e. it is safety critical. The initial focus should be on employees with a growth mindset. These employees tend to embrace and be the advocates of change, keen to adopt the new skills and behaviours. They believe that basic skills and behaviours are qualities you can cultivate through your own efforts. Everyone can grow and change through application and experience within the right environment. The fantastic thing about these growth mindset employees is that their focus is on improving their skills and behaviours to adopt the new change and not on wasting energy by resisting inevitable change.

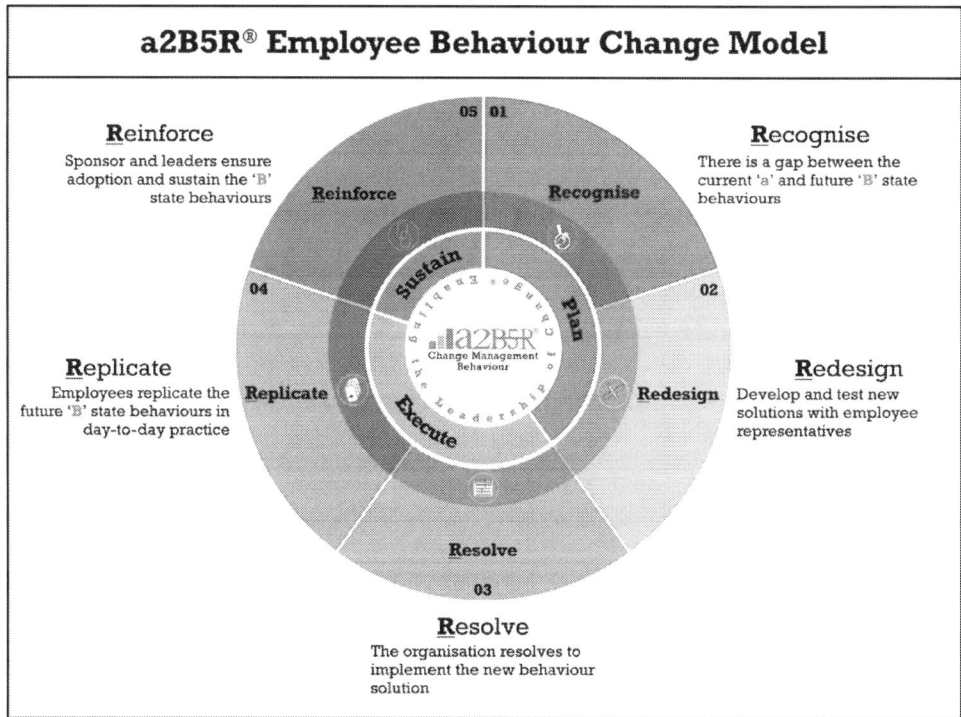

Figure 3.8.2 a2B5R® Behaviour Change Model

Typically, organisations lose focus and energy towards the end of the change cycle and may not achieve either embedded or lasting change because they ignore behaviour change. The **a2B5R® Behaviour Change Model (Figure 3.8.2)** supports the change team to embed the few new behaviours that are critical to change success, to achieve a full return on investment (ROI), adoption and sustainment. The model systematically supports the transition of employee behavioural change from the current '**a**' state to the improved future '**B**' state.

Recognise: To officially accept that there is a problem with the current behaviours within the organisation. This may require analysis of the current behaviours and any challenges this causes. It is important that the change team recognise the current behaviours and the impact they could have on change implementation. Equally, they should also recognise that it is not easy to alter engrained behaviour even when that behaviour is clearly counterproductive to change success (Agryris, 1982).

> **Objective:** Create *consciousness* within the organisation that old behaviours will not deliver the required change.
> **Output:** A gap analysis, based on data, that lists the differences between the current '**a**' and future '**B**' state.

Redesign: As a change team, agree to redesign the new solution and define the few new critical behaviours. A selection of employees should be involved at this stage. If the few new critical behaviours are not developed, then the employees will automatically fall back to the old way and their inherent behaviours.

> **Objective:** Establish how the new behaviours will be defined and how they will *evolve* within the organisation.
> **Output:** Agreed solutions, developed by a sample of employees, that have a high likelihood of achieving the future '**B**' state.

Resolve: The change team, supported by the selected employees, make a resolution to implement the few new critical behaviours. Piloting the new behaviours, collecting feedback and making necessary modifications will increase full implementation success. Sniehotta et al. (2005) provide insights into changing habitual lifestyle patterns. They argue that *"active self-regulation"* is required to break habits that we follow as part of our normal lives.

> **Objective: *Determination,*** both by the organisation and employees, to change. There must be a personal ownership and commitment to behaviour change.

> **Output:** Implementation of the behavioural solutions to achieve the future '**B**' state.

Replicate: Continued implementation of solutions to achieve the future '**B**' state, ensuring they are replicated during normal day-to-day operations to become the new way of working and normal expected behaviour. According to Thaler (2015), *"psychologists tell us that in order to learn from experience, two ingredients are necessary: frequent practice and immediate feedback."*

> **Objective: *Embedding*** the behaviours into normal operations.

> **Output:** A day-to-day practise of the future '**B**' state so it starts to become part of the organisation's culture, *"the way we do things around here."*

Reinforce: Psychologists have long known that behaviour often stems from direct association and reinforcement (Rescorla, 1987). The change agents, leadership team and sponsor should reinforce the new behaviours by first modelling them, as well as intervening to provide feedback to employees when behaviours are not being exhibited, and rewarding them when they are.

> **Objective:** The few new behaviours are part of the ***culture*** and are reinforced by the sponsor and leadership team.

> **Output:** Evidence that the organisation has adopted the new behaviours which will sustain the '**B**' state.

3.8.10 Change Management Training

Organisations with internal change management capability have an advantage over their competitors. They can use this capability to lead the market rather than follow it. Having internal change management capability gives the organisation both agility and expertise to manage internal change. Delivering each change programme or project using the same change methodology and approach is less confusing and more effective for the organisation. Change management programmes will be more effective if the key employees leading the change have similar change management training. Tailored training that suits their specific role would then be additional. Suggested training and development could be:

❖ **Change Team:** Change practitioner training to equip the team with change skills to lead organisational change. Additional training could be provided for specific skills, such as communications, coaching, training delivery, etc.

❖ **Sponsors:** Change management overview workshop and a sponsorship masterclass.

❖ **Leaders:** Change management overview workshop and a leading organisational change masterclass.

❖ **Change Agents:** Change management overview training and coaching skills. On-boarding training should also be considered to cover the specific role of the change agent, this should be aligned with the department or function they are representing.

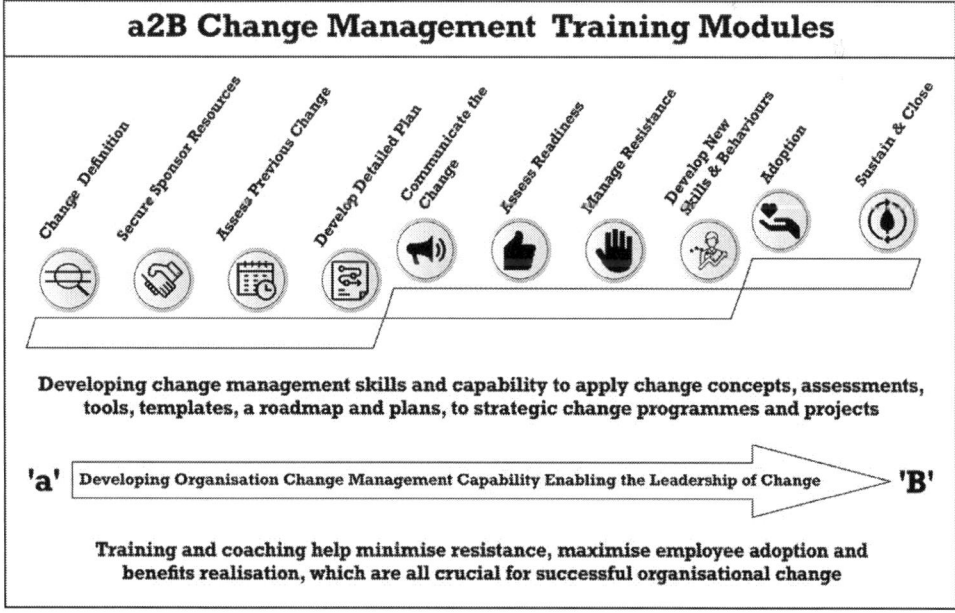

Figure 3.8.3 Change Management Training Modules

3.8.11 Review and Checklist

Develop New Skills and Behaviours: The process of developing the new skills and behaviours, ensuring all impacted employees are prepared for the new way of working. Developing the new skills and behaviours is critical to the organisation in achieving change success.

New Skills and Behaviour Budget: Protecting the skills and development budget against cost, schedule or scope overruns from earlier **a2BCMF®** steps.

Develop the New Skills: An organisation's survival can depend on its ability to learn new skills at the same pace as, or faster than, its external environment.

a2BDNS© Model: There are six process steps for developing the new skills: **Define, Identify, Evaluate, Assess, Deliver** and **Coach**, and **Appraise.**

Develop the New Behaviours: Developing the new behaviours is a critical element of change success and is overlooked by many organisations and its leadership team. If you do not change the employee mindset and behaviour, you will not get organisational change.

Behavioural Challenge: If it is difficult to change the behaviour of people so they become healthier and live longer, how difficult will it be to change employee workplace behaviour?

a2B5R® Model: There are five key life cycle stages to support employee behavioural change. The five stage are: **Recognise, Redesign, Resolve, Replicate** and **Reinforce**.

Coaching: Using coaching to close gaps in skills and behaviours that might have been missed during the initial training.

Leadership Modelling and Reinforcement: Leaders should model the new behaviours and intervene directly to reinforce them when they are not being exhibited by employees.

a2BCMF® Step 8 - Checklist

#	a2BCMF® Questions	Complete Yes/No
1	**Previous Steps:** Have the previous **a2BCMF®** steps been completed?	☐
2	**Developing New Skills and Behaviours:** Does the organisation understand the relationship between this **a2BCMF®** step and change success?	☐
3	**Skills and Behaviour Budget:** Has the initial budget been protected from spend overruns on previous **a2BCMF®** steps?	☐
4	**Skills Development Process:** Has the six-step process with structured analysis been followed to develop the new skills?	☐
5	**New Behaviours:** Has the **a2B5R® Employee Change Behaviour Model** been used as part of changing employee behaviours?	☐
6	**Change Challenge:** Do the leaders understand that people are unlikely to change their behaviour to improve their own health, so the challenge of changing workplace behaviours will be a significant one?	☐
7	**Coaching:** Has coaching been used to close gaps in skills and behaviours that might have been missed during the initial training?	☐
8	**Leadership Modelling and Reinforcement:** Have the leaders modelled and reinforced the new behaviours?	☐

Notes:

Section 3C: Sustain and Close - a2BCMF® Steps 9 - 10

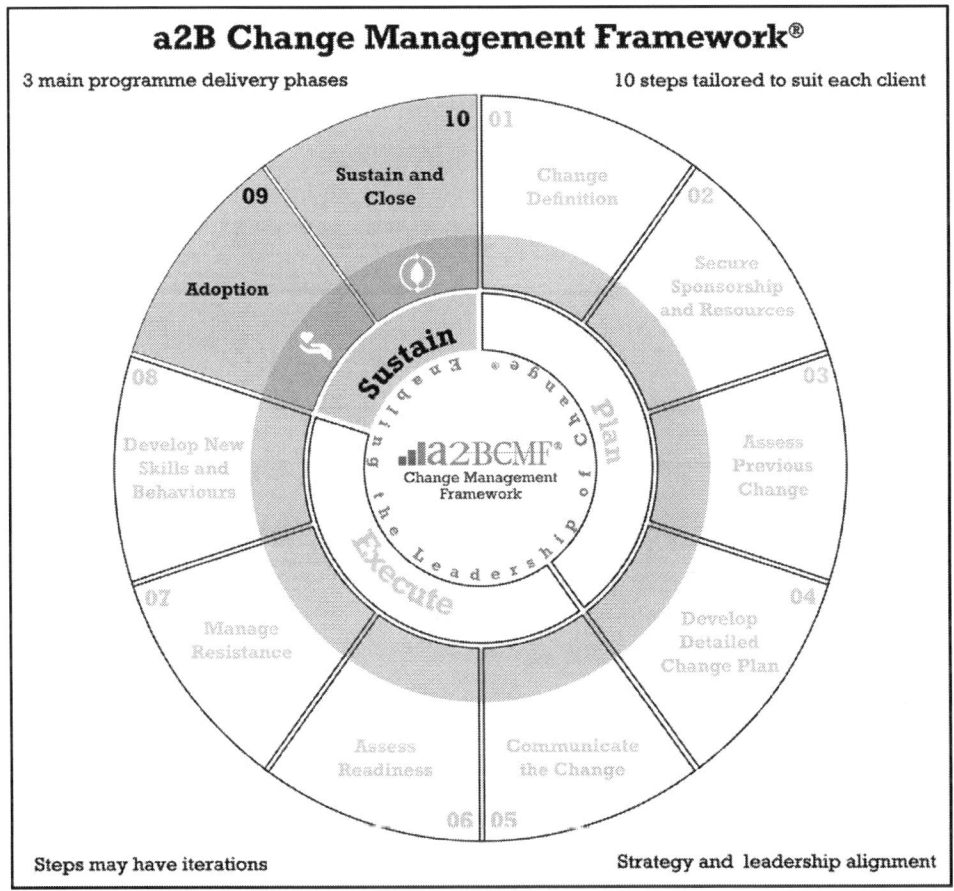

Sustain: Closing the change programme to sustain adoption and ensure benefits realisation.

3.9 Adoption

For change adoption to be successful, leadership needs to ensure employees are supported to develop the new skills, behaviours and motivation that deliver improved future organisation performance.

3.9.1 Adoption - Overview

Definition: This step is about the organisation and employees making the transition from the current state 'a' to the future state 'B', leaving the old ways behind and adopting the new way of working and behaving. It is confirmation that they have fully accepted the change, both in mind and in heart. It is agreement that the new way of working is more efficient and benefits both the organisation and customers, which is part of the organisation's future DNA.

Business Benefits: Without high employee acceptance of change adoption, the benefits of the investment will not be realised, and the organisation's long-term survival may not be as secure.

Key Stakeholders and Elements: Adoption involves all the organisation's key stakeholders and how the change will align with the organisation's processes, systems, leadership and strategy.

Business Objective: To achieve a high level of user adoption of a new system, process or way of working by developing the employee's new skills, behaviours and motivation. This should be supported by the sponsor and leaders, with good communication and ongoing strategic alignment.

Enablers and Barriers

Enablers	Barriers
Understanding the importance of adoption while delivering change success, sustainment and achieving the organisation's ROI.	Sponsors and leaders thinking that well designed training and coaching will ensure adoption.
Aligning the employee with the key elements of the organisation; sponsorship, leadership, processes, systems, communication and strategy.	The leadership team assuming the employees have adopted the change without aligning them with the organisation's processes, systems, etc.
Planning for change adoption during change programme definition at the first **a2BCMF®** step.	The change team only considering change adoption during training design and delivery.
Using the **AUILM® Model** to ensure the employee life cycle stages are in place to achieve change adoption.	Not assessing training effectiveness or following up with coaching to reinforce the new skills and behaviours.
Understanding that involving employees in the change design will help to gain buy-in and support change adoption.	Reducing communication frequency, messaging and not keeping the feedback loop open.
Understanding how the employees feel as they pass through the change transition stages and change disruption.	Ignoring employee's feelings during change disruption and not being aware that they might feel unsettled, resentful of the change or disconnected from the organisation.
Using the **AUILM® Model** and tactics to support the employee to develop competency through learning and incentivising them to keep motivated.	Not understanding that adoption links to employee learning and continued motivation.
Assessing the culture of the organisation to find norms or behaviours that could enable change success.	Ignoring the cultural impact on change, especially if change success is dependent on successful change implementation.

3.9.2 Case Study - Easy Solutions are Not Always Adopted

Part of my role in working for a major global energy organisation was to set up a business improvement function across Europe, specifically in Ireland, the UK, and Norway. The business improvement team was integrated into the leadership and plant management teams to improve operations and support for global initiatives launched from HQ. These would be implemented in over fifty countries.

One of these initiatives was the implementation of an ERP software module into global operations, to ensure that all countries operated using the same systems, processes, and procedures. The obvious advantage of this was that employees could move from country to country with very little training and be able to operate efficiently and effectively within a short period of time. Every country followed the same operational excellence procedures, with the business priority being safe and efficient operations.

During this implementation, I'd received an email from Jaap, one of the business improvement project leads, informing me that he was having people problems with the implementation of one of the ERP software modules. Jaap was in Peterhead, which sits at the easternmost point in mainland Scotland. Peterhead was originally founded by fishermen, and this had strongly influenced the local culture.

He called me later that evening.

"Hi, Jaap. How is it going?" I asked. I'd always admired how well people from the Netherlands spoke in English.

"Peter, all is well with me and the family. And you?"

"Great, Jaap. How are things in the north of Scotland?"

"Peter, I was visiting the plant and control room this morning to assess how the new module was being used. I went to visit the control room and asked one of the control panel operators if he was using the new software module. At first he ignored me, and when I asked him again he was very aggressive and told me to get out of the control room, using what I can only describe as expletives."

I could imagine the scene: a control room operator being interrupted while he was working and being questioned about another new change by someone who was from the Netherlands and not even based at the plant. Although the company had a very good policy on diversity, I'd always personally found that cultural diversity travelled less well in northern Scotland, particularly when the workforce was made up mostly of locals.

"Jaap, I'm sorry that happened. So what did you do?"

"Peter, as per the training, I removed myself from the situation, went back to the main office, and sent you an email, copying in the plant manager."

We chatted further about the incident and I asked him to cut his trip short and meet me back in the regional office the following evening. This was not a major issue, but it had to be corrected quickly, so I started to make arrangements to meet him in Aberdeen the next day.

With a little bit of support from the travel company, and luck in finding an available seat, I was able to rearrange my return flight into Aberdeen Airport. As we landed, I wondered how the culture of Aberdeen and the surrounding region would impact or enhance the change success of this project.

Our planned dinner that evening was both an opportunity to move the project forward, and an excellent chance to build relationships and learn from my team. Jaap had texted to say he was already sitting at the table in the restaurant and Rolf had just arrived.

I walked into the restaurant. Jaap and Rolf stood up and we greeted each other with warm handshakes. We all sat down. Rolf and I caught up and discussed a few issues he faced as the new cross-border business improvement lead, while Jaap perused the wine and food menus.

I reopened the conversation about Jaap's visit to the plant the previous day and asked him to talk us both through it. He shared the same story that I'd heard on the phone but with more detail. He clarified that he'd been alone when he entered the control room but that he'd been respectful and polite at all times, leaving before the situation had got any worse. Jaap had had experience of working throughout Europe, but the eastern point of Scotland and its culture would have been very different to what he would have been used to. I knew that there was resistance in the plant and sometimes felt it myself, but hoped the local leaders would welcome our team's support to change and improve their operations.

Rolf and I both agreed that I should visit the plant the next day, particularly the control room, with one of the shift supervisors. We needed to have a chat with the control panel operator and establish why he was not using the new maintenance module. We also needed to check if there was any fault on our side. Was the new training completed, and was the on-site coaching followed up to close any competency gaps?

In the corner of my eye I could see the waiter bringing the wine and asking Jaap if he wanted to taste it, but he seemed to decline. We looked around to Jaap and Rolf and I asked,

"Are we going to pour the wine?"

Jaap nodded towards the approaching waiter, who was carrying an impressive decanter, and spoke.

"Guys, I asked for it to be decanted. Don't panic. It's not the most expensive wine on the list, but it will taste much better if we aerate it."

Rolf and I looked at each other and rolled our eyes.

Wow, I thought. *Jaap might be great in office environments and some other gas plants, but we might need someone more aligned to the north-eastern Scottish culture to see this task through.*

On my way to the plant the next morning I had plenty of time to think. As planned, I met Keith, the maintenance supervisor, in his office. He had supported me on previous change business improvement initiatives. At first, he was vocally resistant against our team, but as we'd helped him both to uncover and remove inefficiencies, as well as to improve operator behaviour, he'd started to tolerate me. He was aware of why I was on-site, as I had previously called him in confidence to get his take on the situation. He understood that my focus was not on a single operator, but on the impact this could have on wider implementation across other European sites.

I'd visited many oil and gas control rooms in my career and they had always impressed me. In the centre of the room there is a large working area with multiple control panels and a large viewfinder, with multiple TV monitors showing real-time images from the different processing modules and the perimeter fences. The one thing that stood out, however, was Rodney. He was not holding the usual personal access display device (PADD) you would expect. He was holding a laptop. A laptop has no place in the control room, as the room was already fitted with computers in the control panel. But, worse still, Rodney had a dreaded Excel spreadsheet open on the screen. I watched in silence as Rodney read out numbers and text from one of the control panel monitors and typed them into the laptop.

What should happen when a defective part is identified by the system is this: it would be flagged on the monitor with a message indicating the problem, using a predefined code and a short description. Rodney should then hover his mouse cursor over the warning signal and the hyperlink to get more details. The system would usually suggest the required activities so the error could be corrected.

On the monitor I could see the system was indicating that a serviceable part needed to be replaced. Rodney should have been right-clicking the mouse to copy the part number over to the procurement system for automatic ordering (once approved by his supervisor), which would then automatically queue the repair in the maintenance schedule.

Rodney typed the part number and description into the laptop. I surmised he intended to send an email to the shift supervisor to order the part separately. For me, this was too painful to watch. I caught Keith's attention and he nodded, confirming he was aware that I was going to approach Rodney.

"Hello, Rodney. I realise you are extremely busy. I'm Peter. I support the plants with change and business improvement. I think you've seen me before, working on a road safety project, and you showed me some CCTV footage of the roadways." I heard a quiet grunt, which had at least opened up communications. "It would be really great if you could spare me a few minutes to discuss the new maintenance software."

Rodney and I left the control room and started to walk back to the office block to grab a coffee. As we walked, I kept the conversation going with general chit-chat, before mentioning the real reason for my visit.

"Jaap was here a few days ago and he tried to have a chat with you. I'm here to finish what he was trying to do. We will come back to that later. We are implementing this new maintenance module which will benefit everyone in the organisation. At a high level it helps to provide safe and continuous operations for this processing plant."

We arrived at the canteen and sat down in a quiet spot with our coffee. I continued.

"Company-wide benefits of the maintenance software module are; it replaces hard copy logbooks in the control room, it automatically reports on operational events, it provides input into shift handovers and crew handover reports, and it produces a historical event log for each process module on critical equipment."

"I know all this, Peter. I attended the training."

I smiled and took a long sip of my coffee.

"Rodney, which part of the training?"

"All of it," he responded.

To help make my point I continued listing the systems benefits.

"Other specific benefits are the alignment of data and information with other processes and disciplines. It also reduces waste in operator time by avoiding double data or cumbersome data entry, and improves data quality because data is checked automatically and used in other systems where it becomes visible."

Rodney was becoming more impatient and interrupted me.

"I heard this all at the training. Thank you for the coffee. However, you are keeping from my work."

"Rodney. I will be succinct. You may have been to the training, but you are not applying the learning."

"What do you mean?"

"Rodney, entering maintenance part numbers and descriptions in a laptop are absolutely not part of the training, nor, I may add, the desired behaviours. What happens with these details in the laptop when you finish your shift this evening and you are off-site for four or more days? What happens if the part fails and it is not ordered or placed in the maintenance planning queue?"

Rodney responded but with less confidence than before,

"Peter, I was going to send an email to Keith at the end on my shift, like I always do."

"Rodney, there are too many things that are wrong with that statement. One, you are double-entering data into a laptop. Two, the laptop is not connected to the system. And three, the system now takes care of the shift handover, not an email."

Rodney looked sheepish and tried to defend himself.

"Well, that is the way we have always done it."

"Rodney, it is not 'we'. You are one of the few people still doing it the old way. Secondly, nothing will negatively impact this organisation's performance quicker than an employee who believes that the way they work today is the way they will work tomorrow. You are a great operator with vast experience and maintenance knowledge. Everyone talks highly of you, but you will have to adopt the new system and the new way of working."

"Right, Peter, I get it. I will start to use the new system."

"Great, and thank you. Another quick request. Please be nice to Jaap in future."

"But, Peter, he doesn't know how to approach the people here."

I pictured the decanter from last night's dinner, but I had to interrupt him.

"We have a diversity policy and not everyone can be shy, soft, and sensitive like me." The joke broke up the tension and we both laughed.

"Another thing Rodney. When my team and I enter the control room can you please stop giving us that glazed over eye look? The one where your eyes and body language say, 'I will still be here long after you've gone, and I won't be part of any change.'"

Rodney laughed.

"I am going back to work now, Peter."

I shook his hand and waved him goodbye.

As Rodney walked away, I wondered to myself why neither the sponsor nor Keith had had this conversation with Rodney. If this had happened, this issue may never have arisen. I thought to myself that I needed to have a chat with the sponsor and Keith about reinforcement to close this out. This was a learning opportunity. I also needed to check if they had linked their employee's individual performance plans to the change project and the new software module.

Case Study - Insights:

- ❖ **Easy Change Solutions are Not Always Adopted:** The implementation of new, easy to use software does not guarantee user adoption. Some employees will resist change by default and for many reasons. Again, the employee's frame of reference proves to be very important. The change must be communicated in the employee's frame of reference if we want them to adopt the change. Sometimes this can be lost in translation, especially when one person decants wine in the restaurant and the other drink pints in the pub. Cultural differences can also cause confusion, misunderstanding and needless conflict, adding to the complexity of change implementation.

- ❖ **Leader Intervention:** Intervention by leaders is critical to reinforce the new way of working and behaviours to ensure adoption. Leaders need to do this openly, showing that if they are prepared to intervene then the same is expected of their managers and supervisors. Too many leaders and managers fail to intervene to reinforce change, this can result in leaders and managers spending energy on criticising their employees for not changing.
"The only thing necessary for the change adoption to fail are leaders and managers who do not intervene to reinforce change."

3.9.3 The Importance of Adoption

Fundamentally, change management is about getting the employees to adopt the change as the new way of working to ensure the benefits are realised. Thus, successful strategy execution and the organisation achieves a return on investment (ROI).

However, achieving change adoption with a major organisational change has mixed success and the ROI benefits are not always assured. To ensure success, it is imperative that the employees are provided with new skills, behaviours and motivation so they are aligned with the organisation's processes and systems. Some of the key adoption elements (**Figure 3.9.1**) are listed below:

* **Business Processes:** A collection of related structured activities, steps or tasks that produce a specific organisational goal.

* **Systems:** Defined as an organised, purposeful structure that consists of interrelated and interdependent elements.

* **Leadership:** A fundamental element in business success, and achieving organisation change is no different.

* **Communication:** One of the key levers to deliver successful change adoption. Continuous communication should motivate and align employees with the change.

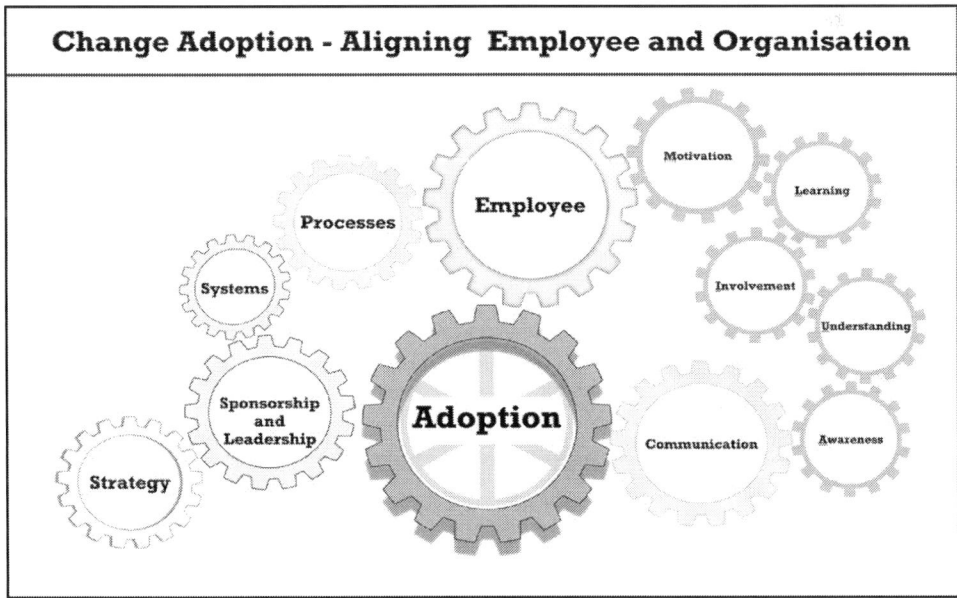

Figure 3.9.1 Change Adoption

3.9.4 Change Adoption - Day One Consideration

Change adoption of the new ways of working, or system user adoption, has to be considered right at the start of the change programme or project when the change is being defined. Adoption is one of the key aims of the change, and you cannot wait until after the training to consider it. The business benefits are clear. Without full change adoption, the benefits of the change investment will not be realised, and the organisation's long-term competitive advantage or survival may be less secure.

To ensure success, it is imperative that the employees are provided with new skills, behaviours, and motivation, so they adopt the organisation's new processes and systems. Central to success are the employees en masse, and the sponsor and leaders who set direction, communicate the change, and ensure positive reinforcement. No single employee or group can be allowed to prevent adoption of the new way of working. Any leader or manager who takes the easy, passive route is acting as an agent for your competitors. Without adoption, the organisation's significant investment in new software or processes will not increase productivity nor achieve the expected ROI.

3.9.5 Employee Change Transition Feelings and Stages

Organisations are in a perpetual state of flux and employees are constantly impacted by this fact. Employees go about performing their normal day-to-day tasks and suddenly they are hit by change disruption. This is likely to impact their role within the organisation and, more widely it may even impact their family. Not all employees will embrace the change, they will offer different levels of resistance and react differently to change. Typical change transition feelings and stages are (**Figure 3.9.2**):

- ❖ **Unsettled:** The change will disrupt the way I perform my role.
- ❖ **Resentment:** I am comfortable with the old way of doing things.
- ❖ **Disconnected to Engaged:** Initially I feel disconnected from the change but if this is the new way of working then I need to take positive steps to become more engaged.
- ❖ **Competent:** I see an opportunity to '**Develop New Skills and Behaviours**' and be a part of the future of my organisation.
- ❖ **Incentivised:** I am motivated to adopt and sustain the new way of working.

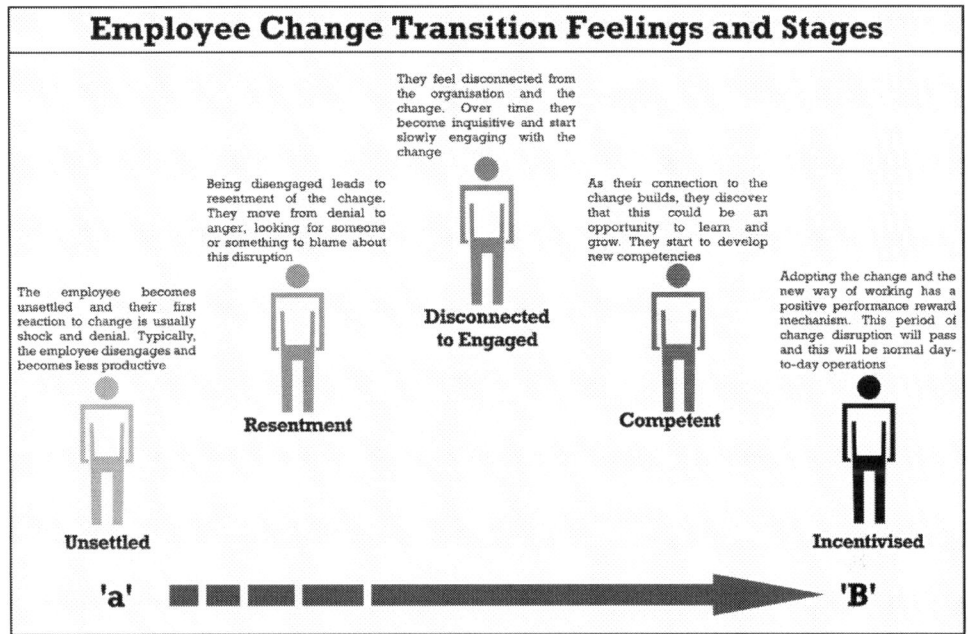

Figure 3.9.2 Employee Change Transition

3.9.6 AUILM® Model and Tactics

The **AUILM® Model** (**Figure 3.9.3**) helps teams driving change to understand how employees might react during a change transition, which they may perceive as a threat to them. Although individual employees will react to change differently, the model highlights some emotions each person may feel at different times during the process. It provides a perspective on why there might be resistance, along with solutions the change team could use to counter resistance along the change transition journey. The **AUILM® Model** outlines the five key life cycle stages the employee goes through in the change transition from the current '**a**' state to the improved future '**B**' state. The tactics for each **AUILM®** step are:

Awareness: The first tactic is to make the employee aware that there is a new change programme coming, and the change could impact them and their role within the organisation. Awareness should start to happen in the early stages of the change, i.e. when it is announced. Getting the change announcement message out simultaneously, through as many communication channels as possible with a feedback loop for questions, is extremely important. Gaps in any change communication will quickly be filled by rumours and resistance.

> **Counteracts Unsettled:** As the employee becomes more aware of the change, they will be less unsettled by it. This should help them avoid or move through the shock and denial stage quickly. Equally, awareness of the change programme helps to stop any disengagement from the organisation or a drop-in productivity.

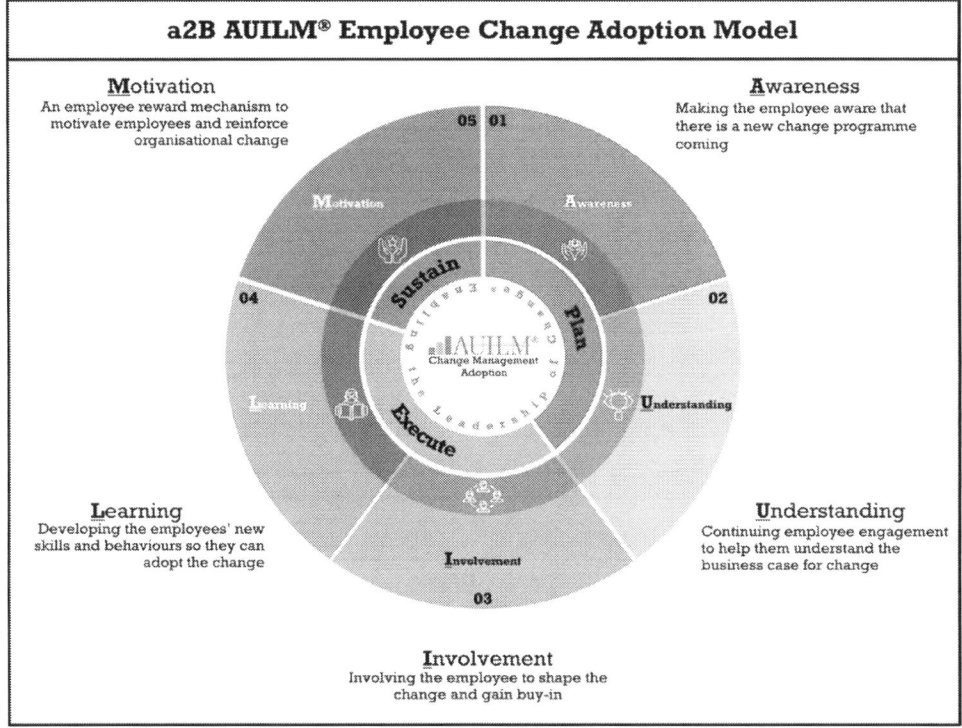

Figure 3.9.3 a2B AUILM® Adoption Model

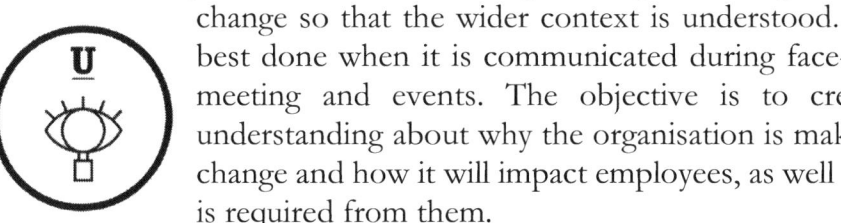**Understanding:** The second tactic is to provide greater insights into the change so that the wider context is understood. This is best done when it is communicated during face-to-face meeting and events. The objective is to create an understanding about why the organisation is making the change and how it will impact employees, as well as what is required from them.

> **Counteracts Resentment:** As the employee starts to understand the change, they will be less likely to disengage or

develop resentment towards it. The aim is to quickly get the employees to understand why the organisation must implement this change, what the changes are to their role and how it will impact them. An employee will worry less when they understand if and how the change will impact them and ultimately their families.

Involvement: The third tactic focuses on involving the employee in the change directly. As mentioned in the CHA© assessment, *"people are never stronger than when they have thought up their own arguments for believing what they believe"* (Vonnegut, 1991). Keeping employees involved in issues that affect them will reduce resistance and start to gain their buy-in to the change.

> **Counteracts Disconnected:** By involving the employees in the change there is less chance of them becoming or feeling disconnected from the organisation and the change.

> **Supports Engaged:** Over time, the employees become inquisitive and slowly start to become involved in the change. They feel confident that the change will be successful now they will have the skills for their new role and develop the new behaviours. Once they are involved in the change design and have provided input into how they would like the change to be implemented, they want it to work.

Learning: The fourth tactic is about getting the employee to see the change as an opportunity for learning and growth. This step focuses on ensuring the employee has developed the new skills and behaviours for the change to be successful. The employee should be competent in their new role and replicating the new behaviours learnt. The support of the sponsor and the leadership team is still required to reinforce the change.

> **Supports Competency:** As the connection to the change builds, the employee discovers an opportunity for learning new skills and behaviours. Being supported to develop the new competencies will equip the employee with the skills, capability and confidence to be a functioning part of the change and the new way of working.

Motivation: The final tactic focuses on ensuring motivation for sustainable change after the change is passed back to operations and the change team has dissolved. With new skills maturing and the new behaviours being reinforced, the final stage is to make sure that employees remain motivated. This will ensure they are positively focused to do their part to improve organisation performance. The individual performance plan (IPP) and a reward mechanism to reinforce positive performance should be put in place. Provision should be made to ensure any remaining resistance is addressed appropriately with timely interventions.

> **Supports Incentivised:** An incentive offered through the organisation's reward mechanism acts as the motivation to adopt and sustain the new way of working. The change disruption will soon pass and the employees should now have the new skills and behaviours that are fast becoming part of normal day-to-day operations.

3.9.7 Culture and Change

An organisation's culture can enable change success or act as a barrier. Culture is a significant factor which needs to be considered when undertaking organisational change. Eldridge and Crombie (1974) state *"the culture of an organisation refers to the unique configuration of norms, values, beliefs, ways of behaving and so on that characterise the manner in which groups and individuals combine to get things done."* Cultural configurations do not always match or support an organisation's change strategy. Culture trumps strategy every time.

Organisational culture is an important part of change management and in many cases makes it much more challenging. There are at least three reasons for this:

❖ **Culture is Hard to Define:** Culture is a soft concept and difficult to define. *"It is obscure and difficult to analyse. You can't see it; you can't count it in any obvious way"* (Ochs, 2002).

❖ **Cultural Norms:** These norms are the agreed-upon expectations and rules that guide behaviour. They vary between professions, organisations, industries, regions and countries.

❖ **Cultural Behaviours:** Behaviour determines the culture. If you think it is difficult to change one employee's behaviour, how difficult will it be to change the behaviour of an entire organisation?

Executives can underestimate how much a strategy's effectiveness and any desired change depends on cultural alignment. Lots of leaders do not connect their desired culture with their change strategy. Leaders often try to implement a strategy or change that is opposed by the deep-rooted practices and attitudes of an organisation's culture. However, for the change team to be successful, they may need to understand and work within the organisation's culture (Steers, et al., 2013). A typical approach could be:

❖ Assess and understand the current organisational culture.

❖ Define what the organisational culture should look like to support change success.

❖ Create and implement changes to reach the desired organisational culture, if required.

❖ Align the new employee behaviours with the new defined culture.

Cultural Awareness

Cultural differences lead to confusion, misunderstanding and needless conflict, and add to the complexity of change implementation. Unless we are regular global travellers it can be very difficult to understand the little cultural idiosyncrasies that could quickly lead you to insult your work colleague who comes from a different country and culture. We can use Hofstede's (2003) cultural analysis framework to explore and understand different cultures and how this might affect change management or cause tension within the organisation. Using the 6-D Model, we can get a good overview of the deep drivers of British culture, relative to the culture of the Dutch and Norwegians. The six dimensions range from 'Power Distance' through to 'Indulgence versus Restraint'.

Erin Meyer's (2016) culture map, provides a first step into understanding a wider and richer array of work styles and how culture influences day-to-day collaboration. She discusses Americans who precede anything negative with three nice comments. The French, Dutch, Israelis, and Germans get straight to the point, while Latin Americans and Asians are steeped in hierarchy. These maps and framework can help with cultural awareness.

3.9.8 Review and Checklist

Adoption: The process of leaving the old ways behind and adopting the new way of working, confirming the employees have fully accepted the change, in mind and heart. It is about the organisation and an employee's transition from the current state 'a' to the future state 'B'.

Day One Consideration: Change adoption should be a consideration whilst the change is being defined, it is too late if it is only being considered as part of the training programme.

Employee and Organisation Alignment: The key elements of the organisation such as sponsorship, leadership, processes, systems, communication and strategy need to align with the employee to achieve adoption.

Employee Change Transition: The change team should be aware of the employee's feelings through each stage of the change transition and period of disruption.

AUILM® Model: The five key life cycle stages of the model support employees through the change to achieve adoption. Its objectives are to provide **A**wareness, **U**nderstanding and **I**nvolvement in the change as well as supporting the **L**earning of new skills and behaviours. The final stage focuses on ensuring employee **M**otivation so the change is sustainable when it becomes normal day-to-day operations.

AUILM® Model Counteracting Tactics: These tactics can counteract the employee's feelings of being unsettled by providing awareness about the change and a deeper understanding of it, this will prevent any resentment from building. By involving employees in the change there is less chance of them feeling disconnected from the organisation.

AUILM® Model Supporting Tactics: These tactics can support the employee to develop their own competency through learning and incentivise them to keep motivated.

Culture and Change: An organisation's culture is a significant factor which needs to be understood, both when undertaking organisational change and in how to achieve results.

a2BCMF® Step 9 - Checklist

#	a2BCMF® Questions	Complete Yes/No
1	**Previous Steps:** Have the previous **a2BCMF®** steps been completed?	☐
2	**Change Adoption:** Has the change team considered change adoption during **a2BCMF® Step 1 - Change Definition**?	☐
3	**Processes and Systems:** Have the organisation's processes and systems been aligned with the employee to enable change adoption?	☐
4	**Leadership:** Has the leadership team continued to focus on adoption after the training has been completed?	☐
5	**AUILM® Model:** Has the model been used to support the employees, from awareness through motivation, to achieve adoption?	☐
6	**AUILM® Counteracting Tactics:** Has the employee been able to counteract any feelings of being unsettled, resentful or disconnected?	☐
7	**AUILM® Supporting Tactics:** Has the employee been supported to learn and develop new competencies and been given an incentive to remain motivated?	☐
8	**Culture and Change:** Has the organisation assessed whether its culture will be an enabler or a barrier to successful change?	☐

Notes:

3.10 Sustain and Close

One of the most difficult tasks in change management is to sustain the change, continuing adoption and aligning new behaviours with the organisation and employee scorecards to ensure benefits realisation.

3.10.1 Sustain and Close - Overview

Definition: This step is about **Sustaining and Closing** the change after the organisation and employees have made the transition to the '**B**' state.

Business Benefits: Even after adoption, the change needs to be sustained. Without sustaining the change, it may not stick or provide long-term benefits realisation. It is important to sustain the change by closing the programme officially with governance approval and by transferring ownership to operations.

Key Stakeholders and Elements: It involves all the key stakeholders but there is a special focus on the stakeholders responsible for governance and the new operations owner after the transfer of ownership.

Business Objective:

Sustain: Ensuring ongoing benefits delivery and measurement:
- ❖ Benefits Delivery, Transition and Sustainment.
- ❖ Balanced Scorecard.
- ❖ Individual Performance Plan.

Close: Completing administrative activities and formal closure:
- ❖ Lessons Learned.
- ❖ Knowledge Transfer.
- ❖ Transfer of Ownership.

Enablers and Barriers

Enablers	Barriers
Sustaining the change by aligning the benefits with organisation performance measures.	Leaders not realising how difficult sustaining the change will be without performance measures.
Using the balanced scorecard to continue measuring change benefits when the change programme becomes normal day-to-day operations.	Not aligning change sustainment and benefits realisation with the organisation's balanced scorecard and thinking that benefits will be delivered by operations.
Formal transfer of benefits realisation responsibility to operations and completing all administrative activities that close the programme.	Not completing all administrative activities that officially close the programme with governance approval.
Using the employee's individual performance plan to link their work performance to change sustainment.	Not using the employee's individual performance plan as a vehicle to ensure long-term benefits realisation.
Officially closing the change programme with governance approval, closing administrative activities and then celebrating.	Not closing the change programme officially with governance approval, hoping there will be employee change adoption and sustainment.
Ensuring there is a controlled and formal process for the transfer of ownership to normal day-to-day operations.	Leadership thinking that the transfer of ownership to operations will be a natural and easy process.
Recording lessons learned from the change programme so they will provide insights and value for future change programmes.	Not seeing the value of investing time and effort in capturing lessons learned that will advise future change teams.
Ensuring there is a structured process for knowledge transfer, that key information is captured and stored for the future.	Not completing knowledge transfer tasks so critical information can be shared within the organisation.

3.10.2 Case Study - 'Tell' Change is More Effective

I was scheduled to work on another offshore business improvement initiative. This visit would provide me with the opportunity to assess some of the previous projects that I had been involved in and give me a chance to perform change sustainment checks to establish whether or not the projects had achieved sustainable change.

I arrived at the offshore terminal for my initial flight to Shetland. I handed over my government identification and my Vantage personnel on board (POB) card. The Vantage POB system is a shared service used by selected oil and gas companies to control and monitor the movements of personnel to, from, and between offshore and onshore facilities. It tracked my travel and basic offshore safety induction emergency training (BOSIET) course, which provided me with a range of knowledge and skills relevant to travelling offshore by helicopter and working offshore, including safety induction, fire safety, and basic firefighting.

I was deliberately the last person in the check-in queue so I could observe the process, as this was to be the first change sustainment check. All employees had the Vantage card, and their certifications were in date. This indicated that the organisation's competency systems seemed to be in order. This process is similar to a passport check on a normal international flight: the photo identification must be current, and the expiry date must not have passed.

I watched as each employee's holdall was thoroughly checked by airport security. This would cover my second change sustainment check, which was: no alcohol or drugs while working or driving. The security employee checked every item in each holdall. This included the toiletries, the holdall lining, and, on several occasions, the holdall straps. As it was November, I was also physically checked to ensure that I had three layers of clothing under my survival suit, a mandatory requirement during the winter months.

The evening flight to Shetland was uneventful, and we landed on time to a wet and windy evening. We were called to board the next flight and I walked out onto the runway towards the helicopter. We were guided to our seats in an orderly, almost military-like fashion.

On the helicopter we took our designated seats, fastened our safety belts, and adjusted our headphones. Once I'd done this, I looked either side of me to access how comfortable the other passengers looked, as well as gauging their health and fitness levels. I was sitting in the middle of the cabin and I would be in this seat, secured by my safety harness, for the duration of the flight. I refocused on the most urgent task at hand. What was my best exit strategy in the unlikely event of the helicopter ditching in the sea? From where I was sitting, I made a quick note of my best exit and fallback options.

I looked around the cabin to make my third change sustainment check, which was to check helicopter seat utilisation. This was the focus and target of a previous change and improvement project and the helicopter was full. The twelve-month baseline data for the four platforms I was now flying towards had just over 70 per cent seat utilisation. The other 30 per cent were cancellations or no-shows, approximately a thousand empty seats. Some of the reasons for this were employee attitudes or behaviour as a passenger. I thought back to the other challenges we'd had on the project, and they were from the leadership and asset management teams, not the employees. There had been a lack of involvement and active sponsorship from both the asset operations leader and his manager, as well as respect for our role, even though the project would have ultimately benefited them and their operational performance.

The flight took less than an hour, and after the usual greetings and health, safety and environment (HSE) briefing, we were allocated our cabins and I unpacked my personal belongings before dinner.

My trip was initially scheduled for seven days, as we didn't know when we would get a time slot to execute the project. After the team completed our planning activities, I waited in my cabin for operations to inform me of the shutdown slot, so we could complete our business improvement project. Luckily, we got the call from the operations team to execute our project during my second night on board. It was about 02:40 in the morning when the operations supervisor called me, and I made my way to the engine area. I observed the team as they performed the shutdown process on one of the engine turbines, and I recorded the main tasks, activities, timing, and made other notes. Back onshore, the following week, we would analyse the data and information with a team of subject matter experts to develop improvements.

I had arranged for the operations installation manager (OIM) to show me around the platform, so I could get his perspective on how our team could help him going forward. The OIM is in charge of the platform and is responsible for ensuring compliance with all appropriate legislative and safety requirements, as well as all local management system processes and procedures. The job requires not only day-to-day management responsibilities for a wide range of functions but also the ability to take the role of the on-scene commander, should an emergency arise.

Gavin was experienced, with over twenty-five years in the oil and gas industry, and he had worked as an OIM in many countries around the world. We met in the control room, put on our safety helmets and gloves, walked outside, and started to make our way down to the lower decks. It was a massive structure, about the height of the London Eye, and had a platform deck space of about the same size as a small football pitch.

I followed Gavin as we made our way from the lower to upper decks. He checked the structure, pipes and anything electrical that he could inspect along the way. I watched Gavin closely to check that this platform walk was not purely for my benefit, but after doing several of these you get to know when it is a genuine walk of the platform. This was the fourth sustainment check, that the safety platform walks were happening on a regular basis by the OIM.

We went up to the drill deck, and as we carefully made our way through the area Gavin appeared to spot some maintenance work going on around one of the large electrical panels adjacent to one of the support pillars on our right. He changed direction and walked directly over to the panel. The panel perimeter was marked off with a white and red plastic chain, supported by two red and white cones that were acting as a safety barrier. Attached to the electrical door panel was the permit to work (PTW). Gavin reached across the safety barrier, removed the permit from the plastic sleeve and began reading it thoroughly, checking that the dates, times, and signatures matched. He told me that it seemed in order and we both smiled. I reached for my notepad again, opened it to a new page and wrote my note about the fifth change sustainment check: Life saver rules (LSR): PTW in order.

The PTW was one of the new LSRs, and my concern was about ensuring it was accurate and that the employees were following its instructions. Having a permit to work is not a failsafe. It must be understood, communicated, and adhered to. Gavin must have been thinking the same thing as he walked around the left-hand side of the electrical panel. I followed behind. He knelt down and looked at the isolation device. He pulled on it to check it was physically isolating the panel, that it was a company-approved device, and that it was in full working order. He looked up at me, gave me a thumbs up and smiled. We both knew that a PTW provided critical safety guidance, but it is the electrical isolation that prevents electrocution. As usual, out came my notepad. I opened it to a new page and wrote my sixth change sustainment check - LSR: electrical isolation in order.

When he finished, we continued our walk, away from the drilling area and into the next passageway. As we did, I spotted the storage of many different types of lubricants and detergents. This area stood out from most other areas on the platform as it was in the middle of a 5S exercise, and I was pleased. I inspected the area. Oil drums were correctly positioned on their painted floor spots, each clearly labelled with the oil type, and there were also clear floor markings segregating the different oil types, the storage area, and the walkways. At a glance, I was able to see if one of the oil drums was sitting on the red painted circle it should be sitting on. Gavin could see the big smile on my face but looked impatiently at me as he wanted to keep going. I pulled out my notepad again and wrote, somewhat untidily, my seventh change sustainment check - 5S: lubricant area (still work in progress across the platform, so check ownership).

Essentially, 5S is a simple system for organising spaces, so work can be performed efficiently, effectively, and safely. This system focuses on putting everything where it belongs and keeping the workplace clean, which makes it easier for people to do their jobs without wasting time or risking injury.

Early on in my career, I was a manufacturing engineer, working for the largest aerospace company in the world at the time, and I was introduced to the 5S system. There I learned about the importance of operator efficiency, and we introduced the twenty-second rule into our manufacturing processes. 'Wherever you are working as an operator, you will be able to locate the correct tool, process instructions, and drawing within twenty seconds, even if you walk into the area as a new employee.' When I moved to the energy sector, the absence of this simple, effective, and efficient rule was a shock and, to me, reflected an industry and its leaders devoid of basic business improvement skills.

We made our way to the nearest stairwell to reach the upper deck and came upon more maintenance work on the ceiling area. Again, the area was clearly marked with a white and red plastic chain supported by lots of red and white tape and safety cones. As before, Gavin reached for the PTW, which was easily accessible for inspection, and started to read through it. Behind the tape and chain was a raised portable scaffolding platform reaching more than two metres in height and about two by three metres in area. It was jacked up with the wheels locked in place but, more importantly, the raised area had a safety rail to secure the worker from falling. Gavin finished reading the permit and reached past the safety chain to shake the scaffolding platform for rigidness, to check that it had an attachment cable and to ensure that it did not move easily. As usual, he gave me the thumbs up and put the permit back into the plastic sleeve. I pulled out my notepad and wrote my eighth change sustainment check - LSR: working at height. This life-saving rule was to ensure that any employee or contractor working above a height of 1.8 metres was to be protected from a fall by being attached to the raised surface.

As we climbed the staircase to the open upper deck we heard the engines of an offshore supply vessel nearing the platform. I told Gavin that I was interested in seeing this, as I had been involved in several logistics change and improvement projects. He smiled at me and led me towards the perimeter safety rails, so we could overlook the loading and unloading operation.

The first phase of the logistics project looked at improving the delivery and collection of supplies from a large number of offshore platforms in the North Sea. The logistics model was based on a milk run concept, to increase a vessel's utilisation and reduce turnaround time at both the platform and the port. Utilising fewer boats to deliver materials more efficiently was one of the keys to operating a well-orchestrated logistics support plan. Our first set of improvements was to change the behaviour of the vessel captains and for the platform to record any reasons for not docking. The change management project focused on communication and on training the platform and the vessel crews to record activities and work together as one team.

After several months we had recorded more data. The analysis showed that the vessels were in transit for just over 40 per cent of the time. Offshore waiting on the platform to unload was about 25 per cent of the time, and offshore loading was 20 per cent of the total vessel time. The remainder was on-shore loading activities and other issues such as delays due to bad weather. With this data, the change team was able to compare times with different assets. Over time, the number of vessels required to complete the milk run was reduced, and offloading became more efficient. I asked Gavin whether the milk runs had improved the delivery and collection of supplies. He told me 'Yes,' and pointed out that by the time we had taken our forty-five-minute walk this supply vessel had sailed up to the platform and was now unloading. As usual, I recorded the notes of my ninth change sustainment check - supply vessel: milk run still more effective.

The vessel's cargo deck probably took up 75 per cent of the ship's surface area. It was flat and open, like a small ferry that does island hops. Even from high up, it was easy to see how well the deck was laid out. This was the second phase of the logistics project - improving the layout of supplies to ensure safe, effective, and efficient use of deck space. I still had my notebook out, so turned to a new page for my tenth change sustainment check - supply vessel: safe, effective, and efficient deck utilisation.

"Peter, I really don't care about how well you utilise deck space. It is not a priority for me. I just want the supplies loaded on and off the ship as quickly as possible, with the least amount of disruption to normal day-to-day operations. You might think that you are saving millions of pounds on logistics but imagine if we had rough seas while trying to create that deck space."

Wow, I thought. He had a great point and I nodded respectfully.

"Peter, I fully support critical safety changes, and I have some capacity for the other changes and improvements. But just remember, I am responsible for the safety and well-being of over a hundred people and this is my priority. The next is day-to-day oil and gas operations. Yes, we need to continually change and improve, but my paradox is safe normal day-to-day operations versus change."

Gavin looked at his watch and told me it was time to get back. I thanked him for taking the time to share his insights and coaching as we walked back towards the control room.

As the helicopter lifted away from the helideck I thought about what Gavin had said about the leadership paradox. One thing is certain. With the technology revolution showing no sign of slowing, more organisational change will come. It will be imperative to achieve a balance between implementing organisational change management versus delivering normal day-to-day operations.

Case Study - Insights:
- **Eventually Everything Changes:** With four platforms in the UK North Sea, the Brent field is among the largest oil and gas fields ever found. The Delta platform is 300m high, double the height of the London Eye and

equal to the height of the Eiffel Tower. Brent is famous for its oil barrels that help to set an international benchmark price for two-thirds of the world's oil. While the Brent Blend will still be used for pricing, there is little Brent crude left and the platforms will soon be decommissioned. Over the years, the oil and gas source has been depleted and this is now being quickly replaced by wind energy, with offshore turbines rising up to 195m high. A lot of the learning and knowledge gained from the global oil and gas industry is transferrable and can now be used in the renewable energy sector for constructing and installing offshore wind farms.

- **Sustainable Change:** The good news was that most of the sustainment checks provided positive evidence that the changes were being sustained. However, it should also be noted and reflected on that most of these changes were HSE 'Tell' compliance changes with consequences for non-adherence. Part of the LSR implementation to save workers lives, started as a 'Sell', but did not achieve the expected results and the change approach was therefore changed to a 'Tell'.

- **Unwanted Change and Improvement:** The customers of change don't always want the changes or improvements that corporate HQ imposes. Employees have other priorities; there is too much change, I am not interested, etc. Some changes are critical and even if we don't like them, they have to be implemented, especially if they are about employee safety or compliance. Others are about improving business performance with small incremental enhancements.

Four of the sustainment checks were based on business improvement, removing waste and making daily operations more effective and efficient. While there was evidence that the improvements had worked and were being sustained, the OIM did not see the benefit of them. While business or continuous improvement offers so much value across the complete organisation, the vast majority of leaders and managers fail to implement or understand the concepts.

When I ask leaders or managers about how effective their processes and services are, I am very often told they are very effective and efficient. These leaders and managers delude themselves into thinking that their operations are like a Formula 1 pit stop. The car zooms into the pit, stops on the marked line, four tyres are replaced, and the car is refuelled in a matter of seconds. A more accurate account would be, the car pulls into the pit stop and some of the mechanics are at their stations ready to perform their tasks. However, others are still in the garage getting a cup of coffee or chatting on social media. They quickly realise the car is in the pits, lift their tyre and run to the car to change it. But by now the competition has the advantage.

The reality is worse. It takes two and a half years to get a large metal structure from Norway to Kazakhstan and it still then has to be transported to an off-shore island. An offshore platform in the North Sea is shut down for maintenance and then the team starts to look for their equipment. Every morning over a hundred people are waiting for their printed permit to work certificate before they can start work at an on-shore gas processing plant. The application of 5-why quickly establishes that of the three available printers, only one is working. The second printer is broken and needs to be replaced but the manager won't approve the expense request. The third printer uses a more expensive ink cartridge and the expense request was also not signed off. Coincidently, this was the same manager who told me that he did not need corporate help to improve his operations because they were already setting an example of operational excellence. The same manager who, under duress, only let me assess this improvement opportunity because he thought the maintenance contractors waiting for their permits to be printed were slacking. The opportunities to remove waste and TIM H WOOD are endless.

3.10.3 The Importance of Sustain and Close

'**Sustain and Close**' are the final two stages of the **a2BCMF®** that should be coordinated at the end of the change programme or project. There should be a seamless connection between the two, without this, success and benefits sustainment is unlikely. The challenges at this point in the change programme are:

- ❖ **Change Fatigue:** Usually by this point, the change team, the organisation and the employees have been involved in the change programme for quite a while. Everyone has gone through the change and now just wants to move on as quickly as possible. This creates a lack of energy and focus on the final administrative activities and tasks to close the change programme officially.

- ❖ **Next Change:** We are now living through the fourth industrial revolution (4IR) and the rate of change hitting organisations is immense. Barely one change programme is complete when another one starts. The challenge is to keep enough people on the programme to satisfactorily close it and ensure it is sustainable going forward.

- ❖ **Lack of Completer Finisher:** Belbin (2010) defines nine different team roles ranging from a resource investigator through to a completer finisher. He argues that, *"a team is not a bunch of people with job titles, but a congregation of individuals, each of whom has a role which is understood by other members."* All the roles play an important part in the team. The completer finisher role is one not often valued in programmes or projects, however, the traits of a completer finisher in this **a2BCMF®** step are invaluable. They can be effectively used to polish and scrutinise the team's final tasks for completion, subjecting them to the highest quality standards to ensure that the team and the change cross the finish line. Without having this role in the team, you may find the change programme is not properly sustained or closed.

3.10.4 Sustain

Sustaining the change programme is the most difficult **a2BCMF®** step. Many organisations embark upon change programmes with the assumption that it will lead to permanent change. However, many attempts often fail to deliver sustained change or realise the intended benefits. Change is not instantaneous and needs to be constructed in a way that ensures it becomes part of the new culture and the organisation's DNA. It needs to be built on solid foundations, as with any structure, in order to be sustainable. The foundations are the previous **a2BCMF®** steps.

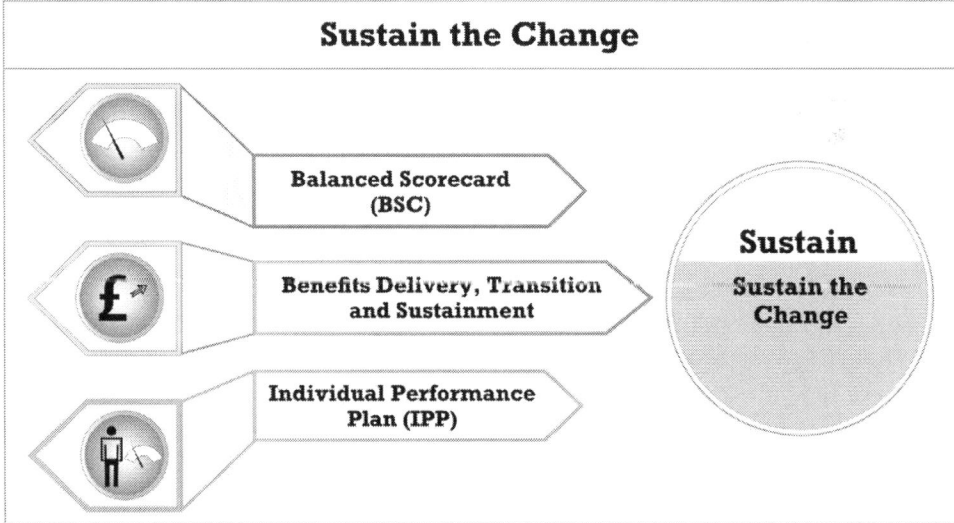

Figure 3.10.1 Sustain the Change

Once change has happened, the focus moves onto how to make it the new normal day-to-day operations so that things don't slip back to how they were. Getting there is only half the battle. Reinforcing the change is essential to make sure adoption sticks.

Topics covered in this **a2BCMF®** sustain step are (**Figure 3.10.1**):
- ❖ Benefits Delivery, Transition and Sustainment.
- ❖ Balanced Scorecard (BSC).
- ❖ Individual Performance Plan (IPP).

3.10.5 Benefits Delivery, Transition and Sustainment

Benefits realisation will have been defined and planned during **a2BCMF® Step 1 - Change Definition**, in the planning phase. The benefits plan and tracker (**Template 3.1.7 Benefits Plan and Tracker**) will have formally documented the activities necessary to achieve the change programme's planned benefits, identifying how and when the benefits are expected to be realised. The timing of benefits delivery will vary from change programme to programme, in some cases starting in the **Execute** phase but in other cases the responsibility for realisation may be transitioned to the operational areas who will be responsible for ongoing sustainment. In this way, responsibility for the change may be with the change team, operations, or a mixture of both.

3.10.6 Balanced Scorecard

The balanced scorecard (BSC) translates a company's vision and strategy into a coherent set of performance measures (Kaplan and Norton, 1996). The BSC helps organisations to spell out their high-level strategy to something actionable and measurable, while helping employees understand how they can contribute to the results the organisation is seeking. The scorecard can also be repositioned as a strategic and change management tool, suiting the purposes of both hard financial and soft behavioural change. The BSC can therefore be used as a change management and organisation learning tool to ensure the alignment of people behind the strategy and the change programme. It has four interdependent elements which can support change adoption and benefits realisation (**Figure 3.10.2**).
- ❖ **Finance:** Typically focuses on sales, expenditures and income.
- ❖ **Business Processes:** Focuses on how well the products are made, or services are delivered.
- ❖ **Learning and Growth:** Focuses on skills, culture and capability.
- ❖ **Customer:** Focuses on the people who buy and their levels of satisfaction.

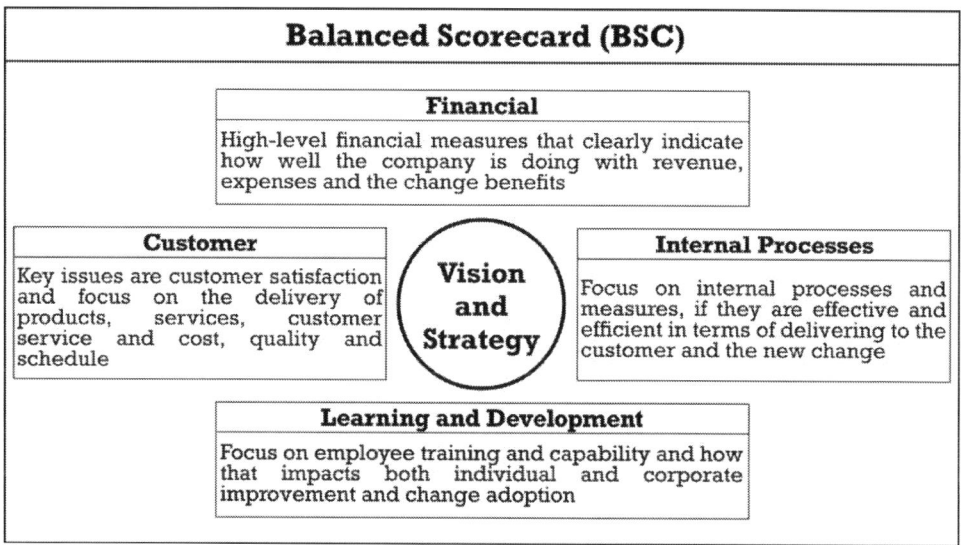

Figure 3.10.2 Balanced Scorecard

3.10.7 Individual Performance Plan

The individual performance plan (IPP) is an instrument used to establish performance expectations and to support performance evaluation, as well as the career development of each employee. It can be a powerful vehicle to support strategy implementation by aligning employee performance to change and benefits realisation. It should define the skills and behaviours expected so that the employee can adopt the change. It should be linked directly to the BSC to show the employee how their individual performance supports the change programme. It can also directly link each individual's performance to their bonus and recognition rewards. It normally contains the following:

❖ Specific goals for learning and development.
❖ Individual key performance measures.
❖ A link to organisation key performance measures.
❖ Actions required to achieve goals.

3.10.8 Close

The change programme closes either because its charter is fulfilled, its benefits have been fully realised, or benefits continue to be realised and managed as part of the transfer of ownership to operations. Conditions may also arise that bring the programme to an early close, such as the change is no longer aligned with the organisation's strategy. Programme governance will have outlined the requirements and criteria to close the change programme during **a2BCMF® Step 1 - Change Definition**. Programme governance usually approves the recommendations for the closure of the change, based on a request from the sponsor. There will be administrative activities to complete as part of formal closure, such as completing the final report. What is in included in the final report will vary for each organisation but typically it will include lessons learned, knowledge transfer and transfer of ownership. The close should be celebrated as this is an important part of change management and the communication process, it acknowledges the successful implementation of the change.

Topics covered in in this **a2BCMF® Sustain** step are (**Figure 3.10.3**):

❖ Transfer of Ownership.

❖ Lessons Learned.

❖ Knowledge Transfer.

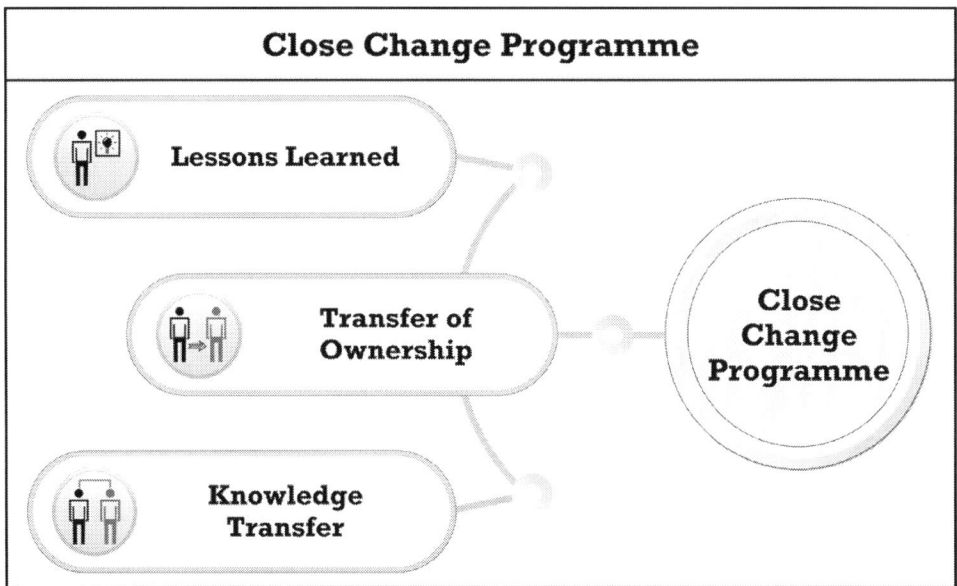

Figure 3.10.3 Close Change Programme

3.10.9 Transfer of Ownership

Organisations invest enormous amounts of financial capital, resources and effort on critical strategic change programmes. However, when it comes to transferring ownership to operations, it is at best a superficial process with little or no hope of the change being sustained.

In some change programmes the benefits may not be realised until after the change team have dissolved, when this happens the responsibility then falls to operations. In this case, there may be some work to transition the resources, responsibilities, knowledge and lessons learned to another sustaining entity. Prior to closing the change programme, the sponsor and change team will coordinate the transfer of ownership to operations and receive approval to formally close out the programme. Benefits transition should ensure that the scope of the transition is defined, the stakeholders in the operational area are identified and they participate in the planning. The change benefits measurement should be defined, the sustainment plans should be developed, ensuring the transition is executed. At the end of the change programme, the benefits should be compared against those stated in the business case, to ensure that the programme has actually delivered the intended benefits and value. Other benefits transition and sustainment activities could include:

❖ Benefits realisation reporting and interventions.

❖ Audit to establish if changes have been successfully integrated.

❖ Activities related to improving acceptance of the change.

❖ Review of training and maintenance materials.

3.10.10 Lessons Learned - Guide

It is important that lessons learned during the change programme are formally recorded before the change team is assigned to other programmes, new roles or leave the organisation. According to Senge (1990[2]) *"the rate at which organisations learn may soon become the only sustainable source of competitive advantage."*

Lessons learned should be identified and documented throughout the programme life cycle. A key component of successful change and project management is the ability to gather key learnings from the experiences throughout the **a2BCMF®** steps or the project life cycle (Williams, 2007). Feedback from all stakeholders involved in the programme should be taken into consideration, as this will provide valuable insights into how the change has been adopted by the organisation. The purpose of this process is to share and use knowledge derived from experience to promote the recurrence of desirable outcomes and prevent the recurrence of undesirable outcomes for future changes. A formal session should be held, and the output should be a document that answers typical questions such as:

- ❖ What went well?
- ❖ What could have gone better?
- ❖ Were the change programme goals or benefits achieved?
- ❖ What obstacles were encountered?
- ❖ What needs to change in the future?

The lessons learned process is one that crosses functional boundaries and allows an organisation to learn from both its mistakes and its successes in implementing change. It is important that lessons learned during the change programme are formally recorded before the change team is assigned to other programmes, new roles or leave the organisation.

Creation Steps: The change lessons learned (**Template 3.10.4 Change Lessons Learned**) should not be created in isolation. The suggested creation steps are:

1. Identify any key stakeholders involved in the change programme, as they will have valuable input.
2. Schedule a lessons learned meeting and send invites.
3. Recreate a draft outline of **Template 3.10.4** to work on.
4. Collate previously collected lessons learned.
5. Appoint a facilitator and prepare for the meeting.
6. Review each lesson, discuss and agree recommendations, actions, owner, etc.
7. Document each lesson learned:
    a. '#' and 'description'.
    b. 'a2BCMF® step #' it was identified.
    c. 'Change impact' (quantify).
    d. 'Identified by' person and 'date'.
    e. 'What went well?' details.
    f. 'What went less well?' details.
    g. 'Recommendations and comments'.
    h. 'Person responsible'.
    i. The 'status' (progress/new owner, etc.).
8. Share the learning with the rest of the organisation.
9. Store on a shared drive/repository for future use.

Template 3.10.4 Change Lessons Learned

#	Lesson Learned Details			Identification Details		Change Lesson Details		Action and Progress		
	Description	a2BCMF® Step #	Change Impact	Identified By	Date	What Went Well?	What Went Less Well?	Recommendation and Comments	Person Responsible	Status
1										
2										
3										
4										
5										
6										
7										
8										
9										
10										

Template 3.10.4 Change Lessons Learned

Lessons Learned - Insights:

❖ Without an accessible repository to store and share these lessons learned, the process is of little value.

❖ This process is made much easier if lessons learned are recorded throughout the change implementation, such as meeting minutes, governance meetings, stakeholder feedback, etc.

An effective lessons learned process can prevent the organisation and change team from repeating the same mistakes and enhance future success. It can be an instrumental part of any organisation's overall continuous improvement process.

3.10.11 Knowledge Transfer

One of the greatest challenges at this stage of the change programme is to ensure that the experiences generated are shared with the rest of the organisation and not lost when the change team dissolves. Knowledge transfer is a practical method of ensuring that key information is captured and stored for the future. Materials, reports, assessments and other documents from the programme should be organised and stored in a central location. This knowledge should be maintained and shared to make the organisation more efficient and effective, especially in the future when the next change comes along. According to Conner and Prahalad, (1996), privately held knowledge is a basic source of competitive advantage, so why would you not transfer this knowledge within the organisation so it can be utilised?

The information should be captured throughout the programme life cycle with the final structuring taking place at the end of the programme to incorporate lessons learned and final reports. The knowledge transfer process is to harvest the knowledge, define the knowledge type, develop the knowledge, provide access and the future management of the information or data (**Figure 3.10.5**).

The objective is to ensure the next change team member, either new or continuing, knows exactly how the previous team made their decisions, or at the very least, is able to identify someone who was centrally involved. It is always a challenge to transfer knowledge from the few experts to the organisation as a whole, and as the programme draws to a close this task becomes even more difficult.

Knowledge Transfer Process

1. Harvest
Define the common process for identifying and selecting the critical person or knowledge

2. Type
(a) Tacit knowledge is the knowledge that is hard to transfer or pass along through writing or verbalisation

(b) Explicit knowledge is the knowledge that is easily shared and transferred through writing or speaking

3. Develop
Develop the knowledge and define the best place to store it (person, function, etc.) within the organisation

4. Access
Define how the employees and, in particular, future change teams can access the information

5. Manage
Define how the knowledge will be managed as part of the organisation's assets

Figure 3.10.5 Knowledge Transfer Process

3.10.12 Celebration

There should be a process to acknowledge all employees who have been instrumental in delivering successful change. The people who have worked on the change should be assigned to other activities and roles that recognise their work, skills and capabilities. What has been achieved, and why it is important, should be celebrated and communicated to all stakeholders right across the organisation.

3.10.13 Review and Checklist

Sustain and Close: The process of sustaining and closing the change after the organisation and employees have adopted the change. '**Sustain and Close**' should have official approval within programme governance, including administrative activities.

Sustain: Sustaining the change by adhering to the benefits plan and tracker, aligning it with organisation and employee measures.

Benefits Delivery: Ensure the benefits plan and tracker has or will deliver benefits realisation and has the required governance approval prior to closure.

Balanced Scorecard (BSC): Use the balanced scorecard (BSC) to align actions and measures with change sustainment after the change team have dissolved to ensure the organisation measures the benefits as part of normal day-to-day operations.

Individual Performance Plan (IPP): Link the employee's individual performance plan (IPP) to ensure change sustainment.

Close: Closing the programme officially with governance approval, completing administrative activities and transferring ownership to operations.

Transfer of Ownership: Ensure there is a controlled process for the transfer of ownership where the change will become part of normal day-to-day operations. It is essential that this ownership is linked to the BSC to ensure ongoing measurement and benefits realisation.

Lessons Learned: Capturing and recording lessons learned to use on future change programmes to ensure the promotion of desirable outcomes and prevent the recurrence of undesirable outcomes.

Knowledge Transfer: Ensure that key information is captured throughout the change programme life cycle and is stored for the future. This information, if captured and shared effectivity, can be very useful for the next change and team.

a2BCMF® Step 10 - Checklist

#	a2BCMF® Questions	Complete Yes/No
1	**Previous Steps:** Have the previous **a2BCMF®** steps been completed?	☐
2	**Sustain:** Have the activities been formally documented to achieve sustainment of the change programme's planned benefits?	☐
3	**Benefits Delivery:** Has the benefits plan and tracker been officially closed or transferred to operations with governance approval?	☐
4	**Balanced Scorecard:** Has change benefits realisation been linked to the organisation's balanced scorecard?	☐
5	**Individual Performance Plan (IPP):** Will the employee's IPP be used to link their performance to sustainable change and benefits delivery?	☐
6	**Close:** Has the change programme been officially closed with governance approval?	☐
7	**Transfer of Ownership:** Has there been a documented and approved process for transferring ownership and benefits realisation to normal day-to-day operations?	☐
8	**Lessons Learned:** Have the lessons learned been captured and recorded for use on future change programmes?	☐
9	**Knowledge Transfer:** Have the change programme information and insights been captured and stored for the future where they can be accessed?	☐

Notes:

Celebration!...........

Section 4: Other Information and Support

4.1 References

Adair, J., 2006. Leadership and motivation. London: Kogan Page.

Agryris, C., 1982. The executive mind and double-loop learning. Organisational Dynamics, 11(2), pp. 5-22.

Belbin, R., 2010. Team roles at work. Oxford: Butterworth-Heinemann.

Boddy, D. and Buchanan, D., 1992. Take the Lead: Interpersonal Skills for Project Managers. New York. Prentice Hall.

Burnes, B., 2009. Managing Change. 5th ed. London: Prentice Hall.

Carnegie, D., 1981. How to win friends and influence people. New York: Simon and Schuster.

Churchill, W., 1931. The World Crisis, New York: Scribner.

Collins, J., 2001. Good to Great. New York, NY: Harper Business.

Conner. K.R., and CK. Prahalad., 1996. A Resource-Based Theory of the Firm: Knowledge Versus Opportunism. Organisation Science, 7.5, 477-501.

Deutschman, A., 2007. Change or Die: The Three Keys to Change at Work and in Life. New York: Harper Business.

Dow, W. and Taylor, B., 2008. Project Management Communications Bible. Indianapolis, IN: Wiley Publishing.

Eldridge, J, and Crombie, A., 1974. A sociology of organisations. London: Allen and Unwin.

Freeman, R., 2010. Strategic management. Cambridge: Cambridge University Press.

Gallagher, P. F., 2019[A]. Change Management Fables - Leadership of Change® Volume 1. London: PFG Publishing.

Gallagher, P. F., 2019[B]. Change Management Pocket Guide - Leadership of Change® Volume 2. London: PFG Publishing.

Goldsmith, M. and Reiter, M., 2007. What got you here won't get you there. New York, NY: Hyperion.

Green, C. and Howe, A., 2012. The trusted advisor field book. Hoboken, N.J.: Wiley.

Harrington, H. J. and Voehl, F., 2014. Organisational capacity for change: Increasing change capacity and avoiding change overload. Newtown Square, PA: Project Management Institute.

Hayes, J., 2010. The theory and practice of change management (3rd ed.). Basingstoke, England: Palgrave MacMillan.

Hofstede, G., 2003. Culture's Consequences: Comparing Values, Behaviours, Institutions and Organisations Across Nations. SAGE Publications, Inc.

Ishikawa, K., 1990. Introduction to quality control. Tokyo: 3A Corp.

4.1 References

Kanter, R. M., B. Stein, and T. D. Jick., 2001. Challenge of Organisational Change. New York: Free Press.

Kaplan, R. S., and Norton, D. P., 1996. The balanced scorecard: Translating strategy into action. Boston, Mass: Harvard Business School Press.

Kearney, E., Gebert, D. and Voelpel, S., 2009. When and How Diversity Benefits Teams: The Importance of Team Members' Need For Cognition. Academy of Management Journal, 52(3), pp.581-598.

Kennedy, J. F., 1963. Address in the Assembly Hall at the Paulskirche in Frankfurt (266), June 25, 1963, Public Papers of the Presidents: John F. Kennedy.

Kirkpatrick, D.L., and Kirkpatrick, J.D., 2006. Evaluating Training Programs: The Four Levels (3rd ed). San Francisco: Berrett-Koehler Publishers.

Kolb, D., 1984. Experiential learning: experience as the source of learning and development. Englewood Cliffs, New Jersey: Prentice Hall.

Kotter, J. P., 1999. John P. Kotter on what Leaders Really do. Boston, MA: Harvard Business School Press.

Kruger, W., 1996. 'Implementation: The Core Task of Change Management. CEMS Business Review, Vol. 1. Kluwer Academic/Plenum Publishers.

Lewin, K., 1946. Action Research and Minority Problems. In GW Lewin and GW Allport (eds) (1948): Resolving Social Conflict. London: Harper and Row.

Lewin, K., 1997. Resolving social conflicts: Field theory in social science. Washington, D.C.: American Psychological Association.

Likert, R., 1932. A Technique for the Measurement of Attitudes. Archives of Psychology, 140, 1-55.

Lock, D., 2013. Project management. 10th ed. Farnham, Surrey: Gower Publishing Limited.

Loosemore, M., 2006. Risk management in projects. 1st edition. London: Tayor and Francis.

Ochs, Elinor., 2002. Becoming a speaker of culture. In C. Kramsch (ed.), Language acquisition and language socialisation. London: Continuum.

Owen, D., 2012, The Hubris Syndrome. Grantham. UK: Methuen Publishing Limited.

Maccoby, M., 2003. The Productive Narcissist: The Promise and Peril of Visionary Leadership. New York: Broadway.

Martin, R., 2010. The Execution Trap. [online] HBR. Available at: https://hbr.org/2010/07/the-execution-trap [Accessed 6 Jun. 2019].

Mendelow, A, 1991. Stakeholder Mapping, Proceedings of the 2nd International Conference on Information Systems, Cambridge, MA.

Meyer, R., 2016. The Culture Map: Decoding How People Think, Lead, and Get Things Done Across Cultures. New York: Public Affairs.

Moore, S., 2010. Strategic Project Portfolio Management: Enabling a Productive Organisation. Hoboken, N.J: John Wiley and Sons, Inc.

Mornell, P., 2015. Hiring Smart: Hiring Smart. How to Predict Winners and Losers in the Incredibly Expensive. Berkeley: Ten Speed Press.

Northouse, P, G., 2015. Leadership Theory and Practice. Thousand Oaks, California: Sage.

Pettigrew, A. and Whipp, R., 1991. Managing Change for Competitive Success. Oxford: Blackwell.

PMI, 2017. A Guide to the Project Management Body of Knowledge (PMBOK Guide). 6th ed.

Prahalad, C, K. and Hamel, G., 1990. The Core Competence of the Corporation. https://hbr.org/1990/05/the-core-competence-of-the-corporation. [Accessed Jun. 2019].

Rescorla, R. A., 1987. "Pavlovian Analysis of Goal Directed Behaviour", American Psychologist, 42 (2), 1 19—29.

Schwab, K., 2017. The Fourth Industrial Revolution. New York: Currency.

Senge, P., 1990[1]. The Fifth Discipline: The Art and Practice of The Learning Organisation: Second Edition. New York: Doubleday.

Senge, P., 1990[2]. The Leader's New Work. Building Learning Organisations. Sloan Management Review, 32(1), pp.7-22.

Shaw, B., and Bentley, E. 1960. @Plays by George Bernard Shaw. New York: Penguin Books.

Simon, P., 2015. Message not received: Why business communication is broken and how to fix it. Hoboken, NJ: Wiley.

Sirkin, H., Keenan, P. and Jackson, A., 2005. The Hard Side of Change Management. Harvard Business Review. Available at: https://hbr.org/2005/10/the-hard-side-of-change-management [Accessed Jun. 2019].

Sniehotta, F.F., Scholz, U and Schwarzer R., 2005. Bridging the Intention-Behaviour Gap: Planning, Self-Efficacy, And Action Control in The Adoption and Maintenance of Physical Exercise. Psychology and Health.

Steers, R., Nardon, L. and Sanchez-Runde, C., 2013. Management across Cultures: Developing Global Competencies. 2nd ed. Cambridge: Cambridge University Press.

Thaler, H. T. Sunstein, C. R., 2009. Nudge: Improving Decisions About Health, Wealth, and Happiness. London: Penguin Books.

4.1 References

Thaler, H. T., 2015. Misbehaving: The Making of Behavioural Economics. London: Allen Lane.

Thomas, R., 2008. Crucibles of leadership. Boston, Mass.: Harvard Business Press.

Tourish, D. and Robson, P., 2004. Critical Upward Feedback in Organisations: Processes, Problems and Implications For Communication Management. Journal of Communication Management, 8(2), pp.150-167.

Ulrich, D., 1997. Human resource champions. Boston: Harvard Business School Press.

Ulrich, D. and Ulrich, W., and Goldsmith, M., 2010. The Why of Work: How Great Leaders Build Abundant Organisations That Win. Boston: McGraw-Hill Education.

Vonnegut, K., 1991. Hocus Pocus. 2nd ed. Olympia, WA, U.S.A: Berkley.

Weiner, B. J., 2009. A Theory of Organisational Readiness for Change. Implementation Science 2009, 4(67). doi:10.1186/1748-5908-4-67.

Whitmore, J., 2002. Coaching for Performance: Growing People, and Purpose. Third Edition. London: Nicholas Brealey Publishing.

Williams, T., 2007. Post-Project Reviews to Gain Effective Lessons Learned. Newtown Square, PA. Project Management Institute.

Yukl, G.A., 2012. Leadership in Organisations Global Edition. Boston: Pearson.

4.2 Glossary

4IR: See 'Fourth Industrial Revolution'.

5S: The approach organises the workplace, keeps it neat and clean, establishes standardised conditions and maintains discipline to sustain the effort. The name comes from the five steps required to implement the process into the workplace. The words used to describe each step: **S**ort, **S**et in order, **S**hine, **S**tandardise, and **S**ustain. This is sometimes referred to as 6S when **S**afety is included.

5 Whys: A lean technique that refers to the practice of asking, five times, why the failure has occurred in order to get to the root cause of the problem.

a2B5R® Model: Our systematic model to change employee behaviour and promote change adoption. The model has five stages: **R**ecognise, **R**edesign, **R**esolve, **R**eplicate and **R**einforce.

a2B Change Management Framework®: Our **a2B Change Management Framework® (a2BCMF®)** is a structured and disciplined approach to support organisations, leadership teams and individuals going through a change, the transition from the current 'a' state to the improved future 'B' state. It has ten key steps but iterations between the steps are usually necessary and some can be worked in parallel.

a2BCMF® Model: See 'a2B Change Management Framework®'.

a2BDNS© Developing the New Skills Model: The six-step process for developing the new skills and behaviours so employees are prepared for the new way of working. The model has six process steps: **Define, Identify, Evaluate, Assess, Deliver Coach** and **Appraise**.

Actionee(s): Person(s) responsible for carrying out an action within the change programme or project.

Adoption: Change adoption is the way that the organisation and employees make the transition from the current 'a' state to the improved future 'B' state, leaving the old ways behind and adopting the new way of working and behaving. It is confirmation that they have fully accepted the change, both in mind and in heart. It is agreement that the new way of working is more efficient and benefits both the organisation and customers and is part of the organisation's future DNA.

Advocates: One of three employee change standpoints during change implementation. '**Advocates**' are similar to the change agents with their positivity towards change. Their energy should be harnessed as they can play an effective role in leading and implementing the change.

Alternative Solutions: Assessing other possible courses of action and solutions during the discussion and creation of the business case. Are there alternatives to this change programme?

4.2 Glossary

Articulate: The first element of a leader's role in organisational change. Leaders are expected to '**Articulate**' the organisation's change vision.

AUILM® Model: This model outlines the five key life cycle stages the employee goes through in the change transition from the current '**a**' state to the improved future '**B**' state. **AUILM®** is an acronym that represents: **A**wareness, **U**nderstanding, **I**nvolvement, **L**earning and **M**otivation.

Backfire: The tendency of some leaders and employees to resist accepting evidence that conflicts with their beliefs. It causes people to strengthen their support for their original stance.

Balanced Scorecard (BSC): An integrated set of measures built around the organisation's mission, vision and strategy. Measures address the financial, customer, internal business process and learning and growth perspectives. They provide a balanced view on what is required to enact the strategy and can be used to measure the change programme.

Barrier: An impediment to successful change, these are challenges to overcome when planning, executing and sustaining change programmes. Examples might include individuals actively or passively resisting change or anything that has the potential to stop or weaken the change effort.

Baseline: The reference level against which a project, programme or portfolio is monitored and controlled.

Behaviour: The way in which employees respond to specific circumstances or situations within the workplace environment. While many elements determine an individual's behaviour in the workplace, employees are shaped by their culture and by the organisation's culture.

Behaviour Training: The training that develops the few new employee and organisation behaviours required to support change adoption. It involves defining the critical few behaviours, designing and delivering the training, and leaders modelling the new behaviours. It is supported by our **a2B5R® Model** to embed the new behaviours.

Benefit: The quantifiable and measurable improvement, resulting from completion of the change or deliverables that are perceived as positive by an organisation. It will normally have a tangible value and be expressed in monetary terms that will justify the investment. The quantitative and qualitative, measurable and non-measurable outcomes resulting from a change.

Benefits Plan and Tracker (BPT): The identification, definition, planning, tracking and realisation of business benefits as defined in the **a2BCMF® Step 1 - Change Definition**.

Benefits Realisation: The actual achievement of the change benefits which are usually delivered through the **Execute** and **Sustain** phase. This is usually the reason why most organisations undertake a change programme and is the way an organisation achieves a ROI. It will normally include a tangible value expressed in monetary terms that will justify the investment.

Budget: The sum of money allocated to the change programme. The term may also refer to revenue and expenses.

Business Case: Developed to assess the change programme's balance between costs and benefits. The business case provides business reasons for starting the change programme.

Business Operations: See 'Normal Day-to-Day Operations'.

Business Plan: A document that summarises the operational and financial objectives of an organisation and contains the detailed plans and budgets showing how the objectives are to be realised

Business Process: A system of activities by which a business creates a specific result for its customers.

Change: The transition from the current state 'a' to the future state 'B'.

Change Agent: The individuals or groups whose task it is to effect change. They can be any member of an organisation or an external consultant involved in facilitating, supporting, influencing or implementing change. They might not be called 'change agents' as their official job title may not recognise or formalise their responsibility.

Change Blindness: A condition where people cling to an old belief or way of working, without considering the future or better options.

Change Capable Organisation: An organisation with developed change capability to constantly manage change successfully, maximising employee adoption and delivering sustainable benefits.

Change Capacity: The overall capacity of an organisation to either effectively prepare for, or respond to, an increasingly unpredictable planned change.

Change Communication Plan (CCP): The plan that depicts the key communications, the channels and the timing of these messages or events.

Change Consultant: An individual who has experience and expertise in applying change tools and techniques to resolve change problems and who can advise and facilitate an organisation's change efforts.

Change Control: Unlike the process of organisational change management, this process is about modifications to documents, deliverables, or baselines. It ensures that modifications associated with the project are identified, documented, approved, or rejected. Change control is a major aspect of the broader discipline of change management.

Change Disruption: Irreversible change that affects nearly every organisation as a result of living during the fourth industrial revolution (4IR). A period of disruption while the new change takes effect.

4.2 Glossary

Change Fatigue: A general sense of apathy or passive resignation towards continual organisational changes by individuals, teams or leaders.

Change Freeze: The point at which scope changes to a programme are no longer permissible.

Change History Assessment© (CHA©): This can be used to assess and review the outcomes of earlier change programmes and initiatives. It provides organisational insights that may increase the likelihood of successful implementation through the analysis of lessons learned, mitigation of previous weaknesses and enhancement of future success.

Change Impact: How employees, processes, systems and the organisation are affected during the transition from the current 'a' state to the improved future 'B' state.

Change Initiative: The name given to an organisational change programme or improvement project.

Change Management: A field of management focused on organisational change which is the practice of applying a structured approach to transition an organisation from the current 'a' state to the improved future 'B' state to achieve change adoption and the expected benefits.

Change Management Framework: See 'a2B Change Management Framework'.

Change Management Gamification: The growing trend which helps to engage employees by using gaming methods. Gamification can be used by employees to learn, test and prepare for organisational change.

Change Management Handbook: A book containing instructions or advice about how to do something or the most important and useful information about a subject. A reference book: in this case, practical change management implementation. This handbook contains the ten-step a2B Change Management Framework® (**a2BCMF®**) and is supported by over fifty concepts, figures, assessments, tools, templates and plans, as well as a roadmap and glossary.

Change Management Methodology: A system or approach which guides change implementation.

Change Management Pocket Guide: Typically, a small paperback that can be carried in the pocket which provides help on change management. The pocket guide contains the ten-step a2B Change Management Framework® (**a2BCMF®**) and is supported by over thirty concepts, models, figures, assessments, tools, templates, checklists and plans, as well as a roadmap and glossary.

Change Model: Models to describe and simplify a principle or define a process to develop a change deliverable.

Change Readiness Assessment (CRA): An assessment to establish if the employee and organisation are ready for change implementation. It can also gauge whether resistance will be high or low.

Change Risk: An event or condition that, if it occurs, may have an effect on change adoption and benefits realisation.

Change Saturation: When the amount of change occurring in an organisation is more than can be effectively handled by those affected by the change.

Change Sponsor Assessment (CSA): An assessment used to assess if the sponsor is performing their duties and if they are committed to the success of the change programme. The assessment should be transparent and focus on how the sponsor is performing their role with regards to 'Say', 'Support' and 'Sustain' activities.

Change Vision: The description of the future state 'B'. It describes how the organisation will look after the change is successfully implemented in the time limit specified.

Charter: See 'Programme Charter' and 'Project Charter'.

Checklist: A quality control technique. This may include a set of important elements that the change practitioner uses for requirement verification and validation of key change programme activities.

Coaching: A process that enables learning and development to occur and therefore performance to improve. The role of a coach is to give the employee feedback on observed performance.

Core Competence: An organisation's unique capability that would be greatly appreciated by customers and would be difficult for competitors to quickly duplicate.

Communication Channels: The routes used to send messages, such as social media, emails, verbal presentations, reports, etc.

Competency: The organisation or individual collection of knowledge, skills, behaviours, and other characteristics and abilities to perform the role. Definitions of competencies tend to be broader than just skills.

Competency Dictionary: A tool or data structure that includes all or most of the general competencies needed to cover all job families and competencies that are core or common to all jobs within an organisation.

Competency Framework: Defines the knowledge, skills, and attributes needed for employees within an organisation. Each role will have its own set of competencies needed to perform the job effectively.

Constraint: A limitation on the change programme which could impact schedule, cost or quality of the change.

Continuous and Never-Ending Improvement (CANI): The name given to the process of always needing to improve. It is associated with growth mindset people.

Continuous Improvement (CI): The never-ending improvement of products, services or processes through incremental and breakthrough improvements. The goal is to increase effectiveness by reducing inefficiencies, frustrations, and waste (rework, time, effort, material, etc.).

Cost Overrun: This occurs when unexpected costs cause a change programme's actual cost to go beyond budget.

Critical Success Factor (CSF): A management term for an element that is necessary for an organisation or change programme to achieve its mission.

Culture: A system of shared assumptions, values and beliefs, which govern how people behave. These shared values have a strong influence on the employees in the organisation and dictate how they behave, act and perform their jobs.

Current State: The condition at the time the change is initiated, defined as the current 'a' state. The current state of the organisation's business processes, systems and employees before the change is implemented. It is often used as a baseline before the organisation moves to the future 'B' state.

Day-in-Life-of (DILO): The DILO study provides insights into the employee's daily operational activities, highlighting tasks that add value in day-to-day work and those that do not.

Deluded Leaders: Leaders who prevent true change programme implementation because they believe (for various reasons) they are more important than the change.

Dependencies: In the project change plan, dependencies are the relationships between preceding tasks. Tasks may have multiple sub-tasks and multiple succeeding sub-tasks.

Due Diligence: One of the first steps in achieving the change programme's goals by systematically assessing the viability of the change initiative. It is effectively a risk management process designed to enable a decision on whether the change should proceed. It assesses risks, benefits, costs and impacts, providing a go/no go decision on whether the project should proceed.

Eight Wastes of Lean: TIM H WOOD is an acronym for the 8 wastes commonly found within business: **T**ransport, **I**nventory **M**otion, **H**uman, **W**aiting, **O**ver production, **O**ver processing, **D**efects.

Emotional Intelligence: The ability to monitor your emotions or the emotions of others and use this to guide your actions during the change. Leaders of change need to recognise and regulate emotions in themselves and others. As change management professionals, we engage employees and impacted stakeholders, relying on them to adopt the change and ensure benefits realisation.

Employee Behaviour: Refers to the way in which employees respond to specific circumstances or changes in the workplace.

Enabler: A positive facilitator to successful change. These can be individuals actively or passively supporting change or anything that has the potential to improve change implementation success.

Estimated Completion Date (ECD): The expected date an action or deliverable should be complete.

Facilitator: The person responsible to guide and support employees through the change process interactively.

Fixed Mindset: Employees with a fixed mindset will, by default, reject and resist disruption and change. This will prevent true change. Their assumption is that change is usually always bad, and they stick what they know.

Fourth Industrial Revolution (4IR): Describes exponential change in the way we live, work and relate to one another. 4IR includes the adoption of cyber-physical systems, the Internet of Things and the Internet of Systems.

Frame of Reference: A set of criteria or stated values in relation to perceptions and judgements that can be made by employees. How the employee or change target interprets what they see in terms of their own cultural frame of reference.

Future State: The future state 'B', when employees have adopted the new way of working and the benefits have been realised.

Governance: The decision-making processes, applied by authorised individuals or teams, for approving/rejecting, monitoring and adjusting activities of the project change plan (PCP).

Growth Mindset: These employees embrace disruption and change to improve organisation performance. Setbacks are opportunities to learn (CANI) and an individual's effort and attitude determine success.

Hubris: Leaders with excessive pride and over confidence which manifests itself as a major barrier to change implementation success.

Hunch and Launch Syndrome: A name given to the process of coming up with a change idea (hunch) and then introducing (launch) it into the organisation without strategic consideration or a plan on how the benefits will be realised. These ideas rarely deliver strategic change or sustainable benefits and are sometimes referred to as 'pet projects'.

Individual Performance Plan (IPP): An instrument used to establish performance expectations and to support the performance evaluation of each employee, usually linked to the balanced scorecard and an individual's bonus.

Intervene: The third element of a leader's role in organisational change. They should '**Intervene**' when they observe an employee resisting change, or when employees are not adopting the new skills and behaviours.

Intervention: All the planned programme activities that aim to bring changes into an organisation. They are led by the sponsor and the leadership team.

Key Performance Indicators (KPI): A set of quantifiable measures that a company uses to gauge its performance over time. These metrics are used to determine an organisation's progress in achieving its strategic (change) and operational goals. They also compare a company's finances and performance against other businesses within its industry.

Knowledge Transfer: The process of transferring knowledge from the change programme to other parts or systems within the organisation. Like knowledge management, knowledge transfer seeks to capture, organise, create, or distribute knowledge and ensure its availability for future change teams.

Leader: A person in the organisation who is responsible for leading; directing, commanding, or guiding a group or activity. Without a leader leading the change programme it is likely to fail. The leader's role in organisational change is to '**Articulate**' the change vision, '**Model**' the new behaviours and '**Intervene**' to reinforce the change.

Leadership: The leaders of the organisation who are collectively responsible for strategy execution and its inherent change programmes.

Leadership Alignment: This process develops change leadership capability, so the organisation's leaders are aligned, as a high performing team, with change leadership skills and knowledge to successfully lead the organisation's change, transformation or improvement to accelerate employee change adoption and deliver sustainable long-term benefits.

Lean: A process improvement methodology, focused on reducing waste in a system. The term lean is derived from the idea that the approach reduces 'waste' that contributes to inefficient processes and poor outcomes.

Lessons Learned: The sum of knowledge gained from the change programme. This should be used as a reference, input and points of interest for future change programmes or projects.

Master Project Plan: The wider project plan that drives the change or transformation across the organisation and coordinates activities performed by the work streams. The project change plan (PCP) should be aligned with the key milestones on the master project plan and both plans should be updated simultaneously. In some cases, there may only be a single PCP.

Mentoring: A process of providing support, challenge and extension of the learning of one person through the guidance of another who is more knowledgeable and experienced.

Merger: The combination of two or more separate companies into one. Most mergers involve the integration of operations, processes, assets, management and organisations.

Milestone: An important date or deadline, the start or end of significant phases of work shown on the project change plan (PCP). It is usually reflected as a diamond symbol.

Mission: Describes the overall purpose of the organisation. Each organisation's statement can vary widely in terms of content, stretch and scope.

Model: The second element of a leader's role in organisational change. It is an activity expected from the organisation's leader (and sponsor). They should 'Model' the new skills and behaviours, providing a role model to other staff.

Narcissistic Leader: A leader with excessive self-confidence and an obsessive focus on their personal image, accompanied by contempt for anyone who thinks that the organisation's strategic change programme is more important than them.

Normal Day-to-Day Operations: The activities that an organisation and its employees engage in on a daily basis for the purposes of generating a profit and increasing the inherent value of the organisation.

Observers: One of three employee change standpoints during change implementation. '**Observers**' will monitor the '**Advocates**' and assess if the change is benefiting them. If this appears positive, they will tend to move towards being receptive to the change.

Organisation: A social arrangement for achieving controlled performance in pursuit of collective goals.

Organisational Agility: The ability of an organisation to respond to ambiguity, threats, opportunities or uncertainty with flexibility and speed.

Organisational Development (OD): A process for instigating, implementing and sustaining change, it involves activities that impact employees, the team and the organisation.

Outcome: A specific measurable result or effect of an action or situation.

Pet Projects: Projects directed or supported by the CEO or other senior leaders that appeal to their emotions and hubris, they rarely deliver strategic value.

Planned Change: An intentional intervention for bringing about change to an organisation. It is best characterised as deliberate, purposeful and systematic.

Programme: A group of related projects, sub-programmes and programme activities that are managed in a coordinated way to obtain benefits not available by managing them individually. (**a2BCMF®** uses this default name for change initiatives, each client organisation can refer to them as programmes, projects, etc.)

Programme Charter: The programme charter is a document that details the scope, organisation, and objectives of a programme. It authorises the programme sponsor or manager to use the organisational resources to deliver the programme. The programme charter may include various project charters.

Project: A temporary endeavour undertaken to create a unique product, service, change or result.

Project Change Plan (PCP): The plan to deliver the change programme. (The words project and programme can be interchangeable depending on the makeup of the change initiative, it can be either a project or programme).

Project Charter: The project charter is a document that details the scope, organisation, and objectives of a project. It authorises the project sponsor or manager to use the organisational resources to deliver the project.

Project Management: The application of knowledge, skills, tools, and techniques to achieve project activities to meet the project requirements.

Project Management Office (PMO): An organisational unit that oversees project (change) management related activities within an organisation. It seeks to facilitate and expedite project and change work through the use of standard procedures.

Qualitative Data: Collects information that seeks to describe a topic more than measure it, such as opinions, views and reflections. A qualitative survey is less structured, and it seeks to delve deeply into the assessment topics to gain information about stakeholders and employee's motivations, thinking, and attitudes.

Quantitative Data: Designed to collect cold, hard facts. Numbers. Quantitative data is structured and statistical. It provides support when you need to draw general conclusions from your assessment or research.

Rarely Blame the Employee (RBtE): Employees should rarely be blamed, as we don't know their environment or background. Only the behaviours they are exhibiting should be judged.

Readiness: The process of assessing the change readiness of the organisation and the employees prior to change implementation. This will ensure change can be adopted and the benefits can be realised.

Rebels: One of three employee change standpoints during change implementation. 'Rebels' tend to resist change blindly, sometimes this can be a natural reaction even if the change is to their benefit. The default reaction is that change is a bad thing and will put them at a disadvantage.

Reinforce: Reinforcing change is critical to ensure adoption of the new way of working. The sponsor and leaders are expected to intervene when there is resistance, or when the employees are not adopting the new skills and behaviours.

Resistance: The reaction by the organisation, departments or individuals when they perceive that an organisational change coming their way could be a threat to them. Without further awareness and understanding, this resistance will cause fear. It will trigger actions that negatively impact the pace of organisational change implementation, adoption of the new ways of working and benefits delivery.

Resistance Management: The process of addressing stakeholders' opposition to a change.

Resistance Strategy Plan (RSP): This plan provides specific actions to understand and address resistance. The actions and plan focus on the change implementation strategy and vary depending on if it is a '**Tell**' or '**Sell**' change implementation approach. This is a component plan of the PCP and may be needed if the change team foresees high resistance challenges.

Return on Investment (ROI): The benefits that the change delivers. These are dependent on speed of adoption as well as delivering the programme on time, within budget and the specified scope. The ROI can be calculated using the following equation, ROI = (Expected Project Benefits - Project Costs) / Project Costs.

Rework: Correcting a defective, failed, or non-conforming item, service or product prior to customer delivery. Rework includes an organisation's repeat effort, such as disassembly, repair, replacement, reassembly, etc.

Risk: See 'Change Risk'.

Roadmap: A chronological representation of a programme's intended direction, graphically depicting dependencies between major milestones and decision points, while communicating the linkage between the organisation's strategy and the programme's work.

Say: The first key element of sponsorship. '**Say**' is the foundation and is all about communicating the business case for the change to all affected stakeholders.

Skills: The expertise or talent needed in order to do a job or task. Transferable skills are needed by the employee to be able to operate at the new way of working. These will include technical understanding and subject knowledge.

Skills and Behaviours Learning Plan: Identifies skills and behaviours that will be required for the employees to adapt to the new way of working. A training needs analysis (TNA) can be used to identify skill and behaviour gaps. This is a component plan of the PCP and may be needed if the change team foresees learning or training as a major activity in terms of effort and time.

Sponsor: The most senior leader within the programme, reporting to the CEO or a steering committee. They are authorised to mandate the programme, the business case and are responsible for change adoption, benefits realisation and successful change programme delivery.

4.2 Glossary

Sponsorship: The sponsorship role is to communicate the programme's change ('**Say**'), provide resources ('**Support**') and ensure the change lasts ('**Sustain**'), the process of aligning stakeholders to support and own the change.

Sponsorship and Resource Plan: Identifies the change sponsor and defines the strategy and actions to develop the required programme resources; change lead, communication lead, change agents, etc. This is a component plan of the PCP and may be needed if the change team foresees resourcing their team as a challenge.

Sponsor Assessment: An assessment of the organisation's sponsorship that can identify strengths or weaknesses with the change implementation.

Stakeholder: An individual affected or impacted by a change.

Stakeholder Analysis: The systematic examination and evaluation of stakeholders in order to prioritise, manage and engage with them effectively throughout the change programme.

Stakeholder Engagement: The process in which an organisation involves and engages people who may be affected by the decisions it makes or can influence the implementation of the change.

Stakeholder Engagement Plan: Identifies the actions to engage groups and individuals affected by the change and mitigate resistance by enlisting their support, adoption and ownership. This is a component plan of the PCP and may be needed if the change team foresees stakeholder engagement challenges.

Stakeholder Mapping: This involves representing stakeholders on a grid to display their level of influence on one axis from low to high, and their likely level of cooperation '**Rebels**', '**Observers**' and '**Advocates**' toward the change on the other.

Strategic Planning: The process undertaken by an organisation to define its overall purpose, priorities to work towards that purpose and how each priority will be addressed.

Strategy: An approach to achieve an organisation's strategic goals or address strategic issues. A strategy might be a major approach that uses the internal strengths of an organisation to take advantage of external opportunities, while shoring up internal weaknesses to ward off external threats. An organisation's strategies are usually long-term.

Subject Matter Expert (SME): An individual who exhibits the highest level of expertise in performing a specialised job, task, or skill within the organisation and can be an invaluable resource to the change team.

Support: The second key element of sponsorship. '**Support**' builds on '**Say**' and in this element the sponsor starts to actively and overtly support the change, provide resources and coach the organisation.

Sustain[1]: The third phase of **a2BCMF®** change implementation. Closing the change programme to sustain adoption and ensure benefits realisation.

Sustain[2]: The third key element of sponsorship. It builds on '**Say**' and '**Support**'. '**Sustain**' is critical for the organisation to deliver value and achieve its strategic goals.

Sustainability: The ability to maintain the future state '**B**'.

Sustain and Close Plan: The sustain part of the plan provides an approach to sustaining adoption and benefits realisation. The close plan will officially transfer ownership and close off the programme, ensuring administrative activities are completed as per the organisation's procedures. This is a component plan of the PCP and may be needed if the change team foresees sustaining and closing the change as challenging.

System Change: An organisational change that focuses on changing its internal systems which manage and control the internal processes and procedures that deliver its products or services.

Tactic: A series of activities, usually short-term and small in scale, intended to achieve a goal or objective.

Leadership of Change®: The ability to lead, support, influence and enthuse those involved in organisation change to transition from the current '**a**' state to the improved future '**B**' state to achieve change adoption and the expected benefits.

Threat: A negative risk that could adversely affect the change programme's objectives.

TIM H WOOD: See 'Eight Wastes of Lean'.

To-Be State: See 'Future State'.

Training Needs Analysis (TNA): The process in which the organisation identifies the training and development needs of its employees so that they can do their job effectively.

Training Plan: A detailed plan for how the organisation, groups and individuals will be trained and coached so they have the new skills and behaviours to perform the new way of working. It will include the training objectives, how and who will develop the content, the selection process of who will be trained, when they will be trained, who will deliver the training, how the trainers will be trained, assessment criteria and coaching plans.

Transfer of Ownership: Prior to closing the change programme, the sponsor and change team should coordinate the controlled transfer ownership to operations and receive approval to formally close out the programme.

Transformation: Fundamental changes that are significant and considered vital to the future success of the organisation.

4.2 Glossary

Transition State: The state between the current 'a' and future 'B' state. Transition state is the process of equipping the employees with skills and behaviours to adopt the new way of working so the organisation can achieve benefits realisation.

Triple Constraint: The triple constraint is the combination of the three most significant restrictions on any change programme or project; scope, schedule and cost.

Values Statement: Describes the overall, top-level priorities for how an organisation chooses to conduct its activities and to be viewed by the public, for example, integrity, efficiency and reliability.

Value Stream Mapping (VSM): Typically, a pencil and paper lean tool used to remove non-value activities. It maps out the current state of a process, product or service's path from beginning to end and draws a visual representation so that value add, non-value add and business non-value add activities can be identified. A more efficient and effective improved future state can then be developed. A VSM can be the source of many potential improvement and change projects.

Vision: See 'Change Vision'.

Vision Statement: A vivid and compelling description of the organisation and its customers at some time in the future. It depicts a long-term, inspirational and strategic vision, which depicts the organisation and customers shortly after the strategic plan has been implemented.

WIIFM (What's In It For Me): This concept focuses on the likelihood of employee acceptance. The basic premise of this acronym is that when the result of an action is in the best interests of an employee, they are more likely to choose to do it.

Work Stream: A team or group of individuals who complete a common set of activities or tasks as part of a bigger change programme.

Yes Men and Women: Employees who agree with deluded leaders when they know that this will damage or delay change implementation.

4.3 Bibliography

Abrahamson, E., 2000. Change without pain. Harvard Business Review, 78(4), 75-79.

Aiken, C. and Keller, S., 2009. The irrational side of change management. Available at: https://www.manageris.com/article-the-irrational-side-of-change-management-23351.html. [Accessed Jul. 2019].

Aldrich, H.E., 1979. Organisations and environments. Englewood Cliffs, NJ: Prentice Hall.

Alvesson, M., and Sveningsson, S., 2008. Changing organisational culture. USA: Routledge Publishing.

Ancient Encyclopaedia, 2018. Heraclitus www.ancient.eu/article/183/heraclitus-life-is-flux/ [Accessed Jul. 2019].

Anderson, J.R., 1987. Methodologies for studying human knowledge. Behaviour and Brain Sciences, 10(3), 467-477.

Ansoff, I., 1988. The new corporate strategy. New York: John Wiley and Sons.

APM, 2015. APMP: The APM Project Management Qualification | APM. [online] Available at: https://www.apm.org.uk/qualifications-and-training/project-management-qualification/ [Accessed Jun. 2019].

Argyris, C., 1993. On organisational learning. Cambridge: Blackwell Business.

Argyris, C., and Schön, D.A. 1974. Theory in practice: Increasing professional effectiveness. San Francisco: Jossey-Bass.

Ash, M., 1984. Mary Kay on people management. New York, N.Y.: Warner Books.

Atkinson, R., 1999. Project management: cost, time and quality, two best guesses and a phenomenon, it's time to accept other success criteria. International Journal of Project Management, 17(6), pp.337-342.

Badiru, A., 2012. Project management Systems, Principles, and Applications (Industrial Innovation Series). Boca Raton, FL: CRC Press.

Bass, B.M., 1985. Leadership and performance beyond expectations. New York: The Free Press.

Bass, B.M., 1990. From transactional to transformational leadership: Learning to share the vision. Organisational Dynamics, 13, 26-40.

Bate, P., 1994. Strategies for cultural change. Oxford: Butterworth-Heinemann Ltd.

Bandura, A., 1977. Social learning theory. Englewood Cliffs, NJ: Prentice Hall.

Barrett, P., 2000. Corporate governance in the public sector context. Canberra: ANAO.

Becker, D., George, M.A., Goolsby, A.E., and Grissom, D.C. 1998. No coordination — all the way down the line: Reorganising Illinois's Department of Human Services: The story of Julie. The McKinsey Quarterly, 1, 17-125.

Beckhard, R., and Pritchard, W., 1992. Changing the essence: The art of creating and leading fundamental changes in organisations. San Francisco: Jossey-Bass.

Beckhard, R., 1969. Organisation Development: Strategies and Models. Reading, MA: Addison-Wesley.

Beer, M., and Eisenstadt, R.A., 2000. The silent killers of strategy implementation and learning. Sloan Management Review, 41(4), 29-40.

Beer, M., Eisenstadt, R.A., and Spector, B., 1990^A. The critical path to corporate renewal, Boston, MA: Harvard Business School Press.

Beer, M., Eisenstadt, R.A., and Spector, B. 1990^B. Why change programs don't produce change. Harvard Business Review, 68(6), 156-166.

Beer, M. and Nohria, N., 2000. Cracking the code of change. Harvard Business Review, May- June 2000, 1-8.

Beer, M., and Nohria, N., 2000. Breaking the code of change. Boston, MA: Harvard Business School Press.

Bennett, J.L., 2001. Change hygiene. HR Magazine, 46(9), 149.

Bennett. M, 2015. Gearing up for the big lift in the North Sea. Available at: https://www.bbc.co.uk/news/uk-scotland-scotland-business-32844552. [Accessed Jun. 2019].

Bennett, R.H., Fadil, P. A., and Greenwood, R.T. 1994. Cultural alignment in response to strategic organisational change: New considerations for a change framework. Journal of Managerial Issues, 6(4), 474-481.

Bennis, W., 1959. Leadership theory and administrative behaviour. Science Quarterly, 4, 259—301.

Best, R., Langton, C. and Devalence, G., 2003. Workplace strategies and facilities management. Oxford: Butterworth-Heinemann.

Binnendijk, H., 2002. Transforming America's military. Washington, D.C.: National Defense University Press.

Blanchard, K., Zigarmi, P. and Zigarmi, D., 2013. Leadership and The One Minute Manager. New York: HarperCollins.

Blanchard, K., 2001. High Five! New York: Morrow.

Boyatzis. R. E., 1982. The Competent Manager: A Model for Effective Performance. New York: John Wiley and Sons.

BS, 9004. British Standard, BS EN ISO 9004:2018 Quality Management. Quality of an Organisation. Guidance to Achieve Sustained Success. London, UK.

Cameron, K. S, and Quinn, R. E., 2006. Diagnosing and changing organisational culture: Based on the competing values framework. San Francisco: Jossey-Bass.

Caroselli, M., 2000. Leadership skills for managers. New York: McGraw-Hill.

Conner, K.R. and Prahalad, C.K., 1996. A Resource-Based Theory of the Firm: Knowledge vs. Opportunism. Organisation Science, 7, 477-501. http://dx.doi.org/10.1287/orsc.7.5.477.

Cullen, S., 2009. The contract scorecard. Farnham, Surrey, England: Gower.

Cullen, The Hon. Lord W. Douglas, 1990. The public inquiry into the Piper Alpha disaster. London: H.M. Stationery Office. ISBN 0101113102. 488 pages, 2 volumes.

Deming, W., 1986. Out of the crisis. Cambridge, Mass.: Massachusetts Institute of Technology, Center for Advanced Engineering Study.

Drucker, P., 1954. The practice of management. New York: Harper and Row.

Drucker, P. F., 2007. The Practice of Management. Collection Edition. London: Routledge.

Duck, J., 2001. The Change Monster. New York: Crown Business.

Goleman, D., 1995. Emotional intelligence. New York: Bantam Books.

Haarman, M. and Delahay, G. 2004. Value driven maintenance. Dordrecht, Netherlands: Mainnovation.

Harrington, H. J., 2014. Organisational Capacity for Change: Increasing Change Capacity and Avoiding Change Overload. PMI White Paper.

Harry, M. and Schroedder, R., 2000. Six Sigma. New York: Currency.

Hayward, M., 2007. Ego check. Chicago: Kaplan Pub.

Howell, W., 1982. The empathic communicator. Belmont, CA: Wadsworth Publishing Company.

Hughes, M., 2011. Do 70 Per Cent of All Organisational Change Initiatives Really Fail? Journal of Change Management, 11:4, 451-464, DOI: 10.1080/14697017.2011.630506.

Investopedia, 2019. Benchmark Oils: Brent Blend, WTI and Dubai. Available at: https://www.investopedia.com/articles/investing/102314/understanding-benchmark-oils-brent-blend-wti-and-dubai.asp. [Accessed Jun. 2019].

Johnson, G. Scholes, K. and Whittington, R., 2009. Exploring corporate strategy. Harlow: Financial Times Prentice Hall.

Katz, R., 2009. Skills of an effective administrator. Boston, Mass: Harvard Business Press.

Katzenbach, J. and Smith, D., 1993. The wisdom of teams. Boston, Mass.: Harvard Business School Press.

Kendrick, T., 2009. Identifying and managing project risk. 1st. New York: Amazon.

Kerzner, H., 2011. Project Management Metrics, KPIs, and Dashboards: A Guide to Measuring and Monitoring Project Performance. Hoboken, N.J.: John Wiley and Sons.

Kolb, D., 2014. Experiential Learning: Experience as the Source of Learning and Development. 2nd ed. New Jersey: Pearson FT Press.

Kotler, P., and Armstrong, G., 2010. Principles of marketing (13th Edn.). Upper Saddle River, New Jersey: Prentice Hall.

Kotter, J., 1996. Leading change. Boston, Mass.: Harvard Business School Press.

Kotter, J., 2007. Leading Change: Why Transformation Efforts Fail. Available at: https://hbr.org/2007/01/leading-change-why-transformation-efforts-fail [Accessed Jun. 2019].

Kotter, J.P., 1989. What effective general managers really do. In H.J. Leavitt, L. Pondy and D.M. Boje (Eds.), Readings in managerial psychology (pp. 534-553). Chicago: University of Chicago Press.

Kotter, J., and Schlesinger, L., 1979. Choosing strategies for change. Harvard Business Review, 57(2), 106-114.

Kotter, J.P., 1995. Leading change: Why transformation efforts fail'. Harvard Business Review, March-April 1-20.

Kotter, J.P., 1996. Leading change. Boston: Harvard Business School Press.

Kotter, J.P., 1997. Leading change: A conversation with John P. Kotter. Strategy and Leadership, 25(1), 18-23.

Kotter, J.P., 1999. Change leadership. Executive Excellence, 16(4), 16-17. 297.

Kotter, J.P., and Cohen, D.S., 2002. The Heart of Change: Real-life stories of how people change their organisations. Boston: Harvard Business School Press.

Kotter, J. and Ratheber, H., 2006. Our Iceberg is Melting. New York: St. Martin's Press.

Kubler-Ross, E., 1997. The wheel of life. New York, NY: Scribner.

Kubler-Ross, E. and Warshaw, M., 1978. To live until we say good-bye. Englewood Cliffs, N.J: Prentice-Hall.

Lewin, K., 1947[A]. Frontiers in group dynamics. Human Relations, 1, 143-153.

Lewin, K., 1947[B]. Feedback problems of social diagnosis and action: Part II-B of frontiers in group dynamics. Human Relations, 1, 147-153. 298.

Lewin, K., 1951. Field theory in social science. New York: Harper and Row.

Lewin, K., 1958. Group decision and social changes. In E. E. Maccoby, T.M. Newcomb, and E.L. Hartley (Eds.), Readings in social psychology (3rd Edn.) (pp. 197-211). New York: Holt.

Lewis, R., 2012. Being When teams collide. London: Nicholas Brealey Publishing.

Maccoby, M., 2004. Narcissistic Leaders: The Incredible Pros, the Inevitable Cons. HBR. Available at: https://hbr.org/2004/01/narcissistic-leaders-the-incredible-pros-the-inevitable-cons [Accessed Jun. 2019].

Malby, B. and Fischer, M., 2006. Tools for Change: An Invitation to Dance. Chichester: Kingsham.

Martin, R., 2010. The Execution Trap. [online] HBR. Available at: https://hbr.org/2010/07/the-execution-trap [Accessed Jul. 2019].

Mcfarlin, D. and Sweeney, P., 2001. Where Egos Dare: The Untold Truth About Narcissistic Leaders and How to Survive Them. Work Study, 50(1).

McGregor, D., 1960. The human side of enterprise. New York: McGraw-Hill.

Merton, R., 1976. Sociological ambivalence and other essays. New York: Free Press.

Mintzberg, H. and Water, J., 1985. Of strategies, deliberate and emergent. Strat. Mgmt. J., 6(3), pp.257-272.

Miredith, J., Mantel, S., Shafer, S. and Sutton, M., 2014. Project Management in Practice. 5th ed. Hoboken, N.J.: John Wiley and Sons, Inc.

Myers, I., Mcaulley, M. and Most, R., 1985. Manual, a guide to the development and use of the Myers-Briggs type indicator. Palo Alto, Ca.: Consulting Psychologists Press.

Orton-Jones, C., 2013. Project managers worth their weight in gold. [online] Raconteur. Available at: http://raconteur.net/business/why-professional-project-managers-are-worth-their-weight-in-gold [Accessed May 2019].

Palmer, I., and Dunford, R., 2008. Managing organisational change: A multiple perspective approach. USA: Mcgraw Hill Higher Education.

Pansesar, S. S. and Markeset, T., 2008. Industrial Service Innovation Through Improved Contractual Relationship: A Case Study in Maintenance. Journal of Quality in Maintenance Engineering, 14(3), pp. 290-305.

Pascale, R., 1999. Managing on the edge: How successful companies use conflict to stay ahead. London: Viking.

Pedler, M., Burgogyne, J. and Boydell, T., 1997. The Learning Company: A Strategy for Sustainable Development. 2nd Ed. London: McGraw-Hill.

Peters, T.J. and Waterman, R.H., 1982. In search of excellence: Lessons from America's best run companies. London: Harper and Row.

Pettigrew, A.M., 1980. The politics of organisational change. In N.B. Anderson (Ed.), The human side of information processing (pp. 45-51). Amsterdam: North Holland.

Pettigrew, A.M., 1990. Longitudinal field research on change: Theory and practice. Organisational Science, 3(1), 267-292. Studies, 11(1), 6-11.

Pettigrew, A.M., and Whipp, R., 1993. Managing change for competitive success. Cambridge: Blackwell.

Pettigrew, A.M., Ferlie, E., and McKee, L., 1992. Shaping strategic change: Making change in large organisations. London: Sage Publications.

Pettigrew, A.M., Woodman, R.W., and Cameron, K.S., 2001. Studying organisational change and development: Challenges for future research. Academy of Management Journal, 44 (4), 697-713.

Pfeffer, J., 1992. Managing with power: Politics and influence in organisations. Boston, MA: Harvard Business School Press.

PMI, 20132. The High Cost of Low Performance: The Essential Role of Communications. Available at: https://www.pmi.org/-/media/pmi/documents/public/pdf/learning/thought-leadership/pulse/the-essential-role-of-communications.pdf [Accessed 6 Jun. 2019].

PMI, 2019. Learn More About Who PMI is and What We Do. Available at: http://www.pmi.org/About-Us.aspx [Accessed Jun. 2019].

PMI, 2019. Project Management Professional Certification | PMP. [online] Available at: http://www.pmi.org/certification/project-management-professional-pmp.aspx [Accessed Jun. 2019].

PRINCE2, 2015. PRINCE2 Download Centre - Communications Plan. Available at: https://www.prince2.com/downloads [Accessed Jun. 2019].

Pryor, M.G., White, J.C., and Toombs, L.A., 1998. Strategic Quality Management: A strategic, systems approach to continuous improvement. United States: Thomson Learning.

Quinn, R. E., 1996. Deep change. San Francisco: Jossey-Bass.

Raven, B. and French, J., 1958. Legitimate Power, Coercive Power, and Observability in Social Influence. Sociometry, 21(2), p.83.

Roda, I. and Garetti M., 2014. Application of a Performance-driven Total Cost of Ownership (TCO). 9th WCEAM Research Papers. Part of the series Lecture Notes in Mechanical Engineering, pp 11-23.

Rutter, D. R., and Quine, L. (Eds.), Social Psychology and Health: European Perspectives (pp. 71-88). Aldershot, England: Avesbury.

Sadler, P., 1996. Managing change. London: Kogan Page Limited.

Scheck, J., Williams, S. and Amiel, G., 2014. How a Giant Kazakh Oil Project Went Awry. WSJ. Available at: http://www.wsj.com/news/articles/SB10001424052702303730804579437492040999738?mod=WSJEUROPE_interactive [Accessed Jun. 2019].

Schein, E.H., 1992. Organisational culture and leadership (2nd Edn.). San Francisco: Jossey- Bass.

Senge, P., Kleiner, A., Roberts, C., Ross, R., Roth, G. and Smith, B., 1999. The dance of change. London: Nicholas Brealey.

Shell, 2019. Brent Field Timeline. Available at: https://www.shell.co.uk/sustainability/decommissioning/brent-field-decommissioning/brent-field-timeline.html. [Accessed 6 June 2019].

Simmank, D., 2013. Using the KANO-model as an approach to evaluate customer satisfaction. München: GRIN Verlag GmbH, p. Kano Model.

Sinek, S. 2009. Start with why. New York: Portfolio.

Stum, D.L., 2001. Maslow revisited: Building the employee commitment pyramid. Strategy and Leadership, 29(4), 4-9.

Sutton, S., 1994. The past predicts the future: Interpreting behaviour- behaviour relationships in social-psychological models of health behaviours. In D. R.

The Economist Insights, 2009. Closing the gap - The link between project management and performance. Available at: http://www.economistinsights.com/business-strategy/analysis/closing-gap [Accessed Jun. 2019].

Tuckman, A., 1994. The yellow brick road: Total quality management and the restructuring of organisational culture. Organisation Studies, 15(5), 727-751.

Tuckman, B., and Jensen, M., 1977. Stages of Small-Group Development Revisited. Group and Organisation Management, 2(4), pp.419-427.

Twidale, S., 2019. World's largest offshore wind farm opens off northwest England. Available at: https://www.reuters.com/article/us-britain-windfarm-orsted/worlds-largest-offshore-wind-farm-opens-off-northwest-england-idUSKCN1LL37G. Accessed Jun. 2019].

Ulrich, D, Huselid, M A. and Becker, B, E., 2001. The HR Scorecard: Linking People, Strategy, and Performance. Boston Harvard Business Press.

Voccola, T., 2006. The Accidental CEO - A Leader's Journey from Ego to Purpose. Thousand Oaks California: Sea Fever Press.

Wang, E., Chou, H.-W., and Jiang, J., 2005. The impacts of charismatic leadership style on team cohesiveness and overall performance during ERP implementation. International Journal of Project Management, 23(3), 173.

Weinkauf, K., and Hoegl, M., 2002. Team leadership activities in different project phases. Team Performance Management, 8(7/8), 171.

Wind, J.W., and Maine, J., 1999. Driving change: How the best companies are preparing for the 21st century. London: Kogan Page.

Worldometers, 2015. Current World Population. [online] Available at: http://www.worldometers.info/world-population/ [Accessed Jun. 2019].

WSJ, 2015. What is the Difference Between Management and Leadership? - Management - WSJ.com. Available at:

http://guides.wsj.com/management/developing-a-leadership-style/what-is-the-difference-between-management-and-leadership/ [Accessed Jun. 2019].

Yergin, D., 1991. The Prize: The Epic Quest for Oil, Money, and Power. New York: Simon and Schuster.

Zander, A.F., 1950. Resistance to change: Its analysis and prevention. Advanced Management, 4(5), 9-11.

Zeffane, R., 1996. Dynamics of strategic change: Critical issues in fostering positive organisational change. Leadership and Organisation Development Journal, 17(7), 36-43.

Zhou, J., and Shalley, C., 2007. Oganisational creativity. New York: Taylor and Francis Group.

Zifcak, S., 1994. The new managerialism: Administrative reform in Whitehall and Canberra. Buckingham: Open University Press.

Zimmermann, J., 1995. The principles of managing change. HR Focus, 2, 15-16.

Zohar, D., 1997. Rewiring the corporate brain: Using the new science to rethink how we structure and lead organisations. New Jersey: Berrett-Koehler Publisher.

4.4 Index

5

5 Why, 39, 258
5S, 236, 237, 258

A

a2B Change Management
  Framework®
  a2BCMF®, viii, xviii, xix, 23, 24, 25,
    26, 28, 29, 33, 34, 43, 47, 48, 49, 53,
    61, 62, 63, 64, 79, 80, 89, 100, 101,
    102, 104, 105, 106, 107, 117, 118,
    119, 120, 121, 124, 126, 127, 129,
    131, 137, 147, 148, 149, 152, 153,
    155, 160, 161, 164, 167, 169, 170,
    171, 177, 179, 182, 183, 184, 185,
    186, 189, 190, 191, 195, 197, 201,
    208, 212, 213, 215, 217, 231, 240,
    241, 242, 244, 245, 246, 247, 251,
    258, 259, 261, 266, 269, 287, 289
a2B5R® Employee Behaviour Change
  Model
  a2B5R®, 5, 29, 35, 79, 119, 161, 197,
    202, 208, 209, 212, 213, 258, 259,
    287
a2BDNS developing the new skills
  model
  a2BDNS, 29, 161, 197, 202, 203, 212,
    258
actionee(s), 107, 117, 118, 258
Adair, 71
adoption
  employee adoption, ix, 5, 12, 53, 79,
    119, 160, 183, 184, 185
  speed up adoption, 130, 137, 186
advocates, 57, 63, 84, 114, 171, 177,
  179, 186, 187, 194, 195, 258, 266,
  269
Agryris, 209
alternative solutions, 35, 46, 258

AUILM® Employee Change
  Adoption Model
  AUILM®, 5, 29, 35, 79, 115, 116, 119,
    147, 148, 161, 170, 183, 184, 185,
    217, 225, 226, 230, 231, 259, 287

B

balanced scorecard, 52, 232, 242, 243,
  250, 251, 259
BSC, 25, 52, 61, 116, 185, 233, 242,
  243, 250, 251, 255, 259, 264
baseline, 52, 53, 78, 235, 259, 263
Belbin, 79, 240
benefits delivery, transition and
  sustainment, 232, 242
benefits plan and tracker, 52, 53, 54,
  113, 120, 242
BPT, 35, 53, 116, 242, 250, 251, 259
benefits realisation, 6, 10, 11, 12, 25,
  52, 53, 63, 90, 102, 106, 108, 117,
  119, 120, 154, 170, 185, 189, 196,
  215, 232, 233, 242, 243, 250, 251,
  259, 261, 263, 268, 269, 270
Bentley, 97, 136
between departments, 82
Boddy, 98
Buchannan, 98
budget, 10, 14, 25, 40, 53, 61, 79, 116,
  125, 197, 201, 212, 213, 262, 267
Burnes, 202
business case, 15, 25, 34, 35, 41, 46,
  47, 52, 61, 62, 63, 72, 81, 83, 99,
  131, 144, 152, 153, 159, 160, 165,
  167, 176, 184, 186, 187, 245, 258,
  260, 268

C

Carnegie, 86
cascading change, 137

celebration, 249, 251
change capacity, 35, 40, 44, 45, 47, 62, 63, 71, 73, 83, 97, 184, 254, 260
change challenges, xviii
change communication plan, 149, 150, 152, 153, 260
   CCP, 29, 104, 105, 131, 137, 144, 148, 149, 152, 153, 177, 178, 182, 191, 260
change consultants, 80
change disruption, xviii, 2, 4, 178, 193, 217, 224, 228, 260
change fatigue, 240, 260
change history assessment
   CHA, 19, 44, 91, 92, 93, 94, 95, 98, 99, 100, 101, 102, 104, 105, 107, 111, 113, 116, 119, 121, 126, 127, 159, 160, 182, 184, 227, 260, 290
change impact, 57, 94, 190, 191, 246, 247, 261
change initiative, 13, 180, 261, 263, 266
change management definition, 4
change management methodology, 99, 261
change model, 5, 13, 161, 208, 209, 261
change readiness, 7, 29, 92, 95, 99, 113, 147, 155, 156, 158, 159, 160, 161, 162, 164, 165, 166, 167, 168, 182, 261, 267
change readiness assessment
   CRA, 7, 29, 113, 155, 156, 158, 159, 164, 182
change resistance plan, 126, 171, 177, 178, 189, 191, 195
change saturation, 261
change sponsor assessment
   CSA, 76, 78, 261
change team resources, 28, 79, 88, 89
change transition, 224, 225, 230
change vision, 6, 16, 71, 131, 137, 144, 152, 153, 165, 259, 262, 265
charter, 47, 76, 92, 108, 109, 110, 243, 262, 266

checklist, 63, 89, 105, 127, 153, 169, 195, 213, 231, 251, 262
Churchill, 20, 143
coaching, 12, 13, 65, 73, 80, 84, 114, 119, 156, 158, 159, 185, 197, 203, 204, 205, 206, 211, 212, 213, 217, 219, 238, 262, 270
Collins, 18, 45, 83, 254
communication
   illusion, 132, 136
communication channels, 131, 137, 142, 145, 148, 149, 152, 153, 225, 262
competency, 111, 114, 183, 185, 203, 217, 219, 227, 230, 234, 262
   dictionary, 262
   framework, 262
Conner, 248
constraint, 46, 47, 62, 262
continuous and never-ending improvement
   CANI, 93, 262, 264
continuous improvement, 239, 248, 262
core competence, 12, 262
cost overrun, 193, 262
CRA, 29, 155, 159, 160, 161, 164, 165, 166, 167, 168, 169, 182, 261
creation steps, xix, 48, 53, 56, 60, 124, 141, 144, 149, 189, 246
critical success factor, 71, 262
Crombie, 228
culture
   cultural awareness, 229
   cultural difference, 222, 229
   culture and change, 203, 228, 230, 231
   culture map, 229
   new culture, 75, 241
current state, 84, 108, 112, 192, 196, 204, 216, 230, 260, 263

D

day in the life of
   DILO, 37, 39, 40, 263
deluded leaders, 19, 197, 263, 271

dependencies, 47, 107, 112, 117, 118, 126, 147, 263, 268
Deutschman, 207
Dow, 138
due diligence, 34, 35, 62

E

Eisenhower, 18
Eldridge, 228
elevator speech, 35, 47, 53, 55, 56, 62, 63, 141, 148, 182, 183
emotional intelligence, 86, 263
employee behaviour, 5, 7, 35, 119, 201, 202, 206, 207, 263
enablers and barriers, xviii, 35, 65, 91, 107, 131, 155, 171, 197, 217, 233
estimated completion date
ECD, 54, 112, 263

F

facilitator, 191, 246, 263
feedback loop, 26, 73, 82, 113, 119, 130, 132, 140, 141, 145, 152, 153, 165, 217, 226
fixed mindset, 18, 19, 93, 95, 102, 181, 192, 194, 264
fourth industrial revolution
4IR, xviii, 2, 3, 74, 240, 260
frame of reference, 136, 182, 222, 264
Freeman, 56
future state, 3, 187, 196, 205, 216, 230, 260, 262, 264, 269, 270

G

Gallagher, 19, 97, 98, 136
Gebert, 79
Goldsmith, 19, 257
governance, 25, 27, 29, 34, 35, 41, 53, 61, 62, 63, 68, 76, 77, 92, 107, 110, 116, 117, 118, 119, 124, 148, 149, 155, 161, 165, 168, 191, 232, 233, 244, 248, 250, 251, 264

Green, 87
growth mindset, 19, 93, 95, 171, 173, 187, 192, 193, 194, 195, 197, 208, 262

H

Hamel, 12
Harrington, 44
Hayes, 15
Hofstede, 229
Howe, 87
hubris, 86, 264, 266
hunch and launch syndrome, 117, 264

I

incremental change, xviii, 20, 21
individual performance plan, 52, 232, 242, 243, 250, 251, 264
IPP, 25, 61, 116, 185, 228, 233, 243, 250
intervention, 16, 17, 75, 78, 99, 154, 166, 167, 222, 264, 266
Ishikawa, 94

J

just-do-it
JDI, 18, 19, 93

K

Kanter, 6
Kaplan, 242
Kearney, 79
Kennedy, 3
key performance indicators, 118, 264
Kirkpatrick, 205
knowledge transfer, 116, 232, 233, 244, 248, 249, 250, 251, 264, 265
Kolb, 205
Kotter, 96
Kruger, 17

L

leader
   change communications leader, 80
   change leader, 17, 79, 201
   change process leader, 79
   change work stream lead, 80
leaders
   'Model', 6, 15, 16, 17, 71, 265
   'Articulate', 6, 15, 71, 259, 265
   'Intervene', 6, 15, 16, 17, 71, 264, 265
leadership, 5, 6, 13, 14, 15, 16, 18, 19, 28, 70, 82, 83, 88, 161, 165, 212, 213, 223, 231, 233, 265
   Illusion, 19
Leadership of Change, viii, 5, 20, 57, 70, 78, 95, 161, 178, 181, 182, 194, 269, 288, 289
lean, 37, 258, 263, 265, 270
learning organisation, 91, 101, 202
lessons learned, 25, 91, 94, 95, 98, 100, 105, 116, 200, 232, 233, 244, 245, 246, 247, 248, 250, 251, 257, 261, 265
level 5 leaders, 18
Lewin, 95
Likert, xix, 77, 99, 165
Lock, 124
Loosemore, 120

M

Maccoby, 19
Martin, 42
master project plan, 7, 29, 107, 117, 124, 125, 126, 127, 265
Mendelow, 60
mentoring, 265
Meyer, 229
milestones, 26, 34, 41, 47, 48, 106, 107, 112, 117, 124, 126, 127, 149, 193, 265, 268
mission, 15, 42, 72, 259, 262, 265
modelling, 16, 76, 88, 89, 161, 165, 197, 210, 259
Moore, 42

Mornell, 98

N

narcissistic
   leader, 19, 86, 191
no vacuum, 74, 82, 89
normal day-to-day operations, 3, 6, 10, 11, 12, 14, 15, 16, 28, 35, 40, 42, 44, 45, 47, 62, 75, 77, 83, 134, 137, 155, 182, 205, 210, 228, 230, 233, 238, 241, 250, 251, 260, 266, 288
Norton, 242

O

observers, 57, 63, 84, 114, 171, 177, 186, 187, 194, 195, 266, 269
Owen, 86

P

pet projects, 264, 266
Pettigrew, 25
planned change, 260, 266
PMI, 125
Prahalad, 248
project change plan
   PCP, 7, 29, 61, 100, 102, 106, 107, 116, 117, 118, 120, 121, 122, 124, 125, 126, 127, 131, 148, 149, 164, 186, 191, 264, 265, 266, 267, 268, 269

Q

qualitative, 19, 92, 93, 100, 111, 155, 164, 168, 169, 259, 266
quantitative, 111, 155, 168, 169, 259, 267

R

rarely blame the employee
   RBtE, 19, 37
rebels, 57, 63, 82, 84, 114, 171, 177, 186, 187, 194, 195, 267, 269

reinforcement, 17, 119, 200, 210, 212, 213, 222, 224
    reinforce, 6, 16, 71, 75, 84, 137, 155, 197, 210, 212, 217, 222, 227, 228, 265, 267

Reiter, 19, 254

Rescorla, 210

resistance
    address resistance, 84, 120, 170, 191, 193, 267
    employee resistance, 15, 29, 107, 155, 171, 175, 176, 188, 192
    manage resistance, xviii, 27, 29, 49, 119, 170, 194
    mitigate resistance, 57, 120, 268
    reduce resistance, 15, 16, 29, 111, 126, 182, 184, 187, 194, 227
    resistance management, 182, 267
    standpoints, 177, 178, 195

resistance strategy plan, 113, 117, 119, 120, 267

return on investment
    ROI, 5, 6, 10, 11, 12, 14, 15, 64, 66, 201, 207, 209, 217, 223, 224, 260, 267, 289

review and checklist, 62, 88, 104, 126, 152, 168, 194, 212, 230, 250

rework, 44, 262, 267

risk, 39, 41, 46, 47, 48, 52, 53, 54, 57, 61, 62, 76, 78, 120, 125, 131, 144, 152, 153, 159, 160, 199, 207, 261, 263, 270

risk management plan, 113, 120

roadmap, viii, ix, xix, 35, 41, 47, 48, 49, 50, 62, 63, 79, 107, 108, 119, 121, 126, 127, 261, 268, 289

S

Schwab, 3

Senge, 94, 202

Shaw, 97, 136

Sirkin, 97

skills and behaviours learning plan, 113, 120, 268

sponsor assessment, 76, 78, 88, 89, 167, 268

sponsorship
    'Say', 65, 69, 70, 72, 73, 75, 76, 77, 78, 88, 89, 184, 262, 268, 269
    'Support', 65, 69, 70, 72, 73, 75, 76, 77, 78, 88, 89, 184, 262, 268, 269
    'Sustain', 65, 69, 70, 72, 74, 75, 76, 77, 78, 88, 89, 116, 184, 262, 268, 269

sponsorship and resource plan, 113, 120, 268

stakeholder analysis, 35, 56, 57, 58, 59, 60, 61, 62, 63, 100, 141, 164, 177, 191, 268

stakeholder engagement plan, 113, 120, 178, 268

stakeholder mapping, 58, 60, 61, 177, 269

Steers, 42

strategic portfolio prioritisation funnel, 35, 42, 43, 62, 63

strategy alignment, 42, 62, 63, 289

subject matter experts, 92, 117, 124, 235, 269

sustain and close plan, 113, 120, 269

T

tactics, 24, 170, 171, 182, 187, 195, 217, 225, 230, 231, 269

Taylor, 138

template, viii, ix, xix, 48, 49, 53, 54, 58, 60, 140, 141, 144, 177, 189, 190, 242, 246, 247, 261, 289

Thaler, 207, 210

Thomas, 16

threat, 19, 114, 115, 170, 181, 194, 225, 267, 270

TIM H WOOD, 240, 263, 270

tipping point, 65, 84, 171, 186, 187, 194, 195

top down, 81

Tourish, 137

training needs analysis, 270
    TNA, 80, 119, 120, 185, 203, 268

transfer of ownership, 25, 29, 116, 232, 233, 243, 244, 245, 250, 251, 270

transformation, xviii, 6, 10, 15, 20, 21, 36, 37, 38, 40, 62, 66, 67, 68, 69, 95, 97, 108, 117, 132, 192, 205, 207, 265, 275
transition state, 270
triple constraint, 76, 108, 112, 270

U

Ulrich, 84, 201

V

values statement, 270
vision statement, 270
Voehl, 44
Voelpel, 79

Vonnegut, 95, 227

W

What's In It For Me
    WIIFM, 73, 77, 141, 183, 270
Whipp, 25
Whitmore, 205
Williams, 245
work stream, 80, 88, 121, 126, 147, 265, 270

Y

yes men, 19, 271
Yukl, 14

4.5 About the Author

Peter is a Change Management Expert, International Speaker, Author, Leadership Alignment Coach and Trusted Adviser to C-suites.

He has a proven track record of complex change and project delivery in multi-disciplinary environments for the world's largest and most successful organisations. He has Big Four external consulting experience, as well as internal and commercial consulting experience, working in over thirty countries over a thirty-year career. Companies he has worked for include: EY, Shell, NCR and Bombardier Aerospace. Peter has also held senior roles in industry and has boardroom experience as a NED. His clients include organisations such as ADNOC, Boeing, BP, GE, Rolls Royce and Aramco.

Peter speaks on the **Leadership of Change**®, change management, change leadership alignment and the benefits of change management gamification. As a speaker, Peter has presented strategic transformations leading practice to Government entities, CEO audiences globally, leadership teams and at professional membership conferences. For over thirty years, Peter has been helping organisations, leaders and employees change, improve and transform through keynotes, masterclasses, change management gamification workshops, projects and programmes. The change question set Peter asks all leaders is:
"Do you have a change vision? Are you aligned on your strategic objectives? Are you a high performing team? Does your team have change leadership skills to lead the change or improvement that your organisation is facing?"
He then works with their leadership team to develop the solution.

Peter has an MBA (Distinction) from the Robert Gordon University. He is an American Society of Quality (ASQ) Certified Manager of Quality, a Certified Change Management Professional™ with the Association of Change Management Professionals (ACMP) and holds three certifications from the Project Management Institute (PMI). He is also a Lean Six Sigma Master Black Belt. He is the Vice President of the Association of Change Management Professionals (ACMP) UK.

4.6 Other Leadership of Change Volumes

Change Management Body of Knowledge Volumes

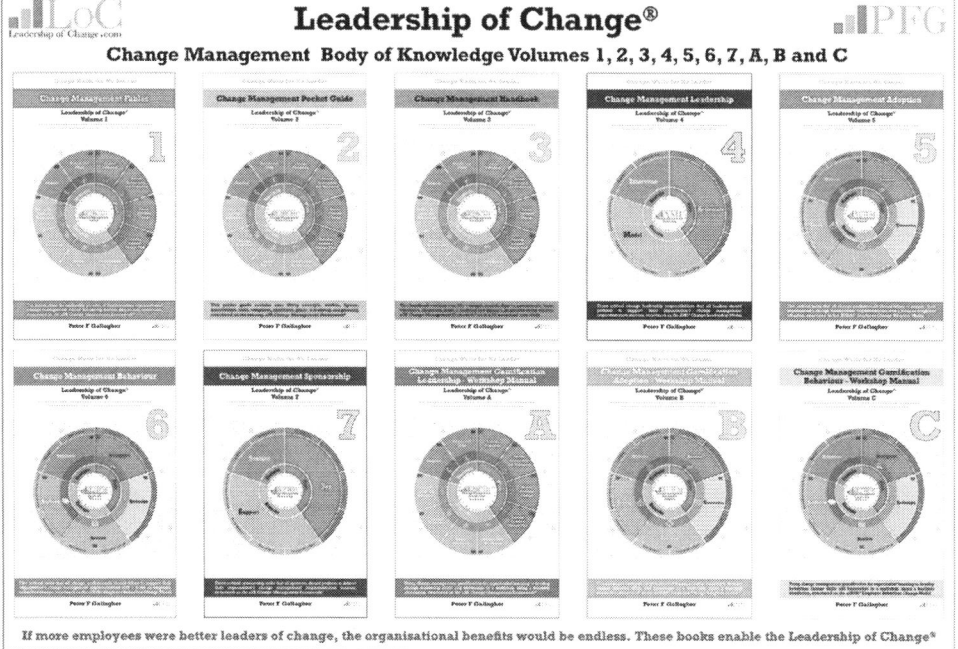

Change Management Fables - Leadership of Change® Volume 1

Ten fables about the leadership paradox of implementing organisational change management versus delivering normal day-to-day operations, structured on the **a2B Change Management Framework®**.

Change Management Pocket Guide - Leadership of Change® Volume 2

This pocket guide contains over thirty concepts, models, figures, assessments, tools, templates, checklists, plans, a roadmap and glossary, structured on the ten-step **a2B Change Management Framework®**.

Change Management Handbook - Leadership of Change® Volume 3

This handbook contains over fifty concepts, models, figures, assessments, tools, templates, checklists, plans, a roadmap and glossary, structured on the ten step **a2B Change Management Framework®** each with a practical case study.

Change Management Leadership - Leadership of Change® Volume 4

Effective and proactive leadership is essential for successful organisational change. This book outlines the three critical leadership responsibilities to implement change: **A**rticulate the vision, **M**odel the new way and **I**ntervene to ensure sustainable change, structured on the **AMI® Change Leadership Model**.

Change Management Adoption - Leadership of Change® Volume 5

Achieving Employee Change Adoption in a major organisation change or transformation has mixed success and the ROI benefits are not always realised. For change adoption to be successful, the leaders, sponsor and change team should support the employees through the change transition by providing **A**wareness, **U**nderstanding, **I**nvolvement, **L**earning, and **M**otivation for the change, structured on the **AUILM® Employee Change Adoption Model**.

Change Management Behaviour - Leadership of Change® Volume 6

Sometimes, in order for an organisation to successfully deliver change or transformation and achieve sustainable change and benefits realisation, employee behaviour change is required. To change these behaviours, the organisation must support employees through the change transition by implementing five key change behaviour stages: **R**ecognise, **R**edesign, **R**esolve, **R**eplicate and **R**einforce, structured on the **a2B5R® Employee Behaviour Change Model**.

Change Management Sponsorship - Leadership of Change® Volume 7

Without a proactive and effective change sponsor, most change programmes or initiatives will fail to achieve the targeted objectives. This book outlines the three critical sponsorship responsibilities to successfully implement change: **Say** - communicating the change, **Support** - providing resources and **Sustain** - embedding the change, structured on the **a2B3S® Change Sponsorship Model**.

Change Management Gamification Leadership - Leadership of Change® Volume A

This change management gamification workshop manual supports organisational leaders to learn about change leadership in a workshop environment using a business simulation. It includes a business case study that enables experiential learning in a safe environment so the skills and knowledge can be immediately applied back in the workplace.

Change Management Gamification Adoption - Leadership of Change® Volume B

This change management gamification workshop manual supports change professionals to learn about change implementation with a focus on employee change adoption in a workshop environment using a business simulation. It includes a business case study that enables experiential learning in a safe environment so the skills and knowledge can be immediately applied back in the workplace.

Change Management Gamification Behaviour - Leadership of Change® Volume C

This change management gamification workshop manual supports change professionals to learn about change implementation with a focus on changing employee behaviours in a workshop environment using a business simulation. It includes a business case study that enables experiential learning in a safe environment so the skills and knowledge can be immediately applied back in the workplace.

4.7 Connect with us online

Connect with me online to learn more about our latest products and services, read our blog, and learn more about how to join the conversation about change management!

We would love to hear your story. If you try something and it works, let us know! Equally, if you tried something and it failed, we would like to hear from you!

www.peterfgallagher.com/leadership-of-change

Join the conversation

 peterfgallagher

 @peterfgallagher

Please contact **Peter** through his website at:

www.peterfgallagher.com

For **Consultancy Services** please contact us through our website at:

www.a2B.consulting

Printed in Great Britain
by Amazon